Exam Ref 70-697 Configuring Windows Devices

Second Edition

Andrew Bettany
Andrew Warren

Exam Ref 70-697 Configuring Windows Devices, Second Edition

Published with the authorization of Microsoft Corporation by:
Pearson Education, Inc.

Copyright © 2018 by Pearson Education

ISBN-13: 978-1-5093-0785-2
ISBN-10: 1-5093-0785-0

Library of Congress Control Number: 2018938485
1 18

Trademarks

Microsoft and the trademarks listed at *https://www.microsoft.com* on the "Trademarks" webpage are trademarks of the Microsoft group of companies. All other marks are property of their respective owners.

Warning and Disclaimer

Special Sales

For information about buying this title in bulk quantities, or for special sales opportunities (which may include electronic versions; custom cover designs; and content particular to your business, training goals, marketing focus, or branding interests), please contact our corporate sales department at corpsales@pearsoned.com or (800) 382-3419.

For government sales inquiries, please contact governmentsales@pearsoned.com.

For questions about sales outside the U.S., please contact intlcs@pearson.com.

Editor-in-Chief	Greg Wiegand
Senior Editor	Trina MacDonald
Development Editor	Mark Renfrow
Managing Editor	Sandra Schroeder
Senior Project Editor	Tracey Croom
Editorial Production	Backstop Media
Copy Editor	Christina Rudloff
Indexer	Julie Grady
Proofreader	Troy Mott
Technical Editor	Byron Wright
Cover Designer	Twist Creative, Seattle

I would like to dedicate this book to Annette and Tommy, for being so supportive and encouraging whenever I work on projects that sometimes eat into our quality time together. This book is also for the reader–having taught thousands of IT Professionals over my career, I hope this book reaches a greater audience and helps you achieve your career aspirations. Work hard and aim for the stars!.

—ANDREW BETTANY

Writing this book has been a team effort, and I am delighted to have been a part of that team. Aside from the folks at Pearson and my co-author, Andrew, I'd like to mention my dog, Lucy. Her enthusiasm for long walks undoubtedly helped me clear my head, and thus to deliver chapters on time to our editor, Trina Macdonald.

—ANDREW WARREN

Contents at a glance

Contents

Chapter 2 Plan desktop and device deployment 37

Chapter 5   Configure storage   163

Chapter 9   Manage updates and recovery   337

About the authors

ANDREW BETTANY, Microsoft Most Valuable Professional (Windows and Devices for IT), Dad, IT Geek, training mentor and consultant, entrepreneur, and author.

As a Microsoft Most Valuable Professional (MVP), Andrew is recognized for his Windows expertise, and is the author of several publications, including Windows exam certification prep, Microsoft official training materials, and an author of video training materials for LinkedIn Learning and Pluralsight.

Having managed the IT Academy at the University of York, UK for years, he now focuses his time training and writing. As a Microsoft Certified Trainer, Andrew delivers learning and consultancy to businesses on many technical areas including Microsoft 365, Azure, and Windows.

He has co-founded the "IT Masterclasses" series of short intensive technical courses, www.itmasterclasses.com, and is passionate about helping others learn technology. He is a frequent speaker and proctor at Microsoft Ignite conferences worldwide.

Active on social media, Andrew can be found on LinkedIn Facebook and Twitter. He lives in a village just outside of the beautiful city of York in Yorkshire (UK).

ANDREW WARREN has over 30 years of experience in IT and has served as subject matter expert for many Microsoft Official Curriculum courses. He is a Microsoft Certified Trainer and runs his own training consultancy in the UK.

Introduction

The Configuring Windows Devices exam (70-697) is separated into nine sets of objectives.

This book contains nine chapters that clearly detail what those objectives are and the content that you can expect to see on the exam. Because each chapter covers a part of the exam, you should concentrate on one chapter at a time and complete the thought experiments and review questions. This book covers the general, high-level knowledge you need to know to answer questions regarding why and when you might perform tasks relating to the exam objectives.

Prior to taking the certification exam, you should fully prepare to the best of your ability and we assume that you have some practical experience supporting Windows devices within the workplace. You are also probably reading this book as part of your final preparations and that you feel almost ready to take the exam. In this book we have included how-to steps and walkthroughs whenever we feel that they are useful, and we hope that you will perform the tasks on your system or within a virtual machine to crystalize your knowledge. Throughout the book there are numerous notes and links to resources on the Internet, which should add even more depth to your preparation. You should expect that Windows 10 will evolve constantly, through Windows upgrades, and you should always supplement your learning with practical experience obtained by using the latest build of the operating system because there are always new things to learn and fresh challenges to master.

This book covers every major topic area found on the exam, but it does not cover every exam question. Only the Microsoft exam team has access to the exam questions, and Microsoft regularly adds new questions to the exam, making it impossible to cover specific questions. You should consider this book a supplement to your relevant real-world experience and other study materials. If you encounter a topic in this book that you do not feel completely comfortable with, use the "Need more review?" links you'll find in the text to find more information and take the time to research and study the topic. Great information is available on *https://docs.microsoft.com* and in blogs and forums.

Organization of this book

This book is organized by the "Skills measured" list published for the exam. The "Skills measured" list is available for each exam on the Microsoft Learning website: *http://aka.ms/examlist*. Each chapter in this book corresponds to a major topic area in the list, and the technical tasks in each topic area determine a chapter's organization. If an exam covers six major topic areas, for example, the book will contain six chapters.

Microsoft certifications

Microsoft certifications distinguish you by proving your command of a broad set of skills and experience with current Microsoft products and technologies. The exams and corresponding certifications are developed to validate your mastery of critical competencies as you design and develop, or implement and support, solutions with Microsoft products and technologies both on-premises and in the cloud. Certification brings a variety of benefits to the individual and to employers and organizations.

> **MORE INFO** **ALL MICROSOFT CERTIFICATIONS**
>
> For information about Microsoft certifications, including a full list of available certifications, go to *http://www.microsoft.com/learning*.

Microsoft Virtual Academy

Build your knowledge of Microsoft technologies with free expert-led online training from Microsoft Virtual Academy (MVA). MVA offers a comprehensive library of videos, live events, and more to help you learn the latest technologies and prepare for certification exams. You'll find what you need here:

http://www.microsoftvirtualacademy.com

Quick access to online references

Throughout this book are addresses to webpages that the author has recommended you visit for more information. Some of these addresses (also known as URLs) can be painstaking to type into a web browser, so we've compiled all of them into a single list that readers of the print edition can refer to while they read.

Download the list at *https://aka.ms/examref697ed2/downloads*

The URLs are organized by chapter and heading. Every time you come across a URL in the book, find the hyperlink in the list to go directly to the webpage.

Errata, updates, & book support

We've made every effort to ensure the accuracy of this book and its companion content. You can access updates to this book—in the form of a list of submitted errata and their related corrections—at:

https://aka.ms/examref697ed2/errata

If you discover an error that is not already listed, please submit it to us at the same page.

If you need additional support, email Microsoft Press Book Support at *mspinput@microsoft.com*.

Please note that product support for Microsoft software and hardware is not offered through the previous addresses. For help with Microsoft software or hardware, go to *http://support.microsoft.com*.

Stay in touch

Let's keep the conversation going! We're on Twitter: *http://twitter.com/MicrosoftPress*.

Important: How to use this book to study for the exam

Certification exams validate your on-the-job experience and product knowledge. To gauge your readiness to take an exam, use this Exam Ref to help you check your understanding of the skills tested by the exam. Determine the topics you know well and the areas in which you need more experience. To help you refresh your skills in specific areas, we have also provided "Need more review?" pointers, which direct you to more in-depth information outside the book.

The Exam Ref is not a substitute for hands-on experience. This book is not designed to teach you new skills.

We recommend that you round out your exam preparation by using a combination of available study materials and courses. Learn more about available classroom training at *http://www.microsoft.com/learning*. Microsoft Official Practice Tests are available for many exams at *http://aka.ms/practicetests*. You can also find free online courses and live events from Microsoft Virtual Academy at *http://www.microsoftvirtualacademy.com*.

This book is organized by the "Skills measured" list published for the exam. The "Skills measured" list for each exam is available on the Microsoft Learning website: *http://aka.ms/examlist*.

Note that this Exam Ref is based on this publicly available information and the author's experience. To safeguard the integrity of the exam, authors do not have access to the exam questions.

CHAPTER 1

Manage Identity

Identity is an important concept in Windows. This chapter tests your understanding of how identities are managed in Windows to provide users with a consistent and secure environment. You'll learn how to support Microsoft Store and Office 365 applications, install applications into images, and support authentication and permissions mechanisms in Windows.

IMPORTANT
Have you read page xxi?
It contains valuable information regarding the skills you need to pass the exam.

Skills in this chapter:

- Skill 1.1: Support Microsoft Store, Microsoft Store for Education, Microsoft Store for Business, and cloud apps
- Skill 1.2: Support authentication and authorization

Skill 1.1: Support Microsoft Store, Microsoft Store for Education, Microsoft Store for Business, and cloud apps

This section covers supporting and installing apps from a variety of sources, including Microsoft Store, Microsoft Store for Education, Microsoft Store for Business, Microsoft Office 365, and Microsoft Intune. You'll see how to use a Microsoft account to synchronize app and Windows settings across multiple devices. You'll also see how to install apps into Windows Imaging Format (WIM) images, and manage the installation and availability of apps, including sideloading and deep linking.

> **This section covers how to:**
> - Integrate Microsoft account and personalization settings
> - Install and manage software with Microsoft Office 365 and Microsoft Store apps
> - Sideload apps into online and offline images
> - Sideload apps by using Microsoft Intune
> - Deep link apps by using Microsoft Intune

Integrate Microsoft account and personalization settings

Using a Microsoft account with Windows 10 is the simplest and quickest way for users to maintain a consistent environment across multiple devices. Windows 10 can use a Microsoft account to save Personalization settings to the cloud and synchronize those settings across devices including PCs, laptops, tablets, and smartphones. In Windows 10, you can associate a Microsoft account with two separate account types:

- **Local account** A local account is stored in the local Security Account Manager (SAM) database on a Windows 10 computer.
- **Domain account** A domain account is stored in the Active Directory Domain Services (AD DS) database on a domain controller. Domain accounts can be used to authenticate a user on Windows computers joined to the domain.

A Microsoft account can provide settings synchronization across local and domain accounts. For example, a user might associate his Microsoft account with a local account on his home computer and a domain account at work. With this configuration, the user can have settings like Internet Explorer favorites or app configuration settings that remain consistent regardless of which computer he is signed in to.

Associating a Microsoft account with a local or domain account

You can associate a Microsoft account with a local or domain account from the Your Info page in the Accounts category of the Settings app, as shown in Figure 1-1.

FIGURE 1-1 The Your Info tab in the Accounts category in the Settings app

To associate a Microsoft account with a local Windows account, complete the following steps:

1. From the Desktop, click the Start button, and then click Settings.
2. In the Settings app, click Accounts.
3. In the left pane of the Accounts page, click Your Info.
4. In the Your Info page, click Sign In With A Microsoft Account Instead.
5. Enter your Microsoft account user name and password, and then click Sign in.
6. You will be asked to verify your identity to be able to associate the account.
7. After verification, click Switch To Start Using Your Microsoft Account to sign in to Windows.

To associate a Microsoft account with a domain account, complete the following steps:

1. When logged in with a domain account, from the Desktop, click the Start button, and then click Settings.
2. In the Settings app, click Accounts.
3. On the Accounts page, click Your info.
4. In the Your info box, click Sign In With A Microsoft Account.
5. On the Connect To A Microsoft Account On This PC page, select the PC settings you want to sync with the domain, and then click Next. The options are:
   - Start Screen
   - App Data
   - Appearance
   - Language Preferences
   - Desktop Personalization
   - Ease Of Access
   - Apps
   - Other Windows Settings
   - Passwords
   - Web Browser
6. Enter your Microsoft account user name and password, and then click Next.
7. You will be asked to verify your identity to continue associating the account.
8. After verification, click Connect to associate your Microsoft account with your domain account.

Configuring Microsoft account synchronization settings

Users can change which items they opt to synchronize by using a Microsoft account. Users can access the options in the Settings app from the Sync Your Settings section of the Accounts page (see Figure 1-2).

FIGURE 1-2 The Sync Your Settings section in the Settings app

Configuring Microsoft account settings by using Group Policy

Network administrators can incorporate Microsoft accounts into the workplace to help users transfer what they've configured with their domain accounts between computers by using a Microsoft account. Network administrators can also disable the ability to associate Microsoft accounts by setting limitations in Group Policy. This section looks at the Group Policy options for controlling the association of Microsoft accounts.

> **NOTE ACCESSING GROUP POLICY**
> To access Group Policy Object settings, click Start, type **gpedit.msc,** and then press Enter. Group Policy cannot be configured on Windows 10 Home edition.

The Group Policy setting used to disable Microsoft account use is named Accounts: Block Microsoft Accounts, and the setting is found in Computer Configuration\Windows Settings\ Security Settings\Local Policies\Security Options (see Figure 1-3). You can choose from three different settings:

- **The policy is disabled**   If you disable or do not configure this policy, users will be able to use Microsoft accounts with Windows.

- **Users can't add Microsoft accounts**   If you select this option, users will not be able to create new Microsoft accounts on this computer, switch a local account to a Microsoft account, or connect a domain account to a Microsoft account. This is the preferred option if you need to limit the use of Microsoft accounts in your enterprise.

- **Users can't add or log on with Microsoft accounts**   If you select this option, existing Microsoft account users will not be able to log on to Windows. Selecting this option might make it impossible for an existing administrator on this computer to log on and manage the system.

FIGURE 1-3 The Accounts: Block Microsoft Accounts Properties dialog box in Local Group Policy Editor

Install and manage software

Although you can install apps using conventional methods, such as choosing Add/Remove Programs in Control Panel , or removable media, you can also perform cloud-based software installation by using Microsoft Store or Microsoft Office 365.

Installing apps by using Microsoft Office 365

Microsoft Office 365 is Microsoft Office in the cloud, accessible by using a user-based paid subscription. Because it's cloud-based, users can access the Microsoft Office products that are licensed to them on up to five compatible devices.

Office 365 updates are applied automatically. There's no need for software maintenance tasks, such as installing updates or upgrading versions, so enterprise administrators don't need to worry about updating devices manually. However, they're still in control of updates and can decide how and when these will be provided to users. Administrators can also decide where users' data should be stored: on the on-premises data servers of a company, in private cloud-based storage, in the public cloud, or a combination of these.

Office 365 is software as a service (SaaS). With SaaS, the user is provided a software product that they can use and consume, on demand. An organization might choose a SaaS product like Office 365 to reduce maintenance and installation workloads, reduce licensing costs, or simplify the organization software portfolio. SaaS products like Office 365 also offer the benefit of access to apps and saved documents from any location or computer, provided an Internet connection is available.

> **MORE INFO** **EXPLORING OFFICE 365**
>
> This Exam Ref focuses on installing Office 365 components. However, there is much more to Office 365, including conferencing, email, secure file sharing, and website hosting. You can learn more about Office 365 at: *https://products.office.com/en-ca/business/explore-office-365-for-business*.

CONFIGURING OFFICE 365

You can obtain a free trial subscription to Office 365 Business Premium by visiting the following link: *https://portal.office.com/Signup/Signup.aspx?OfferId=467eab54-127b-42d3-b046-3844b860bebf&dl=O365_BUSINESS_PREMIUM&culture=en-US&country=US&ali=1&alo=1&lc=1033#0*. After signing up, you can perform the initial configuration steps on the Office 365 Admin Center page, pictured in Figure 1-4.

FIGURE 1-4 The Office 365 Admin Center page

After signing up, you can access the Office 365 Admin Center at: *https://portal.microsofton-line.com/admin/default.aspx*.

INSTALLING OFFICE FROM THE OFFICE 365 PORTAL

You can configure several settings that control the ability to install Office apps from Office 365 Admin Center. From the User Software page under Service Settings in Office 365 Admin Center, you can select the applications that you will enable users to install, one of the options being Office And Skype For Business. If this option is selected, users can install Office on their computers by completing the following steps:

1. Open a web browser and navigate to *https://login.microsoftonline.com*.
2. Sign in with the appropriate user name and password.
3. From the Office 365 Admin Center My account page, click Install Software.
4. Click Run to start the installation, click Yes to continue, and click Next to start the wizard.
5. Select No Thanks to not send updates to Microsoft, and then click Accept.
6. Click Next on the Meet OneDrive page.
7. Click Next to accept defaults, select No Thanks, and then click All Done.

DEPLOYING OFFICE

You can also deploy Office in the enterprise using methods other than the self-service method explained above. The Office Deployment tool enables you to configure information about which language(s) to download, which architecture to use, where the software deployment network share is located, how updates are applied after Office is installed, and which version of the software to install. Deployment methods include Group Policy, startup scripts, or Microsoft System Center Configuration Manager.

Managing software by using Office 365

You can manage all aspects of the Office 365 environment from Office 365 Admin Center. The admin center contains configuration and management pages for all the different features that affect Office app installation:

- **Home**   This page links to commonly used administrative components, such as Users, Billing, Domains, and Service health.
- **Users**   From this page, you can add, remove, and edit user accounts that are part of the Office 365 environment.
- **Groups**   From this page, you can configure groups and shared mailboxes for your organization.
- **Resources**   From this page, you can configure rooms and equipment, sites, and a public website for your organization.
- **Domains**   From this page, you can manage and add domains used by Office 365.
- **Settings**   There are several pages available under the Settings menu, including Services & Add-ins, Security & Privacy, Organization Profile, and Partner Relationships.
- **Admin centers**   This provides a link to each of the management portals for each of the Microsoft cloud-based services to which your organization subscribes, including:
  - Exchange
  - Skype for Business
  - SharePoint
  - OneDrive
  - Azure AD
  - Intune
  - Security & Compliance

IMPORTANT OFFICE 365 FEATURES

There are other important features of Office 365 that you need to consider in preparation for the exam. While these topics are not covered in great detail, they might appear as supporting information for a scenario or question on the exam.

- **Click-to-Run**   You can configure a click-to-run installation of Office that enables a streamed installation process, which gives almost instant access to Office desktop applications, rather than the traditional installation method that requires the user to wait for the entire installation process to complete before using any Office applications.
- **Windows PowerShell**   You can use Windows PowerShell to manage Office 365. You need to be familiar with the common Office 365 management cmdlets. You can find out

more about Office 365 management using Windows PowerShell here: *https://technet. microsoft.com/library/dn568031.aspx.*

Installing apps by using the Microsoft Store

The Microsoft Store is the standard source for Windows 10 apps, and the most common method for installing those apps. The Microsoft Store (Figure 1-5) is installed by default on all Windows 10 computers.

> *NOTE* **NAME CHANGE FOR WINDOWS STORE**
>
> Windows Store was changed to Microsoft Store at the time of writing; however, some elements in the user interface still reference the older name.

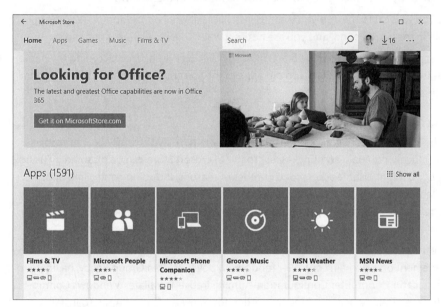

FIGURE 1-5 The Microsoft Store

There are several aspects of the Microsoft Store that you need to be aware of for the exam:

- The Microsoft Store is the primary repository and source for apps that are created and made available to the public, as a free trial or paid app.

- Users must have a Microsoft account associated with their local or domain account in order to download any apps from the Microsoft Store.

- Microsoft Store apps designed for Windows 10 are universal apps. They will function on Windows 10 computers, tablets, and mobile phones or smart devices, as well as Xbox.

- Microsoft Store apps are limited to 10 devices per Microsoft account. A user can install an app on up to 10 devices that are associated with his or her Microsoft account.

- Apps designed for non-public use—that is, for a specific organization—can be submitted through the Microsoft Store and be made available only to members of the organization.

MORE INFO **MICROSOFT STORE APPS VS. WINDOWS DESKTOP APPS**

This Skill domain covers only Microsoft Store apps. Desktop apps, which appear and behave much like traditional Windows programs, are covered in Chapter 8, Managing Apps.

To install a Microsoft Store app, use the following procedure:

1. Open the Microsoft Store while signed in to Windows with a Microsoft account.

2. Navigate the Microsoft Store by browsing the categories provided at the top of the window, or by using the Search toolbar, also at the top of the window.

3. After you've located the app you want to install, click Install on the app page. The app installs in the background, and you are notified when the installation is complete.

Installed apps are available from the Start menu, by clicking All Apps, or by typing the name of the app in the Search field. You can also pin apps to the Start menu or taskbar to make them easier to access.

DISABLING ACCESS TO THE MICROSOFT STORE

By default, the Microsoft Store is accessible to all users who have a Microsoft account associated with their local or domain account. Access to the Microsoft Store can be disabled by using Group Policy. You might disable access for a number of reasons, including controlling apps that are available on certain computers, such as kiosk or terminal computers, satisfying legal or compliance-related requirements, or ensuring that only approved applications of your organization are installed on Windows computers.

To disable access to the Microsoft Store, open either the Local Group Policy Editor, or Group Policy Management on a domain controller for domain policy. Within Group Policy, navigate to the following location: Computer Configuration\Administrative Templates\Windows Components\App Package Deployment. Change the setting for Allow All Trusted Apps To Install to Disabled.

EXAM TIP

Changes to Group Policy do not take place until a Group Policy refresh occurs. By default, this is every 90 minutes. To force a refresh, you can run gpupdate /force from the command prompt.

MICROSOFT STORE FOR BUSINESS AND MICROSOFT STORE FOR EDUCATION

Managing the distribution of line-of-business (LOB) apps can be complex. The IT department might have to handle hundreds of different apps for dozens of departments within an organization. The Microsoft Store for Business and Microsoft Store for Education enable larger organizations to more easily manage their LOB apps.

You can use the Microsoft Store for Business or Microsoft Store for Education as a central location for your organization's LOB apps. By using the Microsoft Store for Business or Microsoft Store for Education, you can provide a single portal for access to these LOB apps. Your users can easily browse the portal, locate the apps they need, and install them.

The Microsoft Store for Business and Microsoft Store for Education both provide public business apps, but also a facility for private LOB apps in a restricted area of the portal. To access the store, users must sign in using credentials from Microsoft Azure.

Sideload apps into offline and online images

Organizations sometimes create their own apps. These apps have the same characteristics as the apps you find in the Microsoft Store (which aren't desktop apps). As noted earlier, enterprise administrators can make these apps available publicly if they want to go through the Microsoft Store certification process, or they can make them available to their enterprise users through a process known as sideloading. Universal apps can also be deployed by using provisioning packages created with the Windows Configuration Designer.

Enabling sideloading in Windows 10

By default, the sideloading option in Windows 10 is disabled. To enable sideloading, you need to use a Group Policy setting. To configure Group Policy so that computers can accept and install sideloaded apps that you created for your organization, navigate to Computer Configuration/ Administrative Templates/ Windows Components/ App Package Deployment. Double-click Allow All Trusted Apps To Install, select Enabled and click OK.

You can also enable sideloading through the Settings app. Click Settings, click Update and Security, and on the For Developers tab, shown in Figure 1-6, click Sideload apps. Click Yes at the security warning message. After sideloading is enabled, any line of business (LOB) Microsoft Store app, signed by a Certification Authority (CA) that the computer trusts, can be installed.

FIGURE 1-6 Enabling sideloading

Sideloading an app

After sideloading is enabled, you can sideload the app using the AppX Windows PowerShell module and the associated cmdlets. To manually sideload an app for the currently logged in user, perform the following steps from a Windows PowerShell prompt:

1. Type **import-module appx**. Press Enter.

2. Type **add-appxpackage** *"path and name of the app"* to add the app. Press Enter. Table 1-1 shows the available AppX cmdlets. If you need to add app dependencies, the command should look more like this: **Add-appxpackage C:\MyApp.appx DependencyPath C:\appplus.appx**.

The app installs, and is then available to the user. This needs to be done for each user if multiple users share a single computer.

EXAM TIP

Some exam questions require you to solve a problem with more than one Windows component or tool. For example, you might be asked how you would deploy an app to all client computers in a domain and configure the app to access network resources. The answer will likely include applying a specific Group Policy Object (Allow All Trusted Apps To Install) and using a Windows PowerShell cmdlet (such as add-appxpackage).

The AppX module for Windows PowerShell includes several cmdlets that you can use to install and manage LOB Microsoft Store apps.

TABLE 1-1 Cmdlets in the AppX module for Windows PowerShell

Cmdlet	Description
Add-AppxPackage	To add a signed app package to a single user account
Get-AppxLastError	To review the last error reported in the app package installation logs
Get-AppxLog	To review the app package installation log
Get-AppxPackage	To view a list of the app packages installed for a user profile
Get-AppxPackageManifest	To read the manifest of an app package
Remove-AppxPackage	To remove an app package from a user account

If you want to sideload the apps to multiple computers, use Deployment Image Servicing and Management (DISM) cmdlets. You can use DISM commands to manage app packages in a Windows image. When you use DISM to provision app packages, those packages are added to a Windows image, and are installed for the desired users when they next log on to their computers.

You need to be familiar with the DISM syntax when servicing a Windows image, whether a computer is offline or online. Table 1-2 lists a few cmdlets to keep in mind.

TABLE 1-2 Cmdlets in the AppX module for Windows PowerShell

Cmdlet	Description
DISM.exe {/Image:<path_to_image_directory> | /Online} [dism_global_options] {servicing_option} [<servicing_argument>]	To service a Windows image with DISM
DISM.exe /Image:<path_to_image_directory> [/Get-ProvisionedAppxPackages | /Add-ProvisionedAppxPackage | /Remove-ProvisionedAppxPackage | /Set-ProvisionedAppxDataFile]	To service an app package (.appx or .appxbundle) for an offline image
DISM.exe /Online [/Get-ProvisionedAppxPackages | /Add-ProvisionedAppxPackage | /Remove-ProvisionedAppxPackage | /Set-ProvisionedAppxDataFile	To service an app package (.appx or .appxbundle) for a running operating system

Other command-line service options include /Get-ProvisionedAppxPackages, /FolderPath, /PackagePath, /LicensePath, and /Add-ProvisionedAppxPackage. Becoming familiar with these is very important because you'll likely be tested on them. You can learn about all available commands and options at *http://technet.microsoft.com/library/hh824882.aspx*. Review this article and make sure that you can make sense of commands you might come across, perhaps one that looks like:

```
Dism /Online /Add-ProvisionedAppxPackage /FolderPath:C:\Test\Apps\MyUnpackedApp /
SkipLicense
```

Or it looks like this:

```
Dism /Image:C:\test\offline /Add-ProvisionedAppxPackage /FolderPath:c:\Test\Apps\
MyUnpackedApp /CustomDataPath:c:\Test\Apps\CustomData.xml
```

Sideload apps by using Microsoft Intune

You can use Microsoft Intune to sideload apps via the cloud and make them available to any authorized, compatible device that's connected to the Internet. The following list outlines the high-level steps that you need to complete to sideload an app using Microsoft Intune.

1. Add users and create groups, if applicable.

2. Upload the app to Microsoft Intune.

3. Choose the users, groups, computers, and devices that can download the app, and link them (user-to-device).

4. For the self-service model in this example, choose how to deploy the app. It can be available, or available and required.

5. Verify that the app is available in the Windows Intune Company Store, and use the Company Store to install the app on devices.

Adding a user and groups

You can add users and groups to assist you in deploying your app to the appropriate audience. In Figure 1-7, you can see the Groups page, where new users and groups can be added to Intune. If you are adding users to a group, the group must be created before the user can be added to the group.

FIGURE 1-7 The Microsoft Intune All Groups page

Uploading an app to Microsoft Intune

You can upload an app by using the Apps page of Microsoft Intune, as shown in Figure 1-8.

FIGURE 1-8 The Microsoft Intune Apps page

To upload an app, complete the following steps:

1. Sign in to Microsoft Intune with an administrative account.
2. Click Mobile Apps and then click Apps.
3. Click Add, and then in the Add app blade, in the App type list, select the type of app. You can choose from:

    - Store app: Android, iOS, Windows Phone 8.1, and Windows
    - Office 365 Suite: Windows 10 and macOS
    - Other: Web app and line-of-business app

4. In this instance, click Line-Of-Business.
5. Click Select file, and then browse to the location of your .appx file. Select the .appx file, as shown in Figure 1-9, and then click OK.
6. Click Configure.
7. Enter a description.
8. Select a Category for the app. Choose from Business, Photos & Media, Collaboration & Social, and others.
9. If you want the app to feature in the Company Portal, next to Display this as a featured app in the Company Portal, and click Yes.
10. Click OK, and then click Add.

FIGURE 1-9 Adding an .appx package to Microsoft Intune

Once uploaded, the app will be available within the administration console to assign to users or groups (see Figure 1-10).

FIGURE 1-10 Assigning apps with the Microsoft Intune console

Choosing the users who can install the app

You can choose the users to whom the app is made available by selecting Assignments on the Mobile Apps – Apps Blade page, as shown in Figure 1-10. When you start the app deployment process, you must choose one or more groups to which the app is assigned, as shown in Figure 1-11. Having selected the group, you must also choose the Type option. Choose from Available, Not applicable, and Available with or without enrollment.

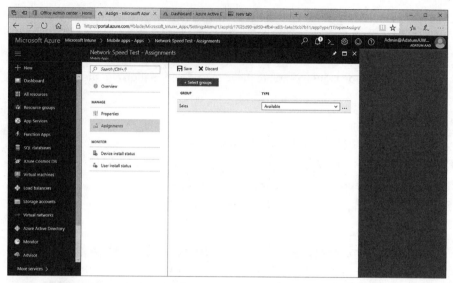

FIGURE 1-11 Choosing deployment groups

Installing the app from the Company Store

To install the app, your users will navigate to the Company Store page, and select the app from the Company Store page. To add an app to the Company Store, choose that option when configuring the app.

Deep link apps using Microsoft Intune

You can make Microsoft Store apps available to in your company portal by using Microsoft Intune or Configuration Manager. This section focuses on Microsoft Intune. The first part of the process requires you to obtain the link to the app you want to add to your company portal. To obtain the link for an app, follow these steps:

1. On Windows 10, open Microsoft Edge and navigate to the Microsoft Store website and click Software: *https://www.microsoft.com/store/apps/windows?icid=CNavAppsWindowsApps*.

2. In the search box, type the name of the app and click Search to locate the app that you want to deep link.

3. Click the app, and then, copy the URL from your web browser.

4. Paste this link to Notepad for use later.

The second part of the deep-linking process involves adding the app to Windows Intune:

1. Sign in to Microsoft Intune with an administrative account.

2. In the Microsoft Azure portal, on the Microsoft Intune blade, click Mobile apps, and then click Apps.

3. Click Add, and then in the Add app blade, in the App type list, select the type of app. Choose Store App and then click Windows.

4. Click Configure.

5. In the App information blade, complete the following information and then click OK:

    - Name and description for the app

    - Publisher

    - Paste in the Appstore URL you copied earlier

    - Category, such as Business, Photos & Media, Collaboration & Social

Click Yes to display the app as a featured app in the Company Portal.

6. Once you have configured the details of the app, click Add.

Skill 1.2: Support authentication and authorization

Users need to be authenticated to access a computer or network before they can be authorized to access the resources on it. Windows 10 supports several authentication mechanisms and methods, and different ways to manage accounts. This chapter will help you to understand the important concepts needed to support Windows 10 authentication and authorization.

This section covers how to:

- Support user authentication, including multi-factor authentication, certificates, virtual smart cards, picture passwords, and biometrics

- Support workgroup, homegroup, and domain membership, including Secure Channel, account policies, credential caching, and Credential Manager

- Know when to use a local account versus a Microsoft account

- Connect a Microsoft account to an AD DS domain account

- Configure Workplace Join

- Implement Azure AD Join

- Configure Windows Hello and Windows Hello for Business

Support user authentication

User authentication can come in many forms in Windows 10. You need to understand the various methods for authentication as well as the different mechanisms for managing and supporting authentication.

Understanding multifactor authentication

Multifactor authentication requires two (or more) types of authentication to gain access to a device or network. Most often, one type is a password, and the other is something else, such as a smart card, fingerprint, or digital certificate. This section focuses a little more on certificates as a means of achieving authentication, but this book has covered this topic in various places, and you need to review those entries when you can (for the most part, certificates have been associated with apps, because apps must be signed to ensure that they can be trusted).

A digital certificate is issued by a Certificate Authority (CA), such as Verisign or Active Directory Certificate Services (AD CS) in Windows Server 2016. The certificate can be used to provide proof that the identity asking for authentication is trusted and true, and that the identity offering it is also trusted and authentic. Authentication with certificates involves a public key and a private key that can be matched to provide that authentication. If no match occurs, no authentication is provided. You can learn more about Certificate Authorities at *http://technet. microsoft.com/library/cc732368.aspx*.

AD CS can issue and manage public key infrastructure (PKI) in a domain, provide public key cryptography and the ability to create digital certificates, and offer digital signature capabilities. For the purposes here, AD CS provides authentication by associating certificate keys with computers, users, and device accounts on a network. This is called binding.

For the exam, you might be asked how to enable users to access a network resource and be given a specific scenario. A scenario that includes AD CS will note that the network has its own PKI infrastructure. You need to understand that the required certificates must be available to the computer and the user, and they need to be stored in the proper location for authentication to be granted. Client certificates are stored in the Personal certificate store for the applicable user account on the client computer. Computer accounts need trusted root certificates to be stored in the Trusted Root Certification Authorities store, again on the client computer.

You can explore many other certificate folders as well. To view these stores on a local computer, type **certmgr.msc** in a Run dialog box, and click OK. Open this console and review the available certificate folders before moving on. Figure 1-12 shows a local computer, not connected to a domain, and the related Personal certificates. Typically, you'll see more certificates than those present in the example.

FIGURE 1-12 The Certmgr console

Understanding virtual smart cards

A virtual smart card works in the same general manner as a physical smart card does, but doesn't require a connected or installed smart card reader. Instead, the virtual smart card works with a Trusted Platform Module (TPM) chip, which protects the virtual card information through encryption, installed on the computer. As with other more advanced security options, you'll need a PKI domain infrastructure, complete with certificates and the ability to create and manage them, to incorporate this technology. Virtual smart cards offer the following:

- Authentication protection
- Confidentiality of the machine and its contents
- Private keys for security
- Encrypted card information that can't be mined or removed (that is, it can't be exported)
- Protection from rogue software that attacks at startup
- Multi-factor protection (smart card and PIN)

To use virtual smart cards, you need to meet more requirements than when you opt to use physical ones. These requirements include, but aren't limited to the following:

- Computers must be running Windows 8 or higher and Windows Server 2012 or higher.
- A compatible TPM must be installed on those computers that adhere to TPM 1.2 or higher standards.

- A limit of ten smart cards (virtual or physical) can be used on a single computer.
- The PIN and the PIN Unlock Key must be a minimum of eight characters. These can include numbers, letters, and special characters.

One very important command that you need to understand for the exam is Tpmvscmgr.exe, the command-line tool you use to configure a virtual smart card. You can use the command locally or remotely. Parameters you can use include Create and Delete. Examples include /name (the name of the smart card), /admin key (administrator key), /PIN (the PIN), /generate (to create the files in storage necessary for the card to function), and others listed at *http://technet. microsoft.com/library/dn593707.aspx*.

To configure a virtual smart card environment from scratch in a domain, you need to follow these steps:

1. Create a certificate template, a sixteen-step process performed on a Windows server in a domain that's installed with and running a CA, as outlined at: *http://technet.microsoft. com/library/dn579260.aspx#BKMK_Step1*.
2. Create the virtual TPM smart card, a four-step process that uses the Tpmvscmgr. exe command with parameters, as outlined at: *http://technet.microsoft.com/library/ dn579260.aspx#BKMK_Step2*.
3. tpmvscmgr.exe create /name tpmvsc /pin default /adminkey random /generate.
4. Enroll the certificate on the TPM virtual smart card, a six-step process, by using the Certmgr.msc console to add the certificate to the Personal store, as outlined at *http:// technet.microsoft.com/library/dn579260.aspx#BKMK_Step3*.

> **MORE INFO VIRTUAL SMART CARDS**
>
> Learn more about virtual smart cards and be sure to explore the additional links on the left side of this page at: *http://technet.microsoft.com/library/dn593708.aspx*.

To configure a Windows 10 virtual smart card on a stand-alone computer if you have the required technology and credentials available, follow these steps:

1. Open an elevated command prompt.
2. Type **tpm.msc**.
3. Verify that a compatible TPM can be found that's at least a TPM 1.2 or later. If you receive an error instead, but are sure a compatible module is available, enable it in the system BIOS before continuing.
4. Close the TPM management console.
5. At the command prompt, enter:

```
TpmVscMgr create /name MyVSC /pin default /adminkey random /generate
```

To provide a custom PIN value when creating the virtual smart card, use /pin prompt instead.

Configuring a picture password

A picture password is a way to sign in to a computer by using a series of three movements consisting of lines, circles, and/or taps. You can pick any picture you want. Picture passwords can't be used to sign in to domains; they are used to sign in to stand-alone computers only. Picture password combinations are limitless because the pictures that can be used are limitless. Although picture passwords are considered more secure for stand-alone computers than typing a PIN or password, a hacker can get into a device by holding the screen up to light to see where most of the gestures are (by following the smudges on the screen). This is especially true if the user touches the screen only to input the password and rarely uses touch for anything else.

You create a picture password (or a four-digit PIN) from the Settings app:

1. Open the Settings app, and then click Accounts.
2. Click Sign-in options.
3. Under Picture password, click Add.
4. Input your current password, and then click Select picture to browse to and select the picture to use.
5. Follow the instructions in the resulting wizard to configure the picture password.

Exploring biometrics

Biometrics, like picture passwords, provides infinite possibilities for securing a computer and can be used as part of a multifactor authentication plan (using it on its own isn't recommended). Biometric options are generally configured by incorporating a person's fingerprint and using a fingerprint reader (you "enroll" the user when configuring this), but you can also use a person's face, the retina of their eye, or even their voice.

Microsoft has made using biometrics easier than ever by including native support for biometrics through the Windows Biometric Framework (WBF), which includes an option in the Settings app for configuring the device on Windows 10 computers. Windows now also includes Group Policy settings related to biometrics, and you can enable or disable this feature as desired. You need to review the information at *http://technet.microsoft.com/library/dn344916.aspx*, and locate the available Group Policy settings, just in case. You can find Local Group Policy options here (and follow the same general path in Group Policy): Computer Configuration/ Administrative Templates/ Windows Components/ Biometrics/, as shown in Figure 1-13.

FIGURE 1-13 The Biometrics Group Policy settings

Support workgroup, homegroup, and domain membership

In this section, you'll review the differences between some similar technologies and network configurations, such as workgroup versus homegroup, workgroup versus domain, and credential caching versus Credential Manager.

Homegroups, workgroups, and domains

In almost all instances and scenarios, using a computer to complete tasks involves connecting to a network of some sort, even if it's just to access the Internet or to back up your work someplace other than your own PC. In homes, networked computers are often configured as homegroups. In a small business, the configuration is generally a workgroup. The purpose of both of these types of networks is frequently to share an Internet connection as well as files, folders, printers, and other resources. Domains are used in larger enterprises, which require more control and good protection of resource access. Domains are the only one of these three that employ AD DS to manage users, computers, and resources.

UNDERSTANDING HOMEGROUPS

A homegroup lets home users easily share documents, printers, and media with others on their private local network. This is the simplest kind of network sharing and is limited in what permissions and restrictions can be placed on the data shared. By default, all users that join a homegroup (only one per network) have read-only access to what's already shared by others.

Users can reconfigure this, however, enabling both read and write access, if desired. When opting for a homegroup, users can:

- Create or join a homegroup from the prompt offered by Windows, assuming the network is configured as Private.

- Create or join a homegroup from the Network And Sharing Center, assuming the computers that want to join are running Windows 7, Windows 8, or Windows 10. Work through the applicable homegroup wizard to create or join a homegroup. Windows generates a random password other users will need to use to join.

- Share files from their original locations and their default libraries.

- Grant read-only or read/write access to the data they've shared.

- Limit access to only those network users who also have an account and password on their computers.

- Configure the same permissions for all network users, or set different permissions for individual users.

> ***MORE INFO*** **UNABLE TO CREATE A HOMEGROUP?**
>
> Creating a homegroup requires IPv6 to be installed on all of the computers in the homegroup. Computers within a homegroup must also be within five minutes of each other's system time in order for the homegroup to function properly. If you have problems with a homegroup, check for these two potential issues.

Because you can create and join a homegroup using a wizard, detailing the steps in this text isn't really necessary. However, you need to create a homegroup on your own local network and let other computers join it, just so that you are familiar with the process. Note that users might already be joined to a homegroup because Windows detects and will prompt you to join existing homegroups automatically during setup.

Understanding workgroups

In businesses where a little more control is required and a homegroup isn't the ideal configuration, a workgroup is used. A workgroup is a manual grouping of computers (almost any operating system will do, including Windows RT) that doesn't include an Active Directory domain controller, but still offers security options. A workgroup exists on a single network segment. Securing data here is a distributed concept similar to a homegroup; each user decides what to share, how to share it, and with whom to share. Note that Windows doesn't create a password for joining the workgroup, nothing is shared automatically by default (except possibly the Public folders), and users join the workgroup from the System Properties dialog box under the Computer Name tab (see Figure 1-14). Click Change in the System Properties dialog box, and then enter the workgroup name in the Computer Name/Domain Changes dialog box.

FIGURE 1-14 The Computer Name/Domain Changes dialog box

Because this section is about authorization, you need to consider that concept with regard to a workgroup. Users decide what to share, and then share it. The person who wants access to shared items must have an account on the sharing computer (or be given one). Accounts are stored in the Security Account Manager (SAM) database in the sharing computer. Because each computer maintains its own local database, users who need to access resources on multiple workgroup computers must be authenticated on each. The problem with this is that as the network grows, so does the amount of work required to maintain and manage these accounts.

Here is an overview of how authorization works:

1. The first time a user tries to access a shared resource, he or she is asked for a user name and password.

2. The user name and password that are entered must be from an approved account on the sharing computer and must be listed in the SAM database. The user can opt to have Windows remember the password for the next time.

3. The Local Security Authority (LSA) looks to the SAM database to see whether the account that was entered is valid.

4. If the account is valid, the user is granted access.

5. The same user who wants to access another shared resource on the same computer during the same session can do so without re-entering the password.

6. If this same user wants to access a shared resource on another computer in the workgroup, the process must be repeated.

UNDERSTANDING DOMAINS

Companies and enterprises configure networks as domains. You couldn't successfully manage 100 computers by using a homegroup or workgroup, so a domain is an obvious choice for enterprise networks.

Domains are configured with at least one AD DS domain controller that authenticates users centrally and secures network resources. These larger networks can contain additional servers that manage data storage, email, faxes, and printers; maintain database replications, and so on. Managing all resources as a whole is important to keeping everything secure and available for users, and enables a simpler management solution for administrators.

A large enterprise can have more than one domain. When multiple domains exist, a Global Catalog is used to locate objects in other domains.

Authentication in a domain is handled by AD DS, a database that contains objects, such as user accounts, computers, groups, and so on. In this case, a network administrator creates user accounts, almost always puts those accounts into groups, and then assigns the desired permissions to the group. This makes managing users simpler than trying to manage users one at a time, and it enables administrators to deal with newly hired or recently fired employees.

The authentication process includes and uses the Kerberos v5 authentication protocol to identify the user or the host. The Kerberos Key Distribution Center (KDC) uses the domain-specific AD DS as its security account database. AD DS is required for default Kerberos implementations within the domain or forest. If you aren't familiar with Kerberos v5, the TechNet article "Kerberos Authentication Overview" at *http://technet.microsoft.com/library/hh831553.aspx* provides a good explanation of how this works and offers links to additional resources.

UNDERSTANDING COMPUTER AND USER AUTHENTICATION

The previous section discusses AD DS and authentication with regard to user accounts. Network administrators create these accounts, users input their account credentials to log on to the domain, and authentication is handled by the applicable AD DS server and Kerberos v5. Computers that join domains acquire a computer account automatically. Like user accounts, computer accounts are used to authenticate the computer to enable it to access network and domain resources. Each computer account must be unique. A user doesn't have to do anything to cause the computer to be authenticated. Note that computers have passwords that are automatically managed, and if a computer password on a client is out of sync with AD DS, then the computer can't authenticate.

Computer accounts are necessary for auditing, for control, and for grouping purposes. You can apply changes to computer accounts that affect whoever logs on to the computer, and not the individual users. For instance, you can force policies regarding the desktop appearance, how updates are applied, and so on, and those policies will affect the computer and anyone who uses it.

Administrators can manage computer accounts in the same way they can user accounts— by adding, deleting, resetting, and disabling them in the Active Directory Users And Computers snap-in.

UNDERSTANDING SECURE CHANNEL

When applications need network or Internet access, you have to ensure that the connection is secure. This is especially true if you are transmitting data over an untrusted network. You can use Transport Layer Security (TLS)/Secure Sockets Layer (SSL) security to authenticate servers and client computers, and then use that to encrypt messages between them. These two protocols are included in the Secure Channel set of security protocols. TLS and SSL aren't interchangeable and SSL is the predecessor to TLS, but both protect against tampering and eavesdropping.

Secure Channel can authenticate an identity as well as provide a secure and private connection to another host by using encryption. It's also called Schannel and is mostly used for applications that require secure HTTP communications. Schannel is a Security Support Provider (SSP), and the TLS/SSL protocol uses a client/server model that's based on certificate authentication. This means you need to also have a PKI configured and available.

> **MORE INFO** **DISCOVERING SECURE CHANNEL**
>
> You can learn more about this feature on TechNet at: *http://technet.microsoft.com/library/hh831381.aspx*.

EXPLORING ACCOUNT POLICIES

The weakest link when protecting computers that use a password as part of the authentication process is most often the password itself. The password could be nonexistent (not likely, especially with the advent of the Microsoft account for stand-alone computers), too short, too simple, too predictable, or the user might simply never change it. Often, users create and use the same password for multiple user IDs. This is a secondary weak link. To protect authentication in both workgroups and domains, you can create local policies and Group Policy Objects (GPOs) defining how passwords should be created, how often they can or must be changed, and what happens when a user fails to log on after attempting a specific number of times that you set. You can configure account policies in the Local Security Policy for a stand-alone computer or for computers in a workgroup, and in Group Policy for domains. In Local Security Policy, Account Policies is listed first. Click Account Policies, and then click Account Lockout Policy to see the options.

You can configure three account lockout policies, and in most instances they must be configured together:

- **Account Lockout Duration** If you've configured an account lockout threshold and if that threshold is met, this setting defines how long (in minutes) the user will be locked out of the computer. A setting of 5 to 15 minutes is common.
- **Account Lockout Threshold** You need to configure this to use the other options. This setting defines how many times a user can try to log on to the computer and fail, before being locked out.

- **Reset Account Counter After** This setting defines the number of minutes that must pass after a failed logon attempt before the failed logon attempt counter is reset to zero. If an account lockout threshold is defined, this must be less than or equal to the number of minutes set there.

EXPLORING CREDENTIAL MANAGER

Using user names and passwords is a common way to authenticate users. Windows 10 includes Credential Manager to help manage and maintain those passwords. Credential Manager saves the credentials that users enter when they use their own computers to access network servers and resources on local networks (Windows credentials), and can be used to back up and restore them. When prompted, users have to check the box Remember My Credentials, or else the credentials won't be saved. Credential Manager also offers Credential Locker, which saves user names and passwords associated with websites and Windows apps (Web Credentials). It saves all of these in an area called the Windows Vault.

> *NOTE* **SAVING CREDENTIALS**
>
> Credentials are saved in encrypted folders on the computer under the user's profile. Applications that support this feature, such as web browsers and Windows apps, can automatically offer up the correct credentials to other computers and websites during the sign-in process.

If the user name or password has been changed since the last time it was saved and access is unsuccessful, the user is prompted to type the new credentials. When access to the resource or website is successful, Credential Manager and Credential Locker overwrite what was there.

The saved user names and passwords follow users when they move from one computer to another in a workgroup or homegroup, presuming they log on with their Microsoft accounts. However, this feature isn't enabled on domains for security reasons. You can open Credential Manager from Control Panel. Figure 1-15 shows Credential Manager.

Here are a few more points to understand about Credential Manager:

- You can program Microsoft Store apps to use Credential Locker.
- Credential roaming requires the Microsoft account for synchronization.
- Credential roaming is enabled by default on non-domain joined computers, and it is disabled on domain-joined computers.
- Credential Locker supports seamless sign in by using Microsoft Store apps that use Web Authentication Broker and remember passwords for services, such as Twitter and LinkedIn.

FIGURE 1-15 Credential Manager

Configure local accounts and Microsoft accounts

The Microsoft account enables users to sync settings to the cloud and to other computers that they log on to using that same Microsoft account. With a Microsoft account, users can also access their own cloud storage, called OneDrive. Windows 10 comes with the OneDrive app, which can be accessed from compatible applications, various web browsers, and File Explorer.

Users are prompted to create a Microsoft account when they set up their Windows 10-based computers. They can opt to do that, or they can decline and create a local account instead. A user might also create a local account if the computer can't access the Internet during setup (because they can't create or confirm the Microsoft account if no Internet access is available). Users generally opt to create a Microsoft account later, even if they start with a local account, because many apps are inaccessible if the user is logged on with a local account. Users also can't get apps from the Store without a Microsoft account.

After a Microsoft account is created, users don't need to be connected to the Internet to log on during subsequent sessions. The account information is cached locally. If an Internet connection isn't available, the last saved settings are also applied because they are also cached locally. You can switch from a local account to a Microsoft account from the Settings app.

A Microsoft account can be used in a domain, if it isn't restricted through Group Policy. If possible at your place of business, when connected, users will see the same desktop background, app settings, browser history, and so on that they see on their main computers at home (or in another office). Again, you can make the change through the Settings app. There, you'll opt to connect your Microsoft account and work through the setup process.

Configure Workplace Join

Personal devices have become part of the enterprise landscape, and if you don't already, at some point you need to be able to enable users to access network resources from them. This is how Workplace Join came about. Workplace Join enables users to have a SSO experience and enables them to get to the resources they need. You can also manage and secure the devices. In Windows Server 2016, you can use Workplace Join with Windows 8.1, Windows 10, and iOS devices.

Workplace Join uses the Device Registration Service (DRS), part of the Active Directory Federation Services (ADFS) role in Windows Server 2016, to create a device object in AD DS and use a certificate to identify the device in the future. If you add Web Application Proxy, users can join your enterprise from any Internet-enabled location.

To enable Workplace Join in Azure AD, use the following procedure:

1. In the Azure AD Admin Center, in the navigation pane, click Azure Active Directory.
2. In the Azure Active Directory blade, click Devices.
3. Click Device settings.
4. Next to Users may register their devices with Azure AD, click All and then click Save.

Because enrollment with Microsoft Intune or Mobile Device Management in Office 365 requires Device Registration, if you have configured either of these services, the option for Users may register their devices with Azure AD will already be selected as All. You are also unable to deselect it.

Configure Azure AD Join

Azure Active Directory (Azure AD) is a cloud-based authentication and authorization platform. It enables your users to enjoy the benefits of single sign-on (SSO) for cloud-based applications, such as Office 365. Users can easily join their devices to your organization's Azure AD once you have enabled device joining in the Azure admin Center.

When joining devices to an AD DS domain in an on-premises environment, the types of device that you can join to the domain are quite restrictive; devices, for example, must be running a supported operating system. This means that users that have devices running Windows 10 Home editions cannot join the company's AD DS domain. However, Azure AD is less restrictive in this respect; you can add almost any tablet, laptop, and desktop computer running a variety of operating systems to Azure AD. Bear in mind when you enable users to add their devices to Azure AD, you cannot manage their enrolled devices by using AD DS Group Policies. Instead, you must use Microsoft Intune to manage and provision your users' devices.

To enable device registration in Azure AD, in the Azure AD admin Center, use the following procedure:

1. In the navigation pane, click Azure Active Directory.
2. In the Azure Active Directory blade, click Devices.

3. Click Device Settings.

4. In the details pane, next to Users may join devices to Azure AD, click either All or else click Selected, as shown in Figure 1-16. If you choose selected, then click the Selected link and choose those users that can join Azure AD. You can select both individual users and groups of users.

5. Click Save.

FIGURE 1-16 Enabling Azure AD join

After you have enabled Azure AD join, you can let your users add their devices. To do this, they must use the following procedure:

1. Open Settings and select System.

2. In the System window, click About.

3. Click Connect to work or school.

4. On the Access work or school page, click Connect.

5. In the Microsoft Account dialog box, click Join this device to Azure Active Directory.

6. In the Let's Get You Signed In dialog box, enter a valid Azure AD user name and click Next. This user must have permissions to join Azure AD.

7. Enter the Azure AD user's password, and then click Sign in.

8. In the Make sure this is your organization dialog box, shown in Figure 1-17, click Join and then click Done.

9. Click Start and click the current user (above the Settings icon). Click Switch Account.

10. Click Other user, and then sign in as the Azure AD user.

11. Depending on organizational settings, your users might be prompted to setup Windows Hello. By default, they will be prompted to setup a PIN. When prompted to setup a PIN, click Set Up PIN.

12. Click Set It Up Now.

13. In the Verify Your Identity dialog box, in the Pick A Verification method list, users can choose a number of methods, including text message. Click Text message and then enter your mobile or cell phone number. Click Next.

14. After receiving the code on your phone, enter it into the Enter Security code box, and then click Next.

15. In the Set Up A PIN dialog box, enter a six digit (by default) PIN in both text boxes and then click OK.

16. Click OK. At this point, the sign on process will complete and you should be presented with the Windows 10 desktop interface.

FIGURE 1-17 Joining Azure AD on Windows 10

In the Azure AD Admin center, you can view joined devices, as shown in Figure 1-18. Use the following procedure:

1. In the Azure AD admin center, click Azure Active Directory.

2. Click Devices, and then click All devices.

FIGURE 1-18 Viewing All devices in Azure AD

Configure Windows Hello

Windows Hello enables your users to sign in by using a biometric authentication system, such as facial recognition or fingerprints. Windows Hello for Business extends this to use a multi-factor authentication to sign in to Windows 10. Users can use a PIN or biometric sign-in system to sign in to a Windows 10 computer. This enables users to authenticate to apps, enterprise content, and online authentication providers.

> **NOTE** **WINDOWS HELLO**
>
> When Windows 10 first shipped, it included two separate authentication technologies: Microsoft Passport and Windows Hello. These two technologies worked together to provide multi-factor authentication. With Windows 10 Creators Update, Microsoft has combined these two technologies under the Windows Hello name.

Windows Hello is designed to be a user-friendly interface for configuring biometric authentication in Windows 10. You can configure Windows Hello from the Settings app, in the Sign-in Options section of the Accounts page. Note that the use of Windows Hello is device-centric, meaning that each of the user's devices might employ a different Windows Hello authentication mechanism, and a different PIN.

> **MORE INFO** **WINDOWS HELLO FOR BUSINESS**
>
> You can learn more about Windows Hello for Business at: *https://docs.microsoft.com/en-gb/windows/access-protection/hello-for-business/hello-identity-verification*.

Thought experiments

In these thought experiments, demonstrate your skills and knowledge of the topics covered in this chapter. You can find the answers to these thought experiments in the next section.

Scenario 1

You manage a small business that has seven employees, and each employee has multiple devices that they use to perform work. You don't have an Active Directory domain. Sometimes the users are at the company, sometimes at home, and often in a hotel. Users don't always have Internet access.

Users complain that they can't always access their work documents and that when they use Microsoft Office on their devices, they get a different user experience on all of them. Their settings and preferences need to be reset repeatedly for each device as they change them. You want to resolve these problems (and others, including mandating Microsoft Office updates), but you don't have a lot of money to spend.

1. What should you set up to resolve all these issues, all without incurring a substantial expense?

2. Where would you store the users' data?

3. If you want to delegate some of the responsibilities for managing your solution, what types of administrator would you create to manage support tickets?

Scenario 2

You've been asked to create and configure a multi-factor authentication solution that can be used to validate users in an enterprise domain. You've also been instructed to include digital certificates in that solution. Your client doesn't want to rely on a third party CA, and instead wants to use the Active Directory Certificate Services (AD CS) in Windows Server 2016. Answer the following questions regarding this task.

1. The network currently doesn't include a PKI infrastructure. Will you need to add it?

2. Where will the client certificates you create be stored?

3. Where will the trusted root certificates you create be stored?

4. What command can you run, from a Run dialog box, on a client computer to view the certificates stored on that machine?

Thought experiment answers

This section provides the solutions for the tasks included in the thought experiment.

Scenario 1

1. Office 365
2. Most likely using the cloud, with options that enable the user to sync that data even when they aren't online
3. Billing; Global; Password; Service; User Management

Scenario 2

1. Yes, AC CS in Windows Server 2012 requires an existing PKI infrastructure
2. Client certificates are stored in the Personal certificate store for the applicable user account on the client computer
3. Trusted root certificates are stored in the Trusted Root Certification Authorities store on the client computer
4. Certmgr.msc can be used to open the Certmgr window

Chapter summary

- You can integrate users' Microsoft accounts into your organization to enable synchronization of settings between multiple devices.
- You can manage apps by using Office 365, DISM, and Microsoft Intune.
- You can configure Group Policy to manage apps, manage access to the Microsoft Store, and enable sideloading.
- You can sideload apps to enable LOB apps without making them available through the Microsoft Store.
- Multi-factor authentication lets you further secure the authentication process with certificates, virtual smart cards, picture passwords, and biometrics, by requiring more than one method of authentication before access is granted.
- Different networks exist for different needs. Homegroups enable simple sharing for home networks; workgroups let you share and manage shared data in a non-domain setting; and domains are used by larger enterprises and include Active Directory Domain Services (AD DS) to secure and manage authentication.
- You can further secure authentication by including Secure Channel, account policies, credential caching, and Credential Manager to help control access and manage logon credentials.

- Local accounts are good for homegroups and workgroups, but now even those networks rely on Microsoft accounts for authorization management. Microsoft accounts can also be incorporated into domains to sync settings, such as desktop backgrounds.

- Workplace Join enables you to enroll and control mobile devices on your domain for the purpose of letting your users bring their own devices to work.

- Windows Hello enables configuration of facial and fingerprint recognition for use with the Windows 10 authentication process.

CHAPTER 2

Plan desktop and device deployment

When deploying Windows 10 devices, it is important to consider who will be using the devices, how the devices will be used, and in what ways you can configure those devices to ensure that you provide users with a functional, flexible, and secure Windows environment. This chapter deals with several aspects of configuring Windows 10 in preparation for deployment to devices serving a variety of roles in the enterprise.

Skills in this chapter:

- Skill 2.1: Migrate and configure user data
- Skill 2.2: Configure Hyper-V
- Skill 2.3: Configure mobility options
- Skill 2.4: Configure security for mobile devices

Skill 2.1: Migrate and configure user data

User data is an important consideration when supporting Windows computers, especially when planning to upgrade or migrate to a new version of Windows. This section covers important topics relating to user profiles, the primary location for user data in Windows 10. You will see the tools and considerations relating to migrating and configuring user data, which you need to be aware of for the exam.

> **This section covers how to:**
> - Configure user profiles
> - Configure folder location
> - Migrate user profiles

Configure user profiles

User profiles hold the majority of user-configurable settings and data in Windows 10. Each user that signs in to a Windows 10 computer is associated with a file-level profile folder, stored by default in the C:\Users folder. This is the default location for user profiles in Windows 10, for all users who sign in, including local and domain accounts. A user profile is automatically created and configured for each user that signs in to a Windows 10 computer.

There are three main profile types in Windows 10: local profiles, roaming profiles, and mandatory profiles.

Local profiles

Local profiles are stored in the C:\Users\%USERNAME% directory on a Windows 10 computer. For example, a user with the username Adam would have his profile stored in the C:\Users\ Adam folder. A local profile is the default profile type in Windows 10, and the data for the profile is located in several files and folders within the C:\Users\%USERNAME% folder, as shown in Figure 2-1. This figure also shows the hidden system files in the folder. These files will not be visible unless the Show Hidden Files option is selected in File Explorer.

FIGURE 2-1 The contents of a user-profile folder

The local profile is defined by a combination of the contents of the folders within a user profile (such as AppData, Documents, Local Settings, and Start Menu) and the NTUSER.DAT file. NTUSER.DAT contains registry settings that pertain to the user. When a user signs out, the HKEY_CURRENT_USER registry hive is saved to NTUSER.DAT, and then applied to the Windows 10 environment the next time the user signs in.

Roaming profiles

While a local profile is available only on the local computer that a user is signed in to, a roaming profile is also stored in a network location. To use roaming profiles, your environment needs to first satisfy specific requirements:

- The Windows 10 computer must be a member of an Active Directory Domain Services (AD DS) domain.
- The user signing in must have a user account object created in the domain.
- The user account must have the Profile path attribute set to a network location to which the user has Read and Write permissions granted.

You can configure a roaming profile for a domain user account in Active Directory Users And Computers, from the Profile tab in the Administrator Properties dialog box, as shown in Figure 2-2.

FIGURE 2-2 Configuring a roaming profile

NOTE **ENVIRONMENT VARIABLES**

In Figure 2-2, the environment variable %USERNAME% is used in place of the user account name. Using this variable inserts the user name for the currently signed in user. Using environment variables can be useful when configuring roaming profiles for multiple user accounts.

When a user account is configured with roaming-profile settings, the local profile is copied to the specified network location when the user signs out. When the user signs in to a computer, the profile is copied from the network location to the local-profile folder.

EXAM TIP

You can also modify domain users, including changing user profile path, with Windows PowerShell. The exam might contain questions about automating profile changes or changing user account properties for multiple users. Windows PowerShell works very well for this. You can read more about using the Set-ADUser cmdlet to modify user accounts at: *https://technet.microsoft.com/en-us/library/hh852287(v=wps.630).aspx*.

Mandatory profiles

A mandatory profile is a special type of roaming profile. Mandatory profiles are copied to a network location, like roaming profiles. However, mandatory profiles are always read-only, which means a mandatory profile cannot be altered by the user. If a user makes changes to the Windows environment when using a mandatory profile, none of the changes are copied to the network location of the profile, so the user will not see those changes reflected in the Windows environment when they next sign in to a Windows computer.

Mandatory profiles are commonly used to provide enforced environment settings for users who perform a specific or specialized task and are set when he or she is signed in to a Windows computer. You can create a mandatory profile by renaming the NTUSER.DAT file in a roaming profile to Ntuser.man. Any time the user signs in after this change has been made, they'll use the mandatory profile.

MORE INFO USER PROFILES

For more information about user profiles, visit: *https://msdn.microsoft.com/en-us/library/windows/desktop/bb776892(v=vs.85).aspx*.

Configure folder location

Although you can use roaming profiles to store user-profile contents in a network location, the entire profile must be copied to and from the network location. You can also configure network locations for specific folders within a user profile. When using an alternate folder location that is stored on the network, all of the files in the folder are not stored locally, but in the network location, by default. Mobile users will have offline versions of the folders available as locally cached files, in case they are disconnected from the network. Changes to files within folders that are redirected to the network are synchronized with the local cache on a file-by-file basis, rather than the entire profile being copied, as happens with roaming profiles.

You can configure folder location in Windows 10, as shown in Figure 2-3, by performing the following steps:

1. Open File Explorer and expand This PC.
2. On any of the folders except Local Disk, right-click the folder and then click Properties. For example, right-click Documents and then click Properties.
3. In the Documents Properties dialog box, click the Location tab, and change the location by performing either of the following steps:
   - Typing a new file location
   - Clicking Move, browsing to the new location, and clicking Select Folder

FIGURE 2-3 Configuring folder location

Migrate user profiles

When upgrading Windows, or moving a user to another computer, user profiles are often the first consideration in the migration process. Migrating user profiles can be a simple process when there's a single user on a single computer, or it can be complicated, involving many users and computers in an enterprise environment.

Use the User State Migration Tool

The User State Migration Tool (USMT) is a collection of command-line tools that enable you to automate and customize the process of migrating user profiles. The USMT can copy user-profile information to a migration store location, from where it can be retrieved and copied to new computers.

You use the USMT to migrate user profiles between Windows computers. The USMT is part of the Windows 10 Assessment and Deployment Toolkit (Windows ADK).

NOTE **USE THE CORRECT VERSION OF WINDOWS ADK**

For each version of Windows 10, there is a corresponding version of the Windows ADK. You must ensure that you download the version of Windows ADK that corresponds to the version of Windows 10 in use within your organization. This book was developed for Windows 10 Version 1703. To check your Windows build, open a command prompt and run winver.exe. A dialog box displays your build number. You can download the Windows 10 ADK, including USMT, from the following URL: *https://msdn.microsoft.com/en-us/windows/hardware/dn913721(v=vs8.5).aspx#winADK*.

MORE INFO **WINDOWS ADK**

For more information about the Windows ADK and the tools it contains, go to: *https://docs.microsoft.com/en-us/windows/deployment/windows-deployment-scenarios-and-tools#sec06l*.

The USMT contains three command line tools:

- **ScanState.exe** Use this tool to scan and copy user-profile data to a migration store for the purpose of copying the profile to new computers.
- **LoadState.exe** Use this tool to locate and copy user-profile data from a migration store to new Windows computers.
- **UsmtUtils.exe** Use this tool to check a migration store for corruption, manage migration stores, and manage encryption during the migration process.

The USMT also includes the following three modifiable .xml files:

- **MigApp.xml** This file includes instructions to migrate supplication settings.
- **MigDocs.xml** This file is used to specify the files and folders that will be migrated by USMT.
- **MigUser.xml** This file includes instructions to migrate user files based on name extensions.

The other file typically used by USMT, but not included with the default USMT files is Config.xml. You can generate Config.xml by using the /genconfig switch with ScanState.exe. Config.xml enables you to specify certain items that are not included in the migration processes of ScanState.exe and LoadState.exe.

USMT AND WINDOWS PE

The USMT command-line tools can be run as an online migration, within Windows, or from Windows Preinstallation Environment (Windows PE), as an offline migration. Windows PE provides a minimal version of Windows that can be used for several tasks on a Windows computer, including deployment and troubleshooting. You can use the Windows 10 installation media to run Windows PE, or you can create a standalone copy of Windows PE to run from bootable media, such as a DVD, removable hard drive, or USB flash drive.

> **MORE INFO** **UNDERSTANDING WINDOWS PE**
>
> For more information about Windows PE, such as benefits, scenarios for use, and limitations, visit: *https://technet.microsoft.com/en-us/library/cc766093(v=ws.10).aspx*.

MIGRATING USER PROFILES WITH USMT

When you're prepared to perform the migration process with USMT, you need to perform the following high-level steps:

1. Install the Windows ADK on a technician computer.

2. Use ScanState.exe to generate Config.xml, if required.

3. Modify Config.xml, MigApp.xml, MigDocs.xml, and MigUser.xml to customize the migration environment, if necessary.

4. Copy the USMT files to a network share or removable drive.

5. Create a folder on a network share or removable drive that can be used as a migration store.

6. On the source computers, run ScanState.exe from the network share or removable drive to collect files and settings,

7. Install Windows 10 on the destination computers that will be part of the migration.

8. On the destination computers, run LoadState.exe from the network drive or removable drive to apply the files and settings in the migration store.

This process is commonly run as part of a Windows PowerShell or startup script to migrate profiles on multiple computers or across an enterprise.

> **EXAM TIP**
>
> While you won't be asked to construct command-line arguments for ScanState.exe or Load-State.exe, you might be asked on the test to choose a command that exhibits proper syntax. To understand the syntax for the USMT commands thoroughly, study the USMT technical reference at: *https://technet.microsoft.com/en-us/library/mt299211(v=vs.85).aspx*.

Skill 2.2: Configure Hyper-V

In Windows 10, Hyper-V provides a virtualization platform that enables you to run virtual machines hosted on a Windows 10 computer. These virtual machines run on the same platform as Hyper-V in Windows Server products, which makes Windows 10 a capable environment for building and testing virtual machines destined for the production virtualization environment. This chapter will familiarize you with the primary functionality and components of Hyper-V.

Create and configure virtual machines

Prior to creating virtual machines, you must ensure that your Windows 10 computer supports Hyper-V and that the Hyper-V feature is installed. To support Hyper-V, your Windows 10 computer must meet the following minimum requirements:

- Windows 10 Professional, Enterprise or Education 64-bit edition
- A processor that supports Second Level Address Translation (SLAT)
- 4 GB of RAM
- BIOS or UEFI-level hardware virtual support

Enabling the Hyper-V feature

To enable the Hyper-V feature, open Programs And Features in Control Panel and click Turn Windows Features On Or Off. In the Windows Features dialog box, expand Hyper-V and select all of the check boxes under the Hyper-V node, as shown in Figure 2-4.

FIGURE 2-4 Enabling the Hyper-V feature

Creating a virtual machine

Hyper-V Manager, shown in Figure 2-5, is the GUI tool that you use to perform Hyper-V configuration tasks.

FIGURE 2-5 The Hyper-V Manager console

To create a virtual machine, perform the following steps:

1. In Hyper-V Manager, on the Action menu, point to New, and then click Virtual Machine.

2. Click Next to start the creation process.

3. Specify the name and location of the new virtual machine. It's best, for now, to keep the default location, so click Next.

4. Choose the Generation option that best suits your needs and click Next:

   - Generation 1 supports the same virtual hardware that the previous version of Hyper-V did. You can use it on operating systems including Windows Server 2008 and Windows 7, among others.

- Generation 2 supports Secure Boot, SCSI boot, and PXE boot using a standard network adapter. Guest operating systems must run at least Windows Server 2012 or a 64-bit version of Windows 8 or later.

5. Enter the amount of startup memory required and choose whether to use dynamic memory for this machine. Click Next.

6. On the Configure Networking page, click Next. You'll only see options here if you've previously created Network Switch settings.

7. Verify that the Create A Virtual Hard Disk option is selected and that the settings are correct. Click Next.

8. For our example here, leave Install An Operating System Later selected and click Next (you could opt to install an operating system now, though).

9. Click Finish (note the new virtual machine in the bottom pane of the Hyper-V Manager).

10. Leave the Hyper-V Manager open.

Configuring a virtual machine

There are several configuration tasks that you can perform on a virtual machine, including the following:

- Change memory and processor settings. The virtual machine must be in a Stopped state to perform either of these on a Generation 1 virtual machine, but memory settings can be modified on a Generation 2 virtual machine while the virtual machine is running.
- Attach or detach virtual hard disk (VHD) files.
- Change network adapter settings.
- Attach virtual DVD or floppy-disk media.

To configure a virtual machine, right-click the virtual machine in Hyper-V Manager, and then click Settings. In the GUI, all settings can be configured in the Settings for Windows dialog box, as shown in Figure 2-6.

FIGURE 2-6 The Settings For dialog box

> **NOTE** **EXPLORING VIRTUAL MACHINE SETTINGS**
>
> It is important that you take the time to explore all of the options in the Settings For dialog box, as shown in Figure 2-6.

Configuring virtual machines by using Windows PowerShell

Windows 10 contains a full set of Windows PowerShell cmdlets that you can use to configure your virtual machine. Windows PowerShell can help to ease administrative effort when performing repetitive configuration tasks or configuration tasks that need to be performed on multiple VMs.

> **NOTE** **HYPER-V CMDLETS IN WINDOWS POWERSHELL**
>
> For a complete list of cmdlets that you can use to configure Hyper-V, visit: *https://technet.microsoft.com/en-us/library/hh848559(v=wps.630).aspx.*

WINDOWS POWERSHELL DIRECT

Windows PowerShell Direct is a new Hyper-V feature in Windows 10. Windows PowerShell Direct enables you to run PowerShell commands remotely on a Windows Hyper-V virtual machine without starting an active Hyper-V console session on the host computer.

The way Windows PowerShell Direct works is similar to Windows PowerShell remoting, except that with Windows PowerShell Direct, you can specify the name of a virtual machine being hosted on the computer rather than on a remote network computer. For example, both of the following commands enable you to run Windows PowerShell cmdlets on a virtual machine:

```
Enter-PSSession -VMName VMName
```

```
Invoke-Command -VMName VMName -ScriptBlock { commands }
```

Create and manage checkpoints

Checkpoints are used to save the state of a virtual machine. A checkpoint includes all of the contents on the hard disk, along with virtual machine configuration settings. If you need to return a virtual machine to a configuration that existed at a previous point in time, you can restore a checkpoint if one has been made. You create checkpoints manually, either through Hyper-V Manager or by using the Checkpoint-VM cmdlet for Windows PowerShell.

CREATE A CHECKPOINT

To create a checkpoint, perform the following steps:

1. In Hyper-V Manager, right-click the VM for which you want to create a checkpoint.

2. In the menu, click Checkpoint.

3. The new checkpoint will appear in the Checkpoints pane, as shown in Figure 2-7.

FIGURE 2-7 A list of checkpoints for a virtual machine in Hyper-V Manager

RESTORE A CHECKPOINT

To restore a checkpoint for a virtual machine, right-click the checkpoint that you want to restore, and then click Apply. After the checkpoint is applied, the virtual machine returns to the state it was in when the checkpoint was taken.

> **NOTE DIFFERENCING DISKS**
>
> A differencing disk is a virtual hard disk (VHD) you create to quarantine changes you've made to a VHD or the guest operating system. You store these changes in a separate file. The differencing disk is associated with another VHD (that already exists) and can be any kind of virtual disk. You choose the disk when you create the differencing disk. This VHD is called the parent disk, and the differencing disk is the child disk.

Create and configure virtual switches

Virtual switches enable you to control how your virtual machines are connected to each other, the host computer, and the rest of your network.

There are three types of virtual switches in Hyper-V:

- **External** Allows the VM to connect to a physical NIC on the computer to communicate with the external network, in the same logical way that the host computer is connected to the network

- **Internal** Allows the VM to communicate with the host computer and other virtual machines connected to the same switch

- **Private** Enables the virtual machine to communicate only with other virtual machines connected to the same switch

> **EXAM TIP**
>
> It is very likely that you'll be asked a question on the exam about the three different types of virtual switches. You need to ensure you understand the functionality of each virtual switch type.

To create a virtual switch, perform the following steps:

1. In the Hyper-V Manager, click Action, and then click Virtual Switch Manager, shown in Figure 2-8.

2. In the Virtual Switch Manager For window, select the type of switch to create (you can select External here, if you're performing these steps).

3. Click Create Virtual Switch.

4. From the drop-down list under What Do You Want To Connect This Virtual Switch To, select the external network to use, if applicable. For now, you need to select an Ethernet-based solution. You can also enable virtual local area network (VLAN) identification if the network switch is going to be used with a specific VLAN.

5. Click OK.

6. If prompted, click Yes to apply the changes.

After you have created the switch, you can test it. If you created an external switch, for example, you can test connectivity to the Internet easily. You can also open the Virtual Switch Manager from the Action pane displayed on the right in the Hyper-V Manager console and rename the new switch.

FIGURE 2-8 The Virtual Switch Manager

Create and configure virtual disks

Virtual machines need VHDs to function. VHDs are files that you can transport on a USB flash drive. These files are in the format of either VHD or VHDX. VHDs reside on the host computer and contain either an operating system or data that is used by the virtual machines. You can boot to a VHD if the host is running Windows 7 or later.

There are two main differences between the two types of VHD formats:

- VHD can be as large as 2048 GB (about 2 TB). You use this format when you know you'll be running the VHD on older operating systems, specifically anything before Windows Server 2012 and Windows 8.

- VHDX can be much larger, up to 64 TB. It is not compatible with versions of Hyper-V or operating systems created before Windows Server 2012 or Windows 8. You use this format when you know you'll be using the VHD on compatible machines. VHDX also provides the following benefits:

  - Protection against data corruption when there is a power failure (because updates are logged effectively)

  - Improved performance on large-sector disks

  - Larger block sizes for dynamic and differencing disks to enhance performance

  - Custom metadata that can be used to record information about the file, such as operating system version, among other things

  - The use of "trim" technology to reduce file size and to access and use free disk space ("trim" requires disks to be directly attached to the VM, and hardware must be compatible)

To create a VHD from the Hyper-V Manager, perform the following steps:

1. In the Action pane, click New, and then click Hard Disk.

2. Select the file type format to use (VHD or VHDX), the Size (Fixed, Dynamically Expanding, or Differencing), Name, and Location, and then opt how to configure the disk. If you want to apply the VM you created in this section, in the Name box you'll need to type the name of the VM to use. When prompted, create a new blank VHD.

3. You can now attach the hard disk to a VM, export it, import it, inspect it, or perform other administrative tasks, as necessary.

Move virtual machine storage

The easiest way to move a VM is to shut it down, export it to the new disk, and then import it to the new location. You might need to export a VM from your production environment, open it somewhere else (perhaps on your desktop with Client Hyper-V), perform any required troubleshooting, and then export it back to the production environment.

To move a virtual machine, follow these steps:

1. In the Hyper-V Manager Wizard, right-click the VM to move and click Shut Down. Click Shut Down again to verify.

2. Wait until the state of the VM shows Off. Then right-click the VM and click Export.

3. Specify where to save the file or click Browse to choose a location. If you receive an Error message, save to a different location or create a subfolder.

4. Click Export.

5. If desired, open the folder that contains the exported VM and note the subfolders: Snapshots, Virtual Hard Disks, and Virtual Machines.

When you import the VM, you work through a similar wizard that prompts you to browse to the VM, select the VM, and provide other necessary details. Once you've specified these details, you are prompted to select an Import Type. The three options are described here:

- **Register The Virtual Machine In-Place (Use The Existing Unique ID For The VM)** If you only need to start using the VM where it is currently stored and you don't want to move it or copy it, choose this option.

- **Restore The Virtual Machine (Use The Existing Unique ID For The VM)** If your VM files are stored on a file share, a removable drive, a network drive, and so on, and you want to move the files, choose this option.

- **Copy The Virtual Machine (Create A New Unique ID For The VM)** If you have a folder of VM files that you want to import multiple times (perhaps you are using them as a template for new VMs), choose this option and copy the files.

To import a VM, perform the following steps:

1. Open Hyper-V on the target computer.
2. In the Actions pane, click Import Virtual Machine.
3. Click Next on the Import Virtual Machine Wizard.
4. Click Browse to locate the top-level folder associated with the export process, and then click Next.
5. Select the VM to import, and then click Next.
6. Read the options available to you and choose how to register the VM. (Here we restore the VM and use the existing unique ID.) Click Next.
7. Accept the default store folder for the VM files, and click Next. If you receive an error message, create a new folder inside the default store to hold the files.
8. Accept the default store folder for the VHDs, and click Next. If you receive an Error message, create a new folder inside the default store to hold the VHD.
9. Click Finish.

Skill 2.3: Configure mobility options

Many Windows 10 computers, such as laptops and tablets will not remain stationary in an office, but be used as mobile devices, moving from location to location. You need to understand the considerations for mobile devices pertaining to power and battery configuration, file synchronization, and network connectivity. This chapter will show you how to configure mobility options in Windows 10.

This section covers how to:

- Configure offline file policies
- Configure sync options
- Configure power policies
- Configure Windows To Go
- Configure Wi-Fi Direct

Configure offline file policies

Remote connectivity for mobile devices has become increasingly more common through virtual private network (VPN) and DirectAccess, in conjunction with Wi-Fi and mobile broadband network connectivity. In a remote connectivity situation, users can connect to network file servers when they are away from the office. However, there are instances when no connection can be made, and users still need access to their files. You can allow offline access for your Windows 10 users by configuring Offline Files and then creating policies to manage it.

When the Offline Files feature is enabled, specified network files are cached locally for offline access when the device isn't connected to the corporate network. A Windows 10 computer will access the local cache in the following scenarios:

- The Always Offline Mode has been enabled. This feature provides faster access to files and uses less bandwidth by letting the user always work offline, even when a connection is available.

- Cost-Aware Synchronization is configured and enabled. This helps users avoid high data-usage costs from synchronization while using metered connections that have usage limits or while roaming on a different network.

- The server is unavailable due to a network outage or server malfunction, or the network connection is slower than a threshold you've configured, and thus working offline could be more efficient for the user.

- The user manually switches to Offline Mode (perhaps to optimize bandwidth usage on a metered connection) by clicking the Work Offline button in File Explorer.

EXAM TIP

To synchronize a Windows 10 computer with a network folder, you can browse to the folder using File Explorer, right-click the folder name, and select Always Available Offline. Windows 10 does the rest and copies the contents of the selected folder to the local hard drive. Along those lines, administrators can prevent users from saving offline copies of files. Administrators use the Advanced Sharing dialog box and click Caching to open the Offline Settings dialog box. There they can configure specific settings.

Administrators create policies that define the use of Offline Files, either in a domain or on the local machine. Those policies can be located in the applicable Group Policy Editor. Two policies are discussed here enabling Always Offline Mode and enabling File Synchronization On Costed Networks, but you need to become familiar with all of the Group Policy options for working with Offline Files.

To enable the Always Offline Mode, use Group Policy to enable the Configure Slow-Link Mode policy setting and set the latency to one (millisecond). Doing so causes client computers running Windows 8 or later and Windows Server 2012 or later to automatically use the Always Offline Mode. Follow these steps:

1. Open Group Policy Management Console.

2. Right-click the Group Policy Object (GPO) you want to use and click Edit.

3. Navigate to Computer Configuration, Policies, Administrative Templates, Network, and Offline Files.

4. Right-click Configure Slow-Link Mode and click Edit.

5. Click Enabled.

6. In the Options box, click Show (you might have to scroll).

7. In the Value Name text box, specify the file share for which you want to enable Always Offline Mode or type *. to enable this for all file shares.

8. In the Value box, type Latency=1, and then click OK.

9. Click OK again.

To enable background file synchronization of Offline Files for a group of users while using metered connections, use Group Policy to enable the Enable File Synchronization On Costed Networks policy setting for the appropriate GPO by following this procedure:

1. Open Group Policy Management Console.

2. Right-click the GPO you want to use and click Edit.

3. Navigate to Computer Configuration, Policies, Administrative Templates, Network, Offline Files.

4. Right-click Enable File Synchronization On Costed Networks, and click Edit.

5. Click Enabled.

6. Click OK, and then click OK again.

EXAM TIP

Explore each entry available from the Offline Files options in Group Policy, including but not limited to Configure Slow Link Speed, Synchronize All Offline Files Before Logging Off, Synchronize All Offline Files When Logging On, and Enable Transparent Caching.

Configure sync options

This Skill focuses on configuring sync options, not on creating sync partnerships. However, you need to know how to create a sync partnership anyway, so we briefly cover that here. With that done, you'll review how to configure sync options in Sync Center, including scheduling when syncing should happen and under what circumstances.

Sync Center and configuring sync options

To practice with Sync Center and configure options you need to first create a sync partnership on a computer running Windows 10. To do this, navigate to a share on a different computer or file server, right-click that share, and click Always Available Offline. After that is done, on that same Windows 10 computer, open Sync Center. You can access Sync Center (shown in Figure 2-9) from Control Panel when viewing in the Large icons or Small icons view. Make a note of the options on the left side before continuing you can use these once after syncing is configured, to manage syncing. One option, Manage Offline Files, lets you view the Offline Files dialog box, where you can disable offline files, view offline files, check disk usage, encrypt your files, and more.

FIGURE 2-9 The Sync Center

In Sync Center, once a sync partnership is available, you can opt to sync everything, or you can select the Offline Files folder, click Schedule (not shown), and follow the wizard to configure sync settings. There are two options:

- At A Scheduled Time; for example, every Monday at 11 A.M. or every day at 2 A.M.
- When An Event Occurs; for example, every time you log on to your computer

Depending on your choice, you can opt for more scheduling options, such as only syncing when the computer has been idle for a specific amount of time or if the computer is running on external power (and not on its battery).

Managing Power Settings

Windows 10 enables users to manage power settings in a number of different ways. These include using the Settings app, configuring power plans in Control Panel, using the powercfg. exe command-line tool, and using group policies.

Using the Settings app

To manage power by using the Settings app, use the following procedure:

1. Click Start, and then click System.

2. In System, click Power & Sleep, as shown in Figure 2-10.

FIGURE 2-10 Configuring Power & sleep options

3. In the details pane, under the Screen heading, set a time interval to manage the On battery power, and turn off after setting. The default is five minutes.

4. Set a time interval to manage the When Plugged In Turn Off After setting. The default is 10 minutes.

You can also configure battery settings. In the System category of the Settings app, click the Battery tab, as shown in Figure 2-11, and then:

1. Select the Turn battery saver on automatically if my battery falls below check box, and then use the slider bar to set a percentage value. The default is enabled for 20%.

2. Select the Lower screen brightness while in battery saver check box.

If you want to know more about which apps are consuming battery, click the Battery Usage By App link.

FIGURE 2-11 Configuring Battery Settings

Configure power plans

You can exert more granular control over your computer's power settings by using the Power Options link in Control Panel. You can switch power plans and you can also configure these options:

- Require a password on wakeup
- Choose what the power buttons do
- Choose what closing the lid does
- Create a power plan
- Choose when to turn off the display
- Change when the computer sleeps

If you aren't already familiar with these features, take some time now to explore them. Make sure to create your own personal power plan by using the Create A Power Plan option in the Tasks pane of the Power Options dialog box, because you might see something about that on the exam. You might also be asked to state how many minutes must pass for each of the three default plans (Balanced, High Performance, Power Saver) before the computer goes to sleep or turns off the display, when running on its battery, or when plugged in. Additionally, and you can explore this on your own, you'll need to know how to monitor battery usage from the No-tification area of the Taskbar and how to change common mobility settings such as the power plan type, display brightness, and so on.

Beyond these end-user tools for managing power, there are other power-related items on which you'll be tested, including how to use the command-line tool Powercfg.exe to view and export power plans and configure power policies using Group Policy. Because these are less common and likely less familiar, these concepts will be covered here.

Using Powercfg.exe

Powercfg.exe is a command-line tool you can use to configure settings that aren't available from Control Panel or Group Policy. One of the things you can do here is to export a power management plan to a file and then import it to another computer. To get a list of the available power plans using this command, type **powercfg.exe list** at a command prompt. If you haven't yet created any custom plans, you'll only see the three default plans that come with Windows 10, as shown in Figure 2-12. Choose the plan to export and note the GUID value. To export the policy, open an elevated command prompt, and run **powercfg.exe export power.pow GUID** (where this is the GUID value for the plan to export).

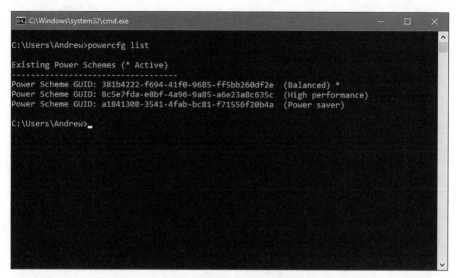

FIGURE 2-12 The default Windows 10 power plans, as shown by Powercfg.exe

MORE INFO **POWERCFG COMMAND-LINE OPTIONS**

For more information about powercfg.exe command line options, visit: *http://technet. microsoft.com/en-us/library/cc748940(v=WS.10).aspx.*

There are some other parameters you can use with Powercfg.exe. You must review these so that you are familiar with everything that's offered. Here are a few you might want to try now, just to get a feel for the command:

- changename
- -delete
- -setactive
- deviceenablewake and devicedisablewake

Creating power policies

As with most Windows 10 components, you can use Group Policy to set policies related to the available power plans. Use the Group Policy Management Editor to navigate to Computer Con-figuration, Administrative Templates, System, Power Management. When you expand Power Management in the left pane you can see the additional containers: Button Settings, Hard Disk Settings, Notification Settings, Sleep Settings, and Video And Display Settings. In the right pane you can see two options: Specify A Custom Active Power Plan and Select An Active Power Plan. The available options from Windows 10, using the Local Group Policy Editor are shown in Figure 2-13. As with any other Group Policy, you double-click the policy to access the options to configure it.

FIGURE 2-13 The Power Management node in the Local Group Policy Editor

When you click one of the five nodes under Power Management, more options appear. You can control every aspect of power management here. For instance, in the Sleep Settings node, you can configure, enable, and disable the following (and more):

- Specify the system sleep timeout (plugged in)
- Specify the system sleep timeout (on battery)
- Require a password when the computer wakes (plugged in)
- Require a password when the computer wakes (on battery)
- Allow standby states (S1 S3) when sleeping (plugged in)
- Allow standby states (S1 S3) when sleeping (on battery)

You need to explore all of the policies in every node before continuing.

Configure Windows To Go

Windows To Go enables users to run Windows 10 from a USB flash drive. Users can plug the Windows To Go flash drive in any computer that supports USB boot. It's like having a PC in your pocket. However, it does have limitations and specific requirements:

- The host PC must meet the Windows 7 Certification requirements, but it can run any operating system. Those requirements are available here: *http://msdn.microsoft.com/en-us/library/windows/hardware/dn423132*. They include, but are not limited to, USB boot compatibility, 1 gigahertz (GHz) or faster processor, 2 GB or more RAM, DirectX 9 graphics device with Windows Display Driver Model (WDDM) 1.2 or greater driver, and an available USB 2.0 port or greater.

- Windows To Go is not intended to replace desktops, laptops, or mobile devices such as tablets. It is meant to support short-term, alternative workplace scenarios.

- Windows To Go is only available for Enterprise customers who are part of the Microsoft Software Assurance program.

- Internal disks are offline to ensure data isn't accessed from the Windows To Go device. Likewise, if a Windows To Go drive is inserted into a running system, the Windows To Go drive will not be listed in File Explorer by default.

- Trusted Platform Module (TPM) can't be used because TPM is tied to a specific computer and Windows To Go drives are associated with multiple computers.

- Hibernate is disabled by default in Windows To Go, although this can be changed in Group Policy settings.

- Windows Recovery Environment isn't available, and neither is refreshing or resetting. If there is a problem with Windows To Go, the drive needs to be reimaged.

- In addition to the USB boot support in the BIOS, the Windows 10 image on the Windows To Go drive must be compatible with the processor architecture and firmware type (32-bit Windows To Go on 32-bit hosts, 64-bit Windows To Go on 64-bit hosts for Unified Extensible Firmware Interface [UEFI] BIOS, and 32-bit Windows To Go on 64-bit Legacy BIOS).

Consider the following Windows To Go features:

- Store apps can roam between multiple PCs on a Windows To Go drive.

- Windows To Go will detect all hardware on the host computer and install necessary drivers. When the Windows To Go workspace is used again on that same computer, it will recognize it's already been used and load the correct set of drivers automatically.

- Administrators can create Windows To Go drives using the same deployment tools they use to deploy Windows in an enterprise, namely DiskPart and the Deployment Image Servicing and Management (DISM) tool. When creating an image, make sure to include everything you'll need, such as device drivers, sync tools, and remote connectivity options if used outside the company network.

- Windows To Go is best configured on certified Windows To Go USB drives. The drives must be USB 3.0, although they can be used in USB 2.0 ports on a host computer.

There are also a few Group Policy settings for Windows To Go. You can find those settings in Computer Configuration, Administrative Templates, Windows Components, and Portable Operating System. You can enable or disable these to manage hibernation options and sleep states, and to set default startup options. To learn more about these settings, double-click an option to review and read the relevant information in the Help window. The Help information for Allow Hibernate (S4) When Starting From A Windows To Go Workspace offers this: specifies whether the PC can use the hibernation sleep state (S4) when started from a Windows To Go workspace. It goes on to explain that if enabled, the PC can hibernate; if disabled, the PC can't hibernate.

On the host side, users can search for Windows To Go from the Start screen and click Change Windows To Go Startup Options. From there, they can enable the host to boot from a

Windows To Go workspace. To boot to the Windows To Go workspace, insert the USB drive and do one of the following:

- If the computer has already been configured to boot to the USB drive and a Windows To Go workspace, the user can simply reboot or turn on the computer.

- If the computer is not USB-boot enabled, the user can reboot the computer, press the required key combination to access the boot menu (perhaps F12 or F2), and choose the USB Drive from the list.

- If the computer is turned on and the operating system is available, the user can use the Advanced Startup options to reboot using a device. You'll find that in the Settings app, under Update And Recovery, Recovery.

Creating a workspace by using the Windows To Go Workspace Wizard

To create a Windows To Go workspace on a USB drive, you need to work through the Create A Windows To Go Workspace Wizard. The basic steps are outlined next.

1. Mount the Windows 10 installation file or image on the Windows 10 Enterprise computer.

2. Insert the certified Windows To Go 3.0 USB drive into an available USB port and start the Create A Windows To Go Workspace Wizard.

3. Work through the wizard to do the following:

- Select the USB flash drive to use.

- Select the image to use.

- Opt whether to protect and encrypt the drive with BitLocker and a password, which is a good idea because USB drives are prone to being misplaced or stolen.

- Opt whether to boot to the new Windows To Go workspace now.

> *MORE INFO* **WINDOWS TO GO: FEATURE OVERVIEW**
>
> For more information about Windows To Go, visit: *https://docs.microsoft.com/en-us/windows/deployment/planning/windows-to-go-overview.*

Creating a workspace by using Windows PowerShell

You can use Windows PowerShell to create a Windows To Go workspace. Although the wizard is easier to use, you'll need to use Windows PowerShell if you want to automate or customize the process or if you want to create multiple workspaces simultaneously. The script required to perform these tasks is quite complex and includes preparing the flash drive with a system partition and a Windows partition and assigning drive letters. You'll have to apply the image using the available Deployment Image Servicing and Management (DISM) tools. You can use the BCDboot command-line tool to install the applicable boot files for both UEFI and BIOS. There are quite a few steps involved, but in an enterprise it's worth the effort.

Configure Wi-Fi Direct

Windows 10 computers can now directly connect to compatible devices one on one, using Wi-Fi Direct, without requiring an intermediary like a router or network access point. Users might use these types of connections to quickly transfer files to other workers using a computer-to-computer connection, or they might even transfer media or perform media streaming to other devices. You'll need to use Netsh to pair the two devices, only one of which has to support Wi-Fi Direct. Once connected, the connected device will appear in the Settings apps in the same way other devices do when they are connected.

You'll combine Netsh with wireless local area network (WLAN) and the desired parameters to connect with Wi-Fi Direct. Here are some of the available parameters you can use with Netsh WLAN at an elevated command prompt:

- **Connect**   This parameter connects to a wireless network. You'll have to use connect name= to input the profile name and service set identifier (SSID)= to input the SSID.
- **Export hostednetworkprofile**   This parameter saves WLAN profiles to Extensible Markup Language (XML) files.
- **Refresh hostednetwork**   This parameter refreshes hosted network settings.
- **Set**   This parameter sets configuration information. You'll have to add tags such as the SSID, name of the profile, and so on.
- **Show all**   This parameter displays information for all networks that are currently visible.
- **Start hostednetwork**   This parameter starts the hosted network.
- **Stop hostednetwork**   This parameter stops the hosted network.

Skill 2.4: Configure security for mobile devices

You can prevent data from being accessed when mobile devices (or hard drives) are lost or stolen. You can use the same technologies to protect against boot attacks, too, like rootkits. There are other ways to secure devices, though, by using Group Policy settings, preventing apps from obtaining a user's location, encrypting data, using VPNs, and more. Here, you'll review only about BitLocker and how to manage startup keys.

This section covers how to:

- Configure BitLocker
- Configure startup key storage

Configure BitLocker

BitLocker Drive Encryption lets you encrypt entire hard disks and disk volumes, which include the Windows operating system drive, user files, and system files. You can use BitLocker to protect 32-bit and 64-bit computers running Windows 10. On computers that have a trusted platform module (TPM) version 1.2 or 2.0, BitLocker can also ensure that data is accessible only if the boot components of the computer haven't been compromised (altered) and if the disk is still installed in the original computer.

EXAM TIP

You can enable BitLocker before you deploy the operating system. When you do, you can opt to encrypt used disk space only or encrypt the entire drive.

When using BitLocker, you have the option of requiring users to enter a password to unlock the drive when they want to use it. You also have the option of requiring multifactor authentication perhaps by adding a smart card or a USB drive with a startup key on it on computers with a compatible TPM. BitLocker can also be managed through Group Policy. For instance, you can require that BitLocker be enabled before the computer can be used to store data.

EXAM TIP

Two partitions are required to run BitLocker because pre-startup authentication and system integrity confirmation have to occur on a separate partition from the drive that is encrypted.

MORE INFO **OVERVIEW AND REQUIREMENTS OF BITLOCKER**

For more information about Windows BitLocker, visit: *http://technet.microsoft.com/en-us/library/hh831507.aspx#BKMK_Overview.*

When configuring BitLocker, you must consider the following:

- **The requirements for hardware and software**   This includes TPM versions, BIOS configuration, firmware requirements, drive size, and so on.
- **How to tell if your computer has a TPM**   An administrator might opt to type **TPM. msc** and click Enter in a Run dialog box. An end user might opt to access Control Panel, All Items, open BitLocker Drive Encryption and see if he can turn on BitLocker. If a TPM isn't found, you'll have to set the required Group Policy to Require Additional Authentication At Startup, which is located in Computer Configuration, Administrative Templates, Windows Components, BitLocker Drive Encryption, Operating System Drives. You need to enable this and then select the Allow BitLocker Without a Compatible TPM check box.
- **What credentials are required to configure BitLocker**   Only Administrators can manage fixed data drives, but Standard users can manage removable data drives (the

latter can be disabled in Group Policy). Standard users can also change the PIN or password on operating system drives to which they have access via BitLocker.

- **How to automate BitLocker deployment in an enterprise** One way is to use the command-line tool Manage-bde.exe. Manage-bde command-line tools you might use in your own work are detailed later in this section. There are other ways, including using Windows Management Instrumentation (WMI) and Windows PowerShell scripts.

- **The reasons why BitLocker might start in recovery mode** Reasons include disabling the TPM, making changes to the TPM firmware, making changes to the master boot record, and so on.

- **How to manage recovery keys** Recovery keys let you access a computer in the event that BitLocker doesn't permit access. There are many ways to store these keys for fixed drives, including saving them to a folder or your Microsoft account online, printing them, and storing the keys on multiple USB drives.

> *NOTE* **USING BITLOCKER WITHOUT TPM**
>
> You can only enable BitLocker on an operating system drive without a compatible TPM if the BIOS or UEFI firmware has the ability to read from a USB flash drive in the boot environment. This is because BitLocker requires a startup key. If you do this, though, you won't be able to take advantage of the pre-startup system integrity verification or multifactor authentication.

Configuring BitLocker in Control Panel

Before you configure BitLocker, there are a few more things to know. The first time you enable BitLocker, you'll be prompted to create a startup key. This is what's used to encrypt and decrypt the drive. The startup key can be stored on a USB drive or the TPM chip. If you opt for USB, you'll have to insert that USB drive every time you want to access the computer, and you'll also have to enter the key. If a compatible TPM chip is used, the key retrieval is automatic. You can also opt for a PIN. This can be created only after BitLocker is enabled. If you lose the startup key, you'll need to unlock the drive using a recovery key. This is a 48-digit number that can be stored in numerous ways, including on a USB drive.

There are five authentication methods for protecting encrypted data using BitLocker, consisting of various combinations of TPM, startup PIN, and startup keys; just a TPM; or just a startup key. Here is a brief summary of these options:

- **TPM + startup PIN + startup key** This is the most secure, but it requires three authentication tasks. The encryption key is stored on the TPM chip, but an administrator needs to type a PIN and insert the startup key (available on a USB drive).

- **TPM + startup key** The encryption key is stored on the TPM chip. In addition to this, the administrator needs to insert a USB flash drive that contains a startup key.

- **TPM + startup PIN** The encryption key is stored on the TPM chip, and an administrator needs to enter a PIN.

- **Startup key only**   An administrator needs to insert a USB flash drive with the startup key on it. The computer doesn't need to have a TPM chip. The BIOS needs to support access to the USB flash drive prior to the operating system loading.

- **TPM only**   The encryption key is stored on the TPM chip, and no administrator login is required. TPM requires that the boot environment has not been modified or compromised.

Additionally, the drive that contains the operating system must have two partitions, the system partition and the operating system partition, both of which need to be formatted with NTFS.

To configure BitLocker and encrypt the operating system drive on a Windows 10 computer, follow these steps:

1. Open Control Panel, change the view to Small Icons or Large Icons, and click BitLocker Drive Encryption.

2. Click Turn On BitLocker (if you receive an error that no TPM chip is available, enable the required Group Policy setting).

3. Choose how to unlock your drive at startup; Enter A Password Is Chosen in this example.

4. Enter the password, re-enter to confirm, and then click Next.

5. Opt to save the password; Save To Your Microsoft Account is selected in this example.

6. Click Next (in this instance, you can perform this step again to perform a secondary backup before moving on).

7. Choose to encrypt either the used disk space or the entire drive. Click Next.

8. Leave Run BitLocker System Check selected, and click Continue.

9. Click Restart Now. If prompted, perform any final tasks, such as removing CDs or DVDs from drive bays, and then click Restart Now again, if necessary.

10. On boot-up, type or provide the startup key.

11. Note the pop-up notification in the Desktop taskbar that encryption is in progress. It will take some time to complete.

Return to Control Panel and review the BitLocker window. Note that from there you can perform additional tasks, including backing up your recovery key, changing your password, removing the passwords, and turning off BitLocker. You can see which actions require administrator approval by the icon next to the options.

Configuring BitLocker by using the Manage-bde tool

You don't have to use Control Panel to manage BitLocker Drive Encryption. You can work from a command line, using commands that can turn on or turn off BitLocker, specify unlock mechanisms, update recovery methods, and unlock BitLocker-protected data drives. Many of these commands are used in large enterprises and are not applicable to this Skill; however, there are several parameters you might use with the Manage-Bde command-line tool, including but not limited to the following:

- **status** Use this parameter to provide information about the attached drives, including their BitLocker status, size, BitLocker version, key protector, lock status, and more.

- **on** This parameter encrypts the drive and turns on BitLocker, used with a drive letter such as C that follows the on parameter.

- **off** This parameter decrypts and then turns off BitLocker, used with a drive letter such as C that follows the off parameter.

- **pause** and **resume** Use pause with a drive letter to pause encryption; use resume with a drive letter to resume encryption.

- **lock** and **unlock** Use these parameters with a drive letter to lock and unlock the drive.

- **changepin** This parameter changes the PIN for the BitLocker-protected drive.

- **recoverypassword** Use this parameter to add a numerical password protector.

- **recoverykey** This parameter adds an external key protector for recovery.

- **password** Use this parameter to add a password key protector.

EXAM TIP

Refer to this article on TechNet to see all of the available parameters: *http://technet.micro-soft.com/en-us/library/dd875513(v=WS.10).aspx*. You can also type **manage-bde /?** at a command prompt to see a list on your own computer.

Configure startup key storage

This section covers how to configure startup key storage. However, to understand what a startup key is, you need to first understand what it isn't. There are several key management terms to contend with:

- **TPM owner password** You need to initialize the TPM before you can use it with BitLocker Drive Encryption. When you do, you create a TPM owner password that is associated only with the TPM. You supply the TPM owner password when you need to enable or disable the TPM or reset the TPM lockout.

- **Recovery password and recovery key** The first time you set up BitLocker, you are prompted to configure how to access BitLocker-protected drives if access is denied. This involves creating a recovery key. You'll need the recovery key if the TPM cannot validate the boot components, but most of the time, a failure to access a BitLocker drive occurs because the end user has forgotten the PIN or password.

- **Password** A password can be used to protect fixed, removable, and operating system drives. It can also be used with operating system drives that do not have a TPM. The password can consist of 8 to 255 characters as specified by the Configure Use Of Passwords For Operating System Drives, Configure Use Of Passwords For Removable Data Drives, and Configure Use Of Passwords For Fixed Data Drives Group Policy settings.

- **PIN and enhanced PIN**   If you use a TPM, you can configure BitLocker with a PIN that the user needs to enter to gain access to the computer. The PIN can consist of 4 to 20 digits as specified by the Configure Minimum PIN Length For Startup Group Policy setting. Enhanced PINs use the full keyboard character set in addition to the numeric set to allow for more possible PIN combinations. You need to enable the Allow Enhanced PINs For Startup Group Policy setting before adding the PIN to the drive.
- **Startup key**   You use a startup key, which is stored on a USB flash drive, with or without a TPM. The USB flash drive must be inserted every time the computer starts. The USB flash drive needs to be formatted by using the NTFS, FAT, or FAT32 file system.

Now that you know what a startup key is, you can save your computer's startup key on a USB flash drive. Right-click the BitLocker-protected drive to get started and then follow the prompts.

Thought experiments

In these thought experiments, demonstrate your skills and knowledge of the topics covered in this chapter. You can find the answers to these thought experiments in the next section.

Scenario 1

You are the network administrator of a 2012 Active Directory domain. All 20 client computers run Windows 10. One of your users purchased her own computer and brought it to work, and it too runs Windows 10 Enterprise. You approve the computer and join it to the domain. There are some issues, though.

1. After logging on to the domain, the user can't access her personal data. What should you do?
2. You want the data the user would normally save to her Documents folder to instead be saved to a share on the network. What should you do?
3. The user wants her local user profile to follow her from computer to computer. What should you do?

Scenario 2

You need to create a VM using a Windows 10 computer as the host that you can move from computer to computer on a USB drive. You'll be using the VM on a Windows Server 2012 computer in the production environment. The VM needs to support Secure Boot and PXE Boot. Answer the following questions:

1. When you create the VM, which Generation option should you choose?
2. Will you need a valid product ID for the operating system you will be installing on the VM?

3. You want the VM to be able to communicate with other VMs on the host computer, but not with any host computer directly. What type of virtual switch should you configure?

4. When you configure your VHD, what file format should you use?

5. To export the VM stored on the USB drive, which export option should you choose?

Scenario 3

You have users who need access to the files stored in the file servers of your company, no matter where they are. You have configured Offline Files to enable this. It's working well except that when the users are on metered connections or are roaming with a cellular connection, the costs are high. You want to reduce or better yet, eliminate these costs. All users are running Windows 10.

1. What feature available with Offline Files would you enable in Group Policy to help users avoid high data-usage costs from synchronization while using metered connections that have usage limits or while roaming on another network?

2. What feature available with Offline Files would you enable in Group Policy to provide fast access to files while also limiting the bandwidth used by having the users work offline even if a connection is available?

3. You also want users to work offline when they aren't on metered networks if the connection is very slow. You've configured a threshold for this in Group Policy. Does the user need to do anything when this threshold is met?

4. Can you configure Offline Files and these settings if your servers are running Windows Server 2008 R2?

Scenario 4

A client wants to enable BitLocker on her laptop and has called you to set it up. She wants to protect the data on the computer if the computer is stolen or if the hard drive is removed. You need to find out if a compatible TPM chip is available, and if not, configure the computer so that BitLocker can be used effectively.

1. What can you type in a Run box to find out if a compatible TPM is available on the computer?

2. If a TPM is not found, what policy do you need to change in Local Group Policy on the computer?

3. If a TPM is not found, what must be true regarding the BIOS or UEFI firmware?

4. If a TPM is found, what is the most secure authentication option to apply during startup?

Thought experiment answers

This section provides the solutions for the tasks included in the thought experiment.

Scenario 1

1. Use USMT to transfer the user's local profile to her domain profile.
2. Configure folder location.
3. Configure a roaming user profile.

Scenario 2

1. Generation 2, because it supports the listed requirements and Generation 1 doesn't.
2. Yes. All installations of an operating system, even those installed on virtual drives, require a product ID.
3. Private. You want the VM to be able to communicate with other VMs on the host computer, but not with any host computer directly. The other options, External and Internal, do not meet these criteria.
4. VHDX. Although you won't likely need the feature that enables the disk to be up to 64 TB, you do use this format when you know you'll be using the VHD on Windows Server 2012 and later or Windows 8 or later.
5. Restore The Virtual Machine (Use The Existing Unique ID For The VM). If your VM files are stored on a file share, a removable drive, a network drive, and so on, and you want to move it, choose this option.

Scenario 3

1. Cost-Aware Synchronization
2. Always Offline Mode
3. No, the computer will go offline when the threshold is met.
4. No. Always Offline and Cost-Aware Synchronization are only available for clients and servers running the latest operating systems.

Scenario 4

1. TPM.msc.
2. You'll need to set the required Group Policy to Require Additional Authentication At Setup, which is located in Computer Configuration, Administrative Templates, Windows

Components, BitLocker Drive Encryption, Operating System Drives. You need to enable this and then select the Allow BitLocker Without A Compatible TPM check box.

3. The BIOS or UEFI firmware must have the ability to read from a USB flash drive in the boot environment.

4. TPM + startup PIN + startup key.

Chapter summary

- You can configure user profiles to support user environments in Windows with local profiles, roaming profiles, and mandatory profiles.

- You can change the default location for several folders in the user profile to another location, including a network location.

- You can use the USMT to migrate user profiles and user files for one or many Windows computers.

- To use Hyper-V in Windows 10, the host computer must:

    - Have Windows 10 Professional, Enterprise or Education 64-bit installed.

    - Have a compatible Second Level Address Translation (SLAT) processor.

    - Have 4 GB of RAM and BIOS-level hardware virtualization support.

- You create VMs in order to use a single computer to house multiple operating systems to test various hardware and software scenarios as well as to save money, resources, space, power consumption, and more.

- Checkpoints let you take snapshots of the configuration of a VM. You can restore to a saved checkpoint at any time.

- Virtual switches can be used to configure the network environment and to separate and secure multiple VMs.

- Virtual disks let you port VMs and are saved as either VHD or VHDX file formats. VHDX is the newer format and is compatible only with Windows Server 2012 or later and Windows 8 or later.

- The Offline Files feature enables users to work with their personal files even when they aren't connected to the network. Administrators can control behavior through Group Policy settings.

- Power plans help users to manage battery life on mobile devices. Administrators can manage power plans by using the Powercfg.exe tool and Group Policy.

- Windows To Go enables users to run Windows 10 from a USB flash drive.

- Wi-Fi Direct lets users share files without an intermediary network device.

- BitLocker can be used to protect mobile devices and mobile drives from theft, loss, or attacks by hackers.

- You need to carefully manage startup keys, recovery keys, and other items related to BitLocker Drive Encryption so that you access the drive if it is compromised or if the user forgets the PIN or password.

- The command-line tool Manage-bde along with applicable parameters lets you manage BitLocker from a command line.

CHAPTER 3

Plan and implement a Microsoft 365 solution

M icrosoft 365 provides enterprises and businesses a comprehensive solution, enabling
user productivity while simplifying the IT management, security and administration for
Windows, Windows 10 Mobile, iOS, and Android devices. You can manage enterprise devices
and bring your own device (BYOD) devices together in the same cloud-based console. Microsoft 365 provides a bundle of essential tools, services, and support, offering a complete
solution for your organization.

Windows 10 and Office 365 are at the heart of Microsoft 365. Complementing the productivity core of Microsoft 365, Intune provides remote policies and device management such
as remote wipe and lock, application and software update deployment, and inventory and
reporting. This chapter reviews how to plan and implement Microsoft 365 in preparation for
the exam.

Skills in this chapter:

- Skill 3.1: Support mobile devices
- Skill 3.2: Deploy software updates by using Microsoft Intune
- Skill 3.3: Manage devices with Microsoft 365 Solution
- Skill 3.4: Configure Information Protection

Skill 3.1: Support mobile devices

Windows 10 supports several features for mobile devices that enable greater control over and
manageability of mobile devices. Devices that are often disconnected from the corporate
network and used in a variety of physical locations warrant special consideration regarding
device security, remote management, data access, connectivity, and administration. In addition, you'll learn how to configure and support standalone Windows 10 devices and devices
that have been enrolled into Microsoft 365.

Support mobile device policies

Unlike traditional device management, modern mobile devices are not necessarily members of an Active Directory domain. Enterprise BYOD and choose your own device (CYOD) allows for diversity in hardware. A modern device can be a smartphone, tablet, laptop, desktop PC, or IoT device.

Mobile Device Management (MDM) requires that administrators manage a wide range of devices and disparate operating systems including Windows, Windows 10 Mobile, iOS, and Android. Only domain-joined Microsoft devices can be managed using Group Policy. So, you must understand how to support other devices that can be configured and controlled using Microsoft Intune policies. If a connected device has been enrolled into your MDM authority, it can be managed remotely using Intune policies.

Think of Intune policies as a group of settings that can be configured to control features on a device. Policy templates are available within the Azure Intune administration portal and can be applied to individual devices, or groups of devices.

Intune provides policies for hundreds of device settings across multiple platforms. Group Policy, however, can configure thousands of settings for Windows and Server operating systems. Vendors add functionality to devices on a regular basis, and Microsoft Intune manages this functionality with available policies.

> **NOTE VENDOR SPECIFIC POLICY**
>
> Mobile device vendors allow certain features to be controlled by the MDM authority. Not every policy or remote feature, such as remote wipe or password reset, will be available on all devices managed by Intune.

The Microsoft Intune policies fall into five categories (described in Table 3-1). These policies can be accessed by signing into the Intune Classic admin portal at *https://manage.microsoft.com/* and then navigating to the Policy node on the left hand side.

TABLE 3-1 Microsoft Intune policies

Intune policy category	Description
Configuration Policies	Manage security settings and features on your devices. Include deploying language settings, or a custom firewall rule
Device Compliance Policies	Define the rules and settings which you want a device to comply with. Can be used with conditional access policy rules so you can monitor whether your devices are compliant.
Conditional Access Policies	Conditional Access Policies (or CAPs) can be used to allow or restrict access to a particular service or resource, such as network access or access to Exchange Online, or a specific app installed on a device. There are specific templates for you to manage access to Microsoft Exchange Online, Microsoft Dynamics CRM Online, Skype for Business Online, and Microsoft SharePoint Online.
Corporate Device Enrollment Policy	Used to specify how devices are to be enrolled and allow administrators to deploy an enrollment profile to Apple devices.
Resource Access Policies	Most commonly deployed policies. Similar to configuration Policies providing access to company files and resources. There are four types of resource access policies available: ■ Wi-Fi profile network settings ■ VPN settings ■ Email client profile settings ■ Certificate profiles

EXAM TIP

Microsoft has stated that the Intune Classic portal will be retired starting on April 2, 2018 for customers using Intune standalone. Therefore, you should familiarize yourself with the modern Azure Intune portal.

Intune Policy Templates

In the Intune classic portal there are a number of templates built into the Intune policy nodethat are used to deliver settings to enrolled devices. The templates are listed in categories and they're split based on the operating system and device type.

For the exam, you should review the available templates and note that not all settings and policies are available for each vendor or device type.

When configuring a device, it is advisable to start with a pre-configured template because they contain recommended settings. It may be more efficient to use an existing template as a starting point, and then customize the settings and deploy them to your managed devices. The list of templates available is shown in Figure 3-1.

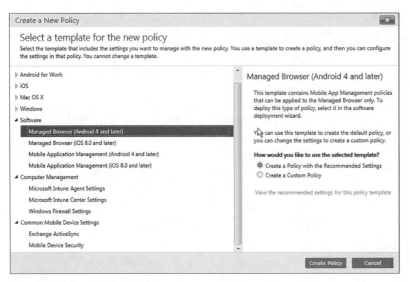

FIGURE 3-1 Intune Policy Templates

All templates allow you to create a new custom policy based on the table of settings within the template. Three of the template types provide recommended settings for you to deploy to your devices. These are: Software, Computer Management and Mobile Device Settings templates. The Software templates are used by Android and iOS devices. The Computer Management templates cater to Windows Intune and Firewall settings on Windows devices. The Mobile Device Settings templates are used for configuring Exchange ActiveSync and also all common security settings such as password length, complexity, and device encryption settings.

Computer management templates

The Computer Management Intune Policies are some of the most used when creating a default configuration on a device running Windows. Within Computer Management you can configure:

- Microsoft Intune Agent Settings
- Microsoft Intune Center Settings
- Windows Firewall Settings

Some of the settings contained in the Microsoft Intune Agent Settings template relate to Windows 8.1 and earlier operating systems. For these devices the Microsoft Intune Agent must be installed. Most of these settings are built into Windows 10 and therefore can be configured using the Windows and Mobile Device Security templates.

The Microsoft Intune Agent Settings template allows you to configure Endpoint Protection, updating and configuring real-time protection settings, including the real-time protection and scan schedules. By default, the service is set to check for and receive updates every 8 hours, but this can be modified.

Since this policy affects the Endpoint Protection service running on the operating system, you can only assign this template to device groups containing computers.

For older devices, you can use the Microsoft Intune Center Settings to provide users of enrolled devices with contact information, such as support contacts, website URL, and support instructions.

With the Windows Firewall Settings template you can configure Windows Firewall settings for each type of network profile: domain, private, and public on a device.

Typical settings include firewall activation, block or allow all incoming connections (overrides existing allowed programs), and notifying whenever Windows Firewall blocks a new program. There are dozens of predefined Windows Firewall exceptions to specific services that you can enable or disable using policy.

Some of the items that can be configured are shown in Table 3-2.

TABLE 3-2 Sample of predefined Windows Firewall exceptions

Exception name	Description
Connect to a Network Projector	Users can connect to projectors over wired or wireless networks to project presentations.
File and Printer Sharing	Users can share local files and printers with other users on the network using NetBIOS, Link Local Multicast Name Resolution (LLMNR), Server Message Block (SMB) protocol, and RPC.
Key Management Service	Provides a license compliance within enterprise environments.
Netlogon Service	Provides a security channel between domain clients and a domain controller for authenticating users and services using RPC.
Network Discovery	Computers can discover other devices on the network. This setting uses FDResPub Services and SSDP, NetBIOS, LLMNR, and UPnP network protocols.
Remote Administration	The remote administration of the computer.
Remote Assistance	Users of managed computers can request remote assistance from other users on the network. Uses SSDP, Peer Name Resolution Protocol (PNRP), Teredo, and UPnP network protocols.
Remote Desktop	The computer can use Remote Desktop to remotely access other computers.
Remote Event Log Management	Client event logs can be viewed and managed remotely. Uses Named Pipes and RPC.
Windows Remote Management (Windows 8 or later)	Enables remote management of managed computers with WS-Management, a Web services-based protocol for remote management of operating systems and devices.

For effective policy you need to apply it to a device, or group of devices. The device receives the policy settings only after it has been configured and connected to the MDM service.

Mobile Device Security Policies

The Mobile Device Security Policy template allows you to define and deploy password lengths and encryption for all supported devices. The settings available are dependent on whether the feature is available on the device and if the vendor allows this to be controlled using MDM.

There are many settings available with this policy. Table 3-3 shows some example settings.

TABLE 3-3 Mobile Device Security Policy

Setting	Example Settings
Security settings	Password length, history, duration, complexity, reuse of previous passwords, picture passwords, allow fingerprint unlock
Encryption settings	Require encryption on mobile device, require encryption on storage cards
Malware settings	Require network firewall, enable SmartScreen
System settings	Require automatic updates, allow screen capture, User Account Control
Cloud settings – documents and data, accounts and synchronization	Allow backup to iCloud, sync to iCloud, Require encrypted backup, Allow Google backup. Allow Microsoft account, Allow Google account auto sync
Application settings – Email, browser, Apps	Make Microsoft account optional in Windows Mail application, Allow custom email accounts. Allow web browser, Allow pop-up blocker, Allow application store
Device capabilities settings – hardware and features	Allow camera, Allow Wi-Fi, Allow Wi-Fi tethering, Allow data roaming, Allow voice assistant, Allow copy and paste

In the new Microsoft Intune portal hosted in Microsoft Azure, you are not offered a set of pre-defined policies to choose from. Instead you are required to create your own policy. The settings available for each policy are platform specific, allowing you to choose from: Android, Android for Work, iOS, macOS, Windows Phone 8.1, Windows 8.1 and later, and Windows 10 and later.

Depending on which platform is chosen, you can build a policy that offers compatible settings that are allowable by the platform vendor as shown in Figure 3-2.

FIGURE 3-2 Policy settings in the Azure Intune portal

Previously, the Mobile Device Security Policy was a useful "catch all" security policy. Intune now includes separate configuration policies for each device platform, which should be used in preference to the Mobile Device Security Policy.

EXAM TIP

Microsoft has stated that the Mobile Device Security Policy will be removed in the future and they will focus their feature development within the platform specific policies.

Support mobile access and data synchronization

Users that have devices disconnected from the corporate network often require access to corporate documents and data. Windows 10 provides features that enable administrators to make corporate data available while a device is disconnected from the network, or completely offline.

Supporting Work Folders

Work Folders provides the ability to synchronize data between a mobile device and a folder hosted on a corporate network file server. Work Folders enable synchronization for devices that are either domain-joined on non-domain-joined, so BYOD users can have access to corporate files without requiring a device that is joined to the domain. You can control the behavior of Work Folders with Group Policy, or configure it from Work Folders in Control Panel, as shown in Figure 3-3.

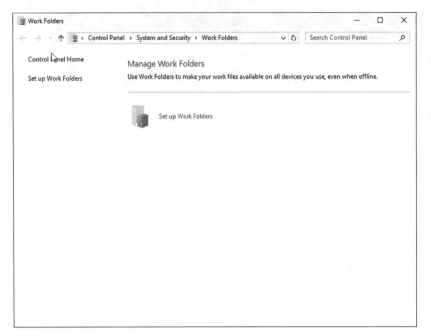

FIGURE 3-3 Work Folders in Control Panel

EXAM TIP

Work Folders was introduced in Windows 8.1 and Windows Server 2012 R2. To use Work Folders, your client and file server operating system must use Windows 8.1 or later and Windows Server 2012 R2 or later. In environments where file servers are older versions of Windows Server, or where users have devices running Windows 8 or earlier, your users can't use Work Folders to provide offline file access for those users.

CONFIGURING WORK FOLDERS IN CONTROL PANEL

To configure Work Folders, users must complete the following steps:

1. If you have an iPad or iPhone, install the Work Folders app from the App Store and then follow the setup instructions.

2. If you have an Android device, install the Work Folders app from the Google Play Store and then follow the setup instructions.

3. On a Windows 8.1 or Windows 10 device click Set Up Work Folders in Control Panel.

4. Enter a corporate email address or a Work Folders universal resource locator (URL).

5. Accept or change the local path for Work Folders storage.

6. Review and accept the security policies.

CONFIGURING WORK FOLDERS BY USING GROUP POLICY

You can also configure domain-joined Windows devices to use Work Folders by using Group Policy. There are two Group Policy settings used to configure Work Folders:

- **Specify Work Folders settings**   This setting is found in User Configuration\Administrative Templates\Windows Components\Work Folders. When you enable this setting, you also specify a Work Folders URL that will be used by Windows to configure Work Folders for the user. You can also select the Force Automatic Setup option, which will set up Work Folders automatically for any users affected by the policy. Users will not be able to choose whether or not they use Work Folders, and the default value for the local Work Folders location (%USERPROFILE%\Work Folders) will be used.

- **Force Automatic Setup For All users**   This setting is found in Computer Configuration\Administrative Templates\Windows Components\Work Folders. When you enable this option, domain-joined computers will use the settings specified in Specify Work Folders settings to configure Work Folders.

When Work Folders is configured for a Windows 10 computer, the Work Folders folder is available in File Explorer under This PC.

> *NOTE* **ADDITIONAL CONFIGURATION**
>
> Work Folders functionality is dependent on server configuration. Work Folders is available for Windows Server 2012 R2 or later, and requires additional configuration of components such as certificates and DNS. To learn more about Work Folders and server configuration, visit: *https://technet.microsoft.com/library/dn265974.aspx*

Supporting mobile access with Sync Center

Sync Center enables domain-joined computers to synchronize local copies of network files for offline use. Sync Center, in combination with Offline Files, can provide offline file access for client computers running any version of Windows as far back as Windows XP.

A sync partnership is the functional component within Sync Center. A sync partnership defines the network location where the files are located along with specific synchronization details. You can define sync partnerships within Sync Center in Control Panel, pictured in Figure 3-4. Sync Center offers several options for configuring and monitoring sync partnerships and Offline Files.

FIGURE 3-4 Sync Center in Control Panel

SCHEDULING SYNCHRONIZATION

In Sync Center, after a sync partnership is configured, you can either synchronize everything by clicking Sync All, or you can select the Offline Files folder, click Schedule, and use the wizard provided to configure sync settings. You can use two scheduling options:

- **At a scheduled time** For example, every Monday at 11 A.M. or every day at 2 A.M.
- **When an event occurs** For example, every time you log on to your computer.

You can configure additional scheduling options, such as preventing syncing, unless the computer has been idle for a specific amount of time or the computer is running on external power. You can also trigger synchronization based on an event in the operating system, such as when the user signs in, when the user locks Windows, or when the user unlocks Windows.

Support broadband connectivity

Windows 10 devices are often connected to corporate networks for access to Internet and corporate network infrastructure. However, as devices become more mobile, users need to connect to resources from locations outside of the corporate network. In many cases, Wi-Fi networks can provide the connectivity required, but in the absence of these, many users opt to use broadband mobile access from personal hotspots or a tethered connection from a mobile phone.

These connections warrant different considerations because data usage is usually tracked and charged back by Internet Service Providers (ISPs). This type of connection is referred to as a *metered network*. Windows 10 offers several options to control data usage when connected to a metered network.

Supporting broadband tethering and metered networks

Some Windows 10 laptop devices now have cellular SIM or LTE functionality, which allows devices to connect to the Internet using their mobile data using a Wi-Fi enabled or a wired network.

Once connected to a mobile data connection you can create a mobile hotspot that can be shared with up to 10 other devices. This transforms the device into an Internet sharing communications hotspot. Nearby devices will be able to connect to your PC or smartphone's data connection via the network center, listed as either an available Wi-Fi or Bluetooth connection. In both cases you will need to provide the correct password or passphrase set by the sharing device, to join to the connection.

> *NOTE* **DATA CHARGES**
>
> Using your Windows 10 device as a Mobile Broadband Hotspot offers great flexibility, especially when away from traditional Wi-Fi and wired Internet connections. Unless you have an unlimited package with your service provider, you should check the details, costs. and limits of your charge plan, and adjust your activity accordingly. Mobile Broadband is typically charged based on the amount of data used.

When a connection has restrictions on the amount of data, such as quotas or limits, it is called a metered Internet connection. If you use a tethered connection, for example, you may want to categorize the connection as metered. Enabling this feature informs Windows that lower priority data requirements such as updates and OneDrive synchronization tasks will be deferred until using a non-metered connection. You can also manually pause OneDrive synchronization for up to 24 hours by right clicking the OneDrive icon in the notification area and selecting pause syncing.

To mark a Wi-Fi network connection as metered, perform these steps while you are online:

1. From the Start menu, select the Settings app.
2. Select Network & Internet.
3. Select the Wi-Fi connection.
4. On the connection properties page, toggle the switch to Set As Metered Connection, as shown in Figure 3-5.

FIGURE 3-5 Configure a network as a metered connection

Support Mobile Device Management by using Microsoft Intune

Mobile Device Management (MDM) enables the administration of remote mobile devices across multiple platforms. Microsoft Intune supports MDM for managing remote mobile devices. Microsoft Intune supports direct management by using MDM for the following devices and associated requirements for enrollment:

Apple

- Apple iOS 9.0 and later
- Mac OS X 10.9 and later
- Obtain an Apple Push Notification service certificate. This enables Microsoft Intune to communicate securely with iOS devices.

Google

- Android 4.4 and later (including Samsung KNOX Standard 4.4 and higher)
- Android for Work

Download the Microsoft Intune Company Portal app from the Google Play store.

Microsoft

- Windows 10 (Home, S, Pro, Education, and Enterprise versions)
- Windows 10 Mobile
- Devices running Windows 10 IoT Enterprise (x86, x64)
- Devices running Windows 10 IoT Mobile Enterprise
- Windows Holographic & Windows Holographic Enterprise
- Windows Phone 8.1, Windows 8.1 RT, PCs running Windows 8.1 (Sustaining mode)

If direct enrollment is not possible, for example with older versions of Windows, you can install the Microsoft Intune software client from the Intune classic portal. The Intune software client can be used to manage Windows 7 and later PCs (except Windows 10 Home edition).

You can use Microsoft Intune to perform several management tasks for these devices in several different areas.

App management

- App deployment
- App restrictions
- Mobile application management

Device security and configuration

- Configuration policies
- Password management
- Remote wipe and lock
- Custom policies

Company resource access

- VPN profiles
- Wi-Fi profiles
- Email profiles
- Certificate profiles
- Conditional access profiles

Inventory and reporting

- Hardware inventory
- Application inventory
- Reporting

Currently different administrative tasks within Intune require that you use one of the following administrative websites:

- Office 365 portal (*https://www.office.com*)
- Azure portal (*https://portal.azure.com*)

The following browsers are supported for these portals:

- Microsoft Edge (latest version)
- Microsoft Internet Explorer 11
- Safari (latest version, Mac only)
- Chrome (latest version)
- Firefox (latest version)

The Intune classic portal requires Silverlight browser support and therefore only these browsers offer Silverlight support:

- Internet Explorer 10 or later
- Google Chrome (versions prior to version 42)
- Mozilla Firefox with Silverlight enabled

Configuring MDM for Microsoft Intune

To support Mobile Device Management (MDM) in Microsoft Intune, you must first configure the MDM authority. Microsoft Intune can provide an MDM authority, or you can use System Center 2012 R2 Configuration Manager or Office 365 as your MDM authority. If MDM has not been previously set to Microsoft Intune, you can configure MDM by performing the following steps:

1. Sign into the Azure portal at *https://portal.azure.com*.
2. Choose More Services then Monitoring + Management, then select Intune.
3. Select the orange banner at the top to open the Mobile Device Management Authority setting.
4. Under Mobile Device Management Authority, choose your MDM authority from the following options as shown in Figure 3-6:
5. Intune MDM Authority
6. Configuration Manager MDM Authority
7. None
8. Click the Intune MDM Authority option.
9. A message indicates that you have successfully set your MDM authority to Intune.

FIGURE 3-6 Configure your MDM authority to Intune

Enrolling devices

You enable MDM management for devices by enrolling them. The enrollment process is different for each platform, and each platform has a specific set of requirements, mentioned earlier
in this chapter.

For Windows devices, there is an existing trust relationship between the device operating
system and Intune, so enrollment can be automatic. For iOS and Android devices, a certificate
must be created and then installed on each device. The following list provides the enrollment
process for each platform:

- **Windows 7 & Windows 8**   Install the Microsoft Intune client. The Company Portal app
  is not available.

- **Windows 8.1 or Windows RT 8.1**   On the device, tap Settings, then PC Settings, then
  Network and Workplace, then enter your credentials and click Join. Turn on device
  management.

- **Windows 10** If users sign into the device using their corporate credentials, their account is added to Azure Active Directory and the device is then managed with Intune.
- **iOS - "bring your own device" or BYOD** iPads, iPhones, and Mac computers. **A** MDM Push certificate is required for Intune to manage iOS and Mac devices. Then install the Company Portal app from the App Store. Open the app and follow the enrollment wizard.
- **iOS - Company-owned devices** For bulk enrollments, you can use the following methods:
  - Apple's Device Enrollment Program (DEP)
  - Apple School Manager
  - Apple Configurator Setup Assistant enrollment
  - Apple Configurator direct enrollment
  - Intune device enrollment manager account
- **Android and Samsung Knox Standard devices** Users must enroll their devices by downloading the Intune Company Portal app from Google Play.

NOTE **ANNUAL CERTIFICATE RENEWAL**

The Apple MDM push certificate is valid for one year and must be renewed annually to maintain iOS and macOS device management. If your certificate expires, enrolled Apple devices cannot be contacted or used.

MORE INFO **MOBILE DEVICE MANAGEMENT**

For more information on MDM in Microsoft Intune and the Azure portal, including signing up for a free trial, to enroll devices and get started using Intune, visit the following URL at: *https://docs.microsoft.com/intune/introduction-intune*.

Skill 3.2: Deploy software by using Microsoft Intune

Microsoft Intune provides you with an alternative method of managing software updates for devices that are outside of the corporate network. You can use Microsoft Intune to approve or decline updates, configure installation methods, deploy updates, or monitor the progress of these deployments.

Use reports and In-Console Monitoring to identify required updates

Microsoft Intune provides dashboard reporting for updates required by managed devices. There are several locations from which you can obtain information about updates, but the Updates page, shown in Figure 3-7, is the most comprehensive.

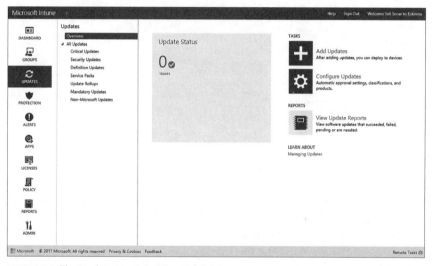

FIGURE 3-7 The Updates page in Microsoft Intune

The classic Intune portal still provides extensive reporting capabilities relating to software updates for operating systems that you install with the Intune client. The client is no longer required for managing devices running Windows 10 because these can be auto enrolled and managed using Azure Active Directory, and reflects the new modern way that Windows 10 receives security and feature updates on an automatic basis.

If you want to manage software updates on Windows 10 devices, using Intune, you will need to install the Intune client and use the classic portal.

The Updates page contains a dashboard view displaying the overall update status for devices managed by Microsoft Intune. It also groups updates according to type and provides links to view updates by those groups. When you click any group, Microsoft Intune displays the updates corresponding to the group. To obtain more detailed information, you can create and view a report by clicking the View Update Reports link in the Overview section of the Updates page. After clicking View Update Reports, you are presented with the Update Reports page, from where you can configure report settings and generate a report to view specific updates as shown in Figure 3-8.

FIGURE 3-8 The Update Reports page in Microsoft Intune

To generate a report, you should specify the specific criteria of updates you want to see, including the following:

- Update classification
- Update status
- Microsoft Security Response Center (MSRC) rating
- Effective approval
- Device group (if configured)

When the parameters of the report have been set, you can generate and view the report by clicking View Report. The report is generated and displayed in a new window and can be printed or exported.

Approve or decline updates

To deploy updates to Microsoft Intune clients, you must approve them in the classic Intune Administration console. To choose how to handle an update, perform the following steps:

1. In the classic Intune Administration console, click the Updates workspace.

2. In the All Updates node, select the update(s) that you want to approve.

3. Click Approve or Decline in the toolbar, depending on how you want the update handled.

4. On the Select Groups page, shown in Figure 3-9, select the groups to which you want the update deployed, click Add, and then click Next.

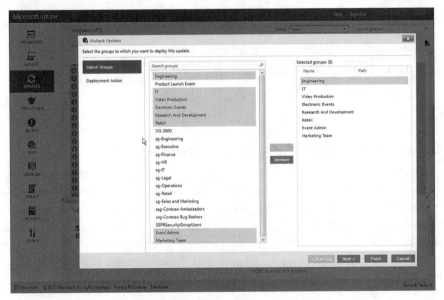

FIGURE 3-9 Selecting groups to which the update will be deployed

5. On the Deployment Action page, shown in Figure 3-10, select the approval status for the update. You can choose from among Required Install, Not applicable, Available Install, and Uninstall.

6. Click Finish.

FIGURE 3-10 Choosing approval status for an update

Configure automatic approval settings

Automatic approval rules enable you to configure Microsoft Intune to approve updates automatically, based on product category and update classification. When you configure an automatic approval rule, the update will be deployed automatically rather than requiring an administrator to perform manual approval. For example, you might configure an automatic approval rule for Windows 10 operating system updates that are classified as critical or security.

Any Windows 10 operating system update that Microsoft publishes that has the critical or security classification will automatically be deployed to Microsoft Intune clients.

EXAM TIP

Remember that approval rules will only apply if Microsoft Intune manages the product and classification that are the subject of the rule. There's no sense in configuring an approval rule for Windows 10 updates if Microsoft Intune isn't configured to manage updates for Windows 10 devices.

To create an automatic approval rule, perform the following steps:

1. Select the Admin workspace of the classic Intune Administration console.
2. Click Updates. Scroll to Automatic Approval Rules, and then click New.
3. On the General page of the Create Automatic Approval Rule Wizard, create a name and provide a description for the rule, and then click Next.
4. On the Product Categories page, select the products to which the automatic approval rule applies, and then click Next.

5. On the Update Classifications page, select the update classifications for which the rule will perform an automatic approval, and then click Next.

6. On the Deployment page, select the Intune groups for which the automatic approval rule will approve the update. If you scroll down, you can also configure an installation deadline for updates approved by this rule. Click Add, and then click Next to proceed.

7. On the Summary page, click Finish to complete the installation of the updates.

Configure deadlines for update installations

In the previous steps for configuring automatic approval, you had the option to choose an installation deadline for updates. In order to choose an installation deadline, you must first select the check box labeled Enforce An installation Deadline For These Updates. Once this check box has been selected, you can choose from the available options to enforce the deadline for installation:

- 1 Day After Approval
- 3 Days After Approval
- 7 Days After Approval
- 14 Days After Approval
- 21 Days After Approval
- 28 Days After Approval

If the update is not installed, or if the computer is not restarted before the deadline configured for the update, the update will be automatically installed when the deadline passes and the computer will be automatically restarted, if required by the update.

Deploy third-party updates

You can also use Microsoft Intune to deploy updates from third parties. You do this by manually uploading the update files, which can be in MSI, MSP, or EXE format. To upload and configure a third-party update to Microsoft Intune, perform the following steps:

1. In the Updates workspace of the classic Intune Administration console, click the Add Updates item on the right side, under Tasks.

2. On the Before You Begin page, click Next.

3. On the Update Files page, select the file you want to upload, and click Next.

4. On the Update Description page, complete the fields describing the update, and then click Next.

5. Select a classification. You can choose from among Updates, Critical Updates, Security Updates, Update Rollups, or Service Packs. Click Next.

6. On the Requirement page, select the operating system and architecture (x86 or x64) requirements for the update, and then click Next.

7. On the Detection Rules page, specify how Microsoft Intune can check whether the update has already been deployed on the Microsoft Intune client. This check can be performed by looking for an existing file, an MSI product code, or a specific registry key. Click Next.

8. On the Prerequisites page, identify any prerequisite software required for update installation and then click Next. You can specify None if no prerequisites are required or specify an existing file, an MSI product code, or a specific registry key.

9. On the Command Line Arguments page, specify any command-line arguments required to deploy the update and then click Next.

10. On the Return Codes page, specify how Intune should interpret return codes the update installation generates. Click Next. Finally, click Upload to complete.

After the update is uploaded to Intune, you can approve it using the same method you use to approve other software updates.

Skill 3.3: Manage devices with Microsoft 365 Solution

You can use Microsoft 365 to extend traditional device management beyond the corporate network and into the public Internet. With the cloud-based nature of the Microsoft 365 components, devices will be secure, productive and manageable from any location, with the only specific requirement being an Internet connection. This skill will review the management capabilities of Microsoft 365 and how you can use those capabilities to manage devices in your organization.

> **This section covers how to:**
> - Provision user accounts
> - Enroll devices
> - View and manage all managed devices
> - Configure the Microsoft Intune subscriptions
> - Configure the Microsoft Service Connection Point role
> - Manage user and computer groups
> - Configure monitoring and alerts
> - Manage policies
> - Manage remote computers

Provision user accounts

Microsoft 365 is a solution that integrates several products providing the combination of Office 365, Windows 10, security, and device management capabilities. With the range of features included, each licensed Microsoft 365 user will be able to be more productive, while at the same time protecting the business from the malicious attacks and potential data loss.

User accounts are an important part of Microsoft 365 functionality. You can control the application of Microsoft 365 management functionality for specific users, depending on how they are configured, and to which groups they belong.

You can add users to Microsoft 365 in several ways including:

- Create users manually in the Microsoft 365 Admin Center.
- Synchronize user accounts with Active Directory Domain Services.
- Import users from a comma-separated values (CSV) file.

> *IMPORTANT* **MICROSOFT 365 USER LICENSES**
>
> A user must have a license to your Microsoft 365 subscription before they can sign in and use the Microsoft 365 service. When a user has a license, they are able to download the latest version of Microsoft Office to their device. They can also enroll up to five devices into Microsoft Intune.

Creating users manually

You can create users manually within the Microsoft 365 Admin Center by entering the information about each user. To create a user account in Microsoft 365 Admin Center, perform the following steps:

1. Sign into Microsoft 365 using *https://www.office.com*, and click the Admin tile.
2. On the Admin center Home page, click Add a User in the Users area.
3. On the New user complete the fields (Display Name and User Name, Product licenses, are required fields) and then click Next.
4. Click Add.

Synchronizing user accounts with Active Directory Domain Services

Microsoft 365 can integrate with Active Directory Domain Services (AD DS) to provide user account synchronization from AD DS to Microsoft 365. This synchronization process enables you to avoid duplicate account creation and information by leveraging the information already stored in your on-premises Windows Server Active Directory (AD DS), and importing it into Microsoft 365 through the synchronization process. Microsoft 365 uses Azure Active Directory (AAD) to store user information, which can also be used with other Microsoft cloud products such as Microsoft Azure and Office 365.

The primary component required by the synchronization process is the Azure Active Directory (AD) Connect tool, which provides integration between AD DS and AAD. Once configured, Azure AD Connect will synchronize selected AD DS user accounts and information to Microsoft 365. You can synchronize Microsoft 365 with AD DS by using Azure AD Connect in two primary ways:

- **Azure AD Connect sync** Azure Active Directory Connect synchronization services (Azure AD Connect sync) synchronizes identity data between your on-premises environment and Azure AD. Optionally, password information is synchronized from AD to AAD to enable the users to maintain a single user account and password. An alternative to password synchronization is passthrough authentication, where authentication requests are forwarded back to Azure AD Connect on-premises.

- **Azure AD Connect and federation** This method of synchronization leverages Active Directory Federation Services (ADFS) to provide a single sign-on environment between Azure Active Directory and your on-premises Active Directory Federation Services (AD FS). With federation sign-in, users can sign in to Azure AD based services with their on-premises passwords.

> *MORE INFO* **DIRSYNC IS NO LONGER SUPPORTED**
>
> Directory Azure AD Connect replaces older versions of identity integration tools such as DirSync and Azure AD Sync, which are now deprecated and DirSync reached the end of support on April 13, 2017.

There are many situations in which you do not have Active Directory Domain Services, or you might have access to user information from another source such as another directory service or a human resources database. In these cases, the information from the source can usually be exported to a comma separated value (CSV) file, which can be used to create the users in Microsoft 365.

To import users from a CSV file, perform the following steps:

1. Sign into Microsoft 365 using *https://www.office.com*, and click the Admin tile.
2. On the Admin center Home page, click Add a User in the Users area.
3. Click Users in the navigation pane.
4. On the Users page, click New, type Import into the search bar and click the Search icon.
5. In the results pane, select Import Multiple Users.
6. In the Import Multiple Users screen click Browse, locate the CSV file you want to use, and optionally click Verify.
7. After the file has been selected, click Next.
8. On the Set User Options page, choose whether the users can sign-in the the account, select their geographical location and allocate any product licenses that need to be allocated to the user. (If you do not want to allocate a product license at this time, select the option to Create user without product license).

9. Click Next.

10. On the View your results page you can choose to download the import results or email them. Read the warning, that the initial system generated passwords for the new users will be contained in the result reports.

11. Click Send and close.

Enroll devices into Microsoft 365 Business

When you enroll devices into Microsoft 365 Business, they must be running Windows 10 Pro, version 1703 (Creators Update) or later. If you have any Windows devices running Windows 7 Pro, Windows 8 Pro, or Windows 8.1 Pro, the Microsoft 365 Business subscription entitles you to upgrade them to Windows 10 Pro.

Microsoft 365 Business includes a set of device management capabilities powered by Microsoft Intune, but not the full Intune solution, which is available with the Microsoft 365 Enterprise subscription.

To enroll a brand new device running Windows 10 Pro into Microsoft 365 Business follow these steps:

1. Go through Windows 10 device setup until you get to the How Would You Like To Set Up? page as shown in Figure 3-11.

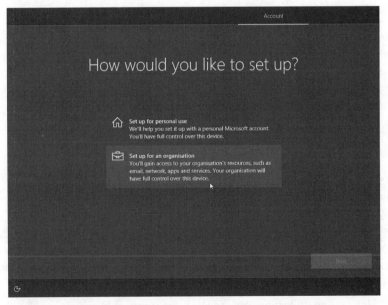

FIGURE 3-11 Windows 10 device setup

2. Choose Set up for an organization and then enter your username and password for Microsoft 365 Business subscription (the new user account not the tenant admin account.)

3. Finish Windows 10 device setup.

4. The device will be registered and connected to your organization's Azure AD.

5. You can verify the device is connected to Azure AD by signing into the device and clicking the Windows logo, and then the Settings icon.

6. In Settings, go to Accounts.

7. On Your info page, click Access Work Or School.

8. You should see that the device is Connected to your organization. Click your organization name to expose the buttons Info and Disconnect.

9. Click on Info to get your synchronization status.

10. To verify that the device has been upgraded to Windows 10 Business edition, clicking the Windows logo, and type **About**.

11. Confirm that the Edition shows Windows 10 Business as highlighted in Figure 3-12.

FIGURE 3-12 Windows 10 device setup

Even though Microsoft 365 Business does not include the full Intune support or provide a link from the Microsoft 365 Business Admin portal, you do have access to Intune App Protection in the Azure portal. This allows you to view app protection settings for Windows 10, Android, and iOS devices.

To access the Intune App Protection blade follow these steps:

1. Sign into the Azure portal at *https://portal.azure.com* with your Microsoft 365 Business admin credentials.

2. Choose More Services, then type **Intune** into the filter, selecting Intune App Protection.

3. Select App Policy.

> **IMPORTANT** **MICROSOFT 365 LICENSE RESTRICTION**
>
> Take care when modifying settings within the Azure Intune portal, because the Microsoft 365 Business subscription provides you with a license to modify only the Intune settings that map to the settings available in Microsoft 365 Business.

Enroll devices into Microsoft 365 Enterprise

For larger organizations, with over 300 users and devices, the Microsoft 365 Enterprise solution includes Microsoft Intune for device & app management. Microsoft Intune supports enrollment in a number of different ways, depending on the device being enrolled as described in the section related to enrolling devices into Intune.

When enrolling devices into Microsoft 365 Enterprise, they must be running Windows 10 Enterprise, version 1703 (Creators Update) or later. Devices running an earlier version of Windows, are able to upgrade to Windows 10 Enterprise as part of the Microsoft 365 Enterprise licensing.

If you want to enroll a large number of devices in an enterprise scenario, you can use the Device Enrollment Manager (DEM) account in Microsoft Intune. The DEM is a special account in Microsoft Intune that allows you to enroll up to 1,000 devices (By default standard users can manage and enroll up to five devices). For security reasons, the DEM user should not also be an Intune administrator. Each enrolled device will require a single Intune license.

By default, there is no device enrollment account user present in Microsoft Intune. You can create a device enrollment account by performing the following steps:

1. In the Azure portal, choose More Services > Monitoring + Management > Intune.

2. On the Intune blade, choose Device Enrollment, and then under Manage, choose Device Enrollment Managers.

3. Select Add.

4. On the Add User blade, enter the username for the DEM user, and select Add. The user is promoted to the DEM role.

5. Close the Add User blade.

6. The list of Device Enrollment Managers now contains the new user as shown in Figure 3-13.

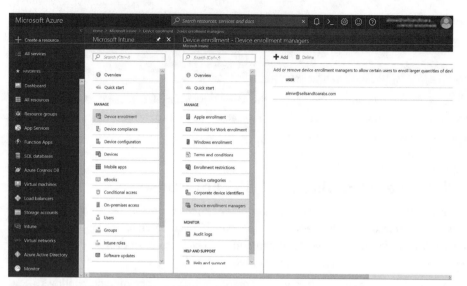

FIGURE 3-13 List of Device Enrollment Managers

> ***MORE INFO* ENROLL DEVICES USING DEVICE ENROLLMENT MANAGER**
>
> For more information on the DEM in Microsoft Intune, together with example scenarios and limitations of devices that are enrolled with a DEM account, visit the following URL at *https://docs.microsoft.com/intune/device-enrollment-manager-enroll.*

View and manage all managed devices

For Microsoft 365 Business subscription administrators, you can manage your enrolled devices directly from the Microsoft 365 Business Admin portal Home screen as shown in Figure 3-14.

On the Microsoft 365 Business Admin portal Home screen, you have tiles available to perform the following tasks related to devices:

- **Manage Device Policies**   Including Add policy, Edit policy and Delete policy.
- **Manage Device Actions**   Including Deploy Windows with Autopilot, Remove company data, Factory reset, and Manage Office Deployment.
- **Perform Windows 10 Upgrade**   Including Install upgrade, Share the download link, create installation media, and troubleshoot installation.

FIGURE 3-14 Microsoft 365 Business Admin portal Home screen

For Microsoft 365 Enterprise and businesses with a Microsoft Intune subscription managed devices can be viewed from several different pages in either the classic Intune portal or from Intune in the Azure portal.

The Groups page, in the classic Intune console, as shown in Figure 3-15, contains views for devices based on Microsoft Intune group membership. The following default views will provide access to a list of devices that correspond with the definition of that view:

- All Devices
- All Corporate Pre-enrolled devices

FIGURE 3-15 List of managed devices in the classic Intune portal

From these views, you can manage and interact with the devices listed, including retire or wipe a device, and perform tasks, such as remotely lock the device.

In the modern Intune portal, in Azure, you can navigate to the devices pane, and view the devices you manage, and perform remote tasks on those devices.

To access the devices workplace perform these steps:

1. Sign into the Azure portal at *https://portal.azure.com*.

2. Choose More Services > Monitoring + Management > Intune.

3. In Intune, choose Devices.

4. View information about devices and perform the remote device actions as follows:

   - **Overview**   A snapshot of the enrolled devices you can manage.

   - **All devices**   A list of the enrolled devices you manage. Select a device to view device inventory.

   - **Azure AD devices**   A list of the devices registered or joined with Azure Active Directory (AD) as shown in Figure 3-16.

FIGURE 3-16 A list of managed Azure AD devices in the modern Intune portal

   - **Device actions**   This option provides a history of the remote actions performed on enrolled devices including the action taken, its status, time and who initiated the action.

Configure Microsoft Intune subscriptions

Microsoft Intune subscriptions dictate the capability and number of users that an instance of Microsoft Intune can support. You configure several options for subscription management on the Microsoft 365 Admin center in the Billings section of the Microsoft 365 Admin center.

- **Subscriptions**   This page displays the active subscriptions and includes a summary of licenses available and assigned for each subscription. For each subscription, the renewal date (or expiration date for trial subscriptions) is shown. There is also an Add subscription link will redirect you to the Purchase Services page where you can purchase additional licenses.

- **Bills**   From the Bills page, you can view bills and charges for your tenant for anytime in the previous 12 months. You can then print or save a PDF copy of the invoice.

- **Licenses**   The Licenses page displays which licenses have been attached to the Microsoft 365 subscription, as shown in Figure 3-17. To add more licenses, you need open the Subscriptions page, then choose the subscription that you want to add licenses to and then the Add/Remove licenses.

FIGURE 3-17 The Licenses page in Microsoft 365

- **Purchase Services**   This page, allows you can purchase additional licenses.

- **Billing notifications**   Allows you to configure how your billing statement is sent. You can configure each administrator to receive a separate email with the billing statement.

Configure the Microsoft Service Connection Point role

The System Center Configuration Manager service connection point is a role that allows an instance of System Center Configuration Manager (Current Branch) to use Microsoft Intune as a management point for Configuration tasks.

The Microsoft Intune Connection Point role is installed on System Center Configuration Manager and communicates with the Microsoft Intune service to enable administration for Microsoft Intune managed devices from the System Center Configuration Manager console, thereby extending the scope of your System Center Configuration Manager environment to the Internet.

The service connection point can operate in either online or offline mode:

- **Online mode**   The service connection point automatically checks every 24 hours for updates. If updates for your current infrastructure and product version are available these are downloaded and made available in the Configuration Manager console.

- **Offline mode**   You must manually use the Service Connection Tool for System Center Configuration Manager to import available updates.

To configure the Microsoft Intune Connection Point role in System Center Configuration Manager, perform the following steps:

1. In the Configuration Manager console, click Administration.

2. In the Administration workspace, expand Sites, and then click Servers and Site System Roles.

3. Add the Service connection point role to a new or existing site system server:

   - **New site system server**   On the Home tab, in the Create group, click Create Site System Server to start the Create Site System Server Wizard.

   - **Existing site system server**   Click the server on which you want to install the service connection point role. On the Home tab, in the Server group, click Add Site System Roles to start the Add Site system Roles Wizard.

4. On the System Role Selection page, select Service connection point, click Next.

5. Complete the wizard.

Manage user and computer groups

Groups are an important organizational component in Microsoft Intune. You can use groups to group computers or users together into logical units for management and administration tasks in a more effective manner.

By default, Intune groups are now managed as groups in the Azure Active Directory in the Azure Portal. Some of the Intune tasks that work with groups include: Alerts, Software Updates, Endpoint Protection, Policies and Software Management.

Group membership can include users or devices, or other existing groups within Azure AD. Once a group has been created, the membership can consist of assigned members, or dynamically assigned members based on their Azure AD properties.

Users and devices can belong to multiple groups. In Azure Active Directory, you can allocate members by using assigned membership or dynamically:

- **Criteria Membership**   These allow you to create advanced rules to enable attribute-based dynamic memberships to include or exclude users or devices as members. These criteria use security groups and other information synchronized from your local Active

Directory. When the security group or data that is synchronized changes, the group membership can change.

- **Assigned Membership**   These are static rules that explicitly add or exclude user or devices as members. The membership list is static.

Creating an Assigned User or Device group

To create a group membership using an assigned membership, use these steps:

1. Sign into the Azure portal at *https://portal.azure.com* with an account that is a global administrator or a user account administrator.
2. Choose More Services > Monitoring + Management > Intune.
3. In Intune, choose Groups.
4. Select All groups, and select New group.
5. On the Group blade, add a name and description for the group.
6. On the membership type drop down box, select Assigned.
7. Under the Members item, click the > and select members.
8. Type the name of users, groups or devices and select them to add members.
9. Select Create on the Group blade to create the group.

Creating a Dynamic User or Device group

To create a group membership using an advanced rule, use these steps:

1. Sign into the Azure portal at *https://portal.azure.com* with an account that is a global administrator or a user account administrator.
2. Choose More Services > Monitoring + Management > Intune.
3. In Intune, choose Groups.
4. Select All groups, and select New group.
5. On the Group blade, choose a name and description for the new group.
6. Select a membership type of either Dynamic User or Dynamic Device (depending on whether you want to create a rule for users or devices).
7. Next select Add dynamic query. (You can use the rule builder to build a simple rule, or enter the advanced rule yourself).
8. After creating the rule, select Add query at the bottom of the blade.
9. Select Create on the Group blade to create the group.

Configure monitoring and alerts

You can use the classic Microsoft Intune portal to monitor your managed devices. There are two primary ways that you can monitor the status of your Microsoft Intune environment:

- **Reports**   You can use reports to monitor the status of devices including software update status, software installed, and certificate compliance.

- **Alerts**   You can use alerts to provide notifications based on Microsoft Intune events or status parameters.

Using reports

Reports can provide information about both past and future events in Microsoft Intune, and they can help to forecast future needs and confirm the current state of your environment.

There are several types of reports available in Microsoft Intune as shown in Figure 3-18:

- **Update reports**   Shows the software updates that succeeded on computers in your organization, in addition to the updates that failed, are pending updates, or if updates are needed.

- **Detected software reports**   Shows software installed on computers in your organization and includes the software versions. You can filter the information that displays based on the software publisher and the software category. You can expand the updates in the list to show more detail (such as the computers on which it is installed) by clicking the directional arrow next to the list item.

- **Computer inventory reports**   Shows information about managed computers in your organization. Use this report to plan hardware purchases and to understand more about the hardware needs of users in your organization.

- **Mobile device inventory reports**   Shows information about the mobile devices in your organization. You can filter the information that displays based on groups, whether the device is a jailbroken or rooted device, and by operating system.

- **License purchase reports**   Shows the software titles for all licensed software in selected license groups, based on their licensing agreements.

- **License installation reports**   Shows reports that compare installed software on computers in your organization with your current license agreement coverage.

- **Terms and conditions reports**   Show whether users accepted terms and conditions you deployed, and which version they accepted. You can specify up to 10 users whose acceptance of any terms and conditions that were deployed to them are shown, or show the acceptance status for a particular term deployed to them.

- **Noncompliant apps reports** Shows information about the users who have apps installed that are not on your lists of compliant appa or on your list of noncompliant apps. Use this report to find users and devices that are not in compliance with your company app policies.

- **Certificate compliance reports** Show which certificates have been issued to users and devices through the Network Device Enrollment Service. Use this report to find certificates that are issued, expired, and revoked.

- **Device history reports** Show a historical log of retire, wipe, and delete actions. Use this report to see who initiated actions on devices in the past.

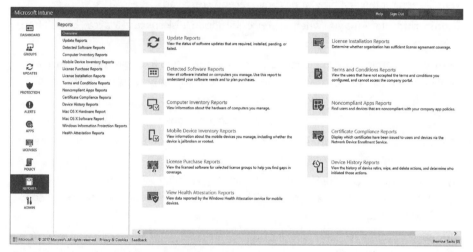

FIGURE 3-18 The Reports workspace in Microsoft Intune

Once a report has been created, it can be saved, printed or exported. The report criteria can also be loaded from a previously saved report.

Creating a report

To create a report use these steps: In the classic Microsoft Intune administrator console, click the Reports workspace.

1. Select the report type you want to generate.

2. On the Create New Report page, accept the default values or customize them to filter the results that will be returned by the report. (For example, you can select that only software published by Microsoft will be displayed in the detected software report).

3. Click View Report to open the report in a new window.

Using alerts

Alerts provide notification based on Microsoft Intune status events. You can use alerts in several ways in Microsoft Intune:

- View all recent alerts to obtain a high-level view of device health.
- Identify specific issues that are occurring in your environment with regard to timing, and scope.
- Use filter alerts to target specific events or issues in your environment.

There are several alert categories available in Microsoft Intune including:

- **Endpoint protection**   Informs you when computers have malware warnings, are not protected, or have malware that requires action. These alerts also notify you when malware is seen for the first time or has been recently resolved.
- **Monitoring**   Informs you when a service is stopped, disk space is too low, or disk fragmentation is high.
- **Notices**   Informs you about configuration tasks that need to be performed (such as configuring automatic approvals for updates) and service announcements that display on the Notice Board on the System Overview page.
- **Policy**   Informs you when a device is unable to apply one or more policy settings.
- **Remote Assistance**   Informs you when a user on a managed computer has initiated a request for remote assistance.
- **System**   Informs you when client deployments have failed. Also contains a sub-category of Mobile Device Management, which informs you when mobile device issues occur, including Exchange connectivity.
- **Updates**   Informs you when specific updates are waiting for approval, such as Security Updates or Critical Updates.

> *NOTE* **ADD RECIPIENT EMAIL ADDRESS**
>
> If you want to be emailed when a notification rule is triggered, you need to enter a recipient email address in the Recipients area within the Admin workspace.

Creating a new notification rule

To create a notification rule use these steps:

1. In the classic Microsoft Intune administrator console, click the Admin workspace.
2. Click Alerts and Notifications, click Notification Rules, and then Create New Rule.
3. In the Create Notification Rule Wizard, enter a Name for the notification rule.
4. Select the Categories and Severity for the notification rule, and then click Next.

5. If presented with the Select Device Groups page, select the device groups to which this rule will apply, then click Next.

6. On the Select Email Recipients page, (if you have previously added a notification recipient), select an email address and then click Save.

7. Close the wizard.

8. The rule now appears in the Notification Rules.

Troubleshoot Microsoft Intune

In addition to reports and alerts, the new Intune portal in Azure allows you to access a troubleshooting portal to view user information to address user help requests.

From the troubleshooting portal, Intune shows useful data including:

- User status
- Assignments
- Compliance issues
- Device not responding
- Device not getting VPN or Wi-Fi settings
- App installation failure

To access and review troubleshooting details for a user, follow these steps:

1. Sign into the Azure portal.

2. Choose More Services > Monitoring + Management > Intune.

3. On the Intune blade, choose Troubleshoot.

4. Click Select user.

5. Select a user by typing the name or email address, and click Select.

6. The troubleshooting information for the user shows in the Troubleshooting blade (Figure 3-19).

FIGURE 3-19 Troubleshooting enrolled users in Intune

Manage policies

You can use Microsoft Intune policies to enforce functionality, compliance, and security related features on enrolled devices. Policies are managed from the Policy workspace in the classic Microsoft Intune and from the Device Compliance blade in the Azure Intune portal. To help understand which portal you should use, consider the guidance:

- In the Azure portal, the compliance policies are created separately for each supported platform.
- In the Intune classic portal, one device compliance policy is common to all supported platforms.

Exploring classic Intune policies

The Microsoft Intune Policy page is broken down into several sections:

- **Overview** The Overview page provides a dashboard view of current policy status, shortcuts to common policy-related tasks, and links to relevant help topics.
- **Policy Conflicts** This page shows conflicts where Intune policy was not applied according to configuration. Each conflict is listed with relevant details including where and when the conflict occurred.
- **Configuration Policies** On this page, you can create and manage policies that configure Windows computers and mobile devices. A large portion of Intune policies are configured from this page.

- **Compliance Policies**   The Compliance Policies page provides the ability to create and manage policies related to compliant devices and enforcing compliance.

- **Conditional Access**   On this page, you can control access to Microsoft Exchange, Exchange Online and SharePoint Online for managed devices.

- **Corporate Device Enrollment**   On this page, you can create a device enrollment profile to enable enrollment for iOS based devices.

- **Terms and Conditions**   On this page, you can create policies to explain how enrollment, access to work resources, and how using the company portal affect devices and users. Users must accept the terms and conditions before they can use the company portal to enroll and access their work resources.

EXAM TIP

Microsoft Intune policies feature similar functionality and some of the same settings as Group Policy. In the case of a settings conflict between Intune policy and Group Policy, Group Policy takes precedence and will be applied instead of the Intune policy.

Configuring Microsoft Intune policies in the Azure Portal

You need to be comfortable with creating policies in both the classic Intune portal and the Azure portal. Unlike the classic portal, when you create a policy in the Azure portal, the process is wizard driven and only the options that are applicable for the platform, setting, or policy are made available in the wizard.

To create a device compliance policy in the Azure portal, follow these steps:

1. Sign into the Azure portal at *https://portal.azure.com* with an account that is a global administrator or a user account administrator.

2. Choose More Services > Monitoring + Management > Intune.

3. In Intune, choose Device compliance.

4. In the Device compliance blade, under Manage, choose Create Policy.

   A. Type a name, description and choose the platform that you want this policy to apply to.

   B. Click the Settings and then choose the compliance requirements required. Depending on which platform you choose, you can specify various options that may include Email, Device Health, Device Properties and System Security settings.

   C. When you are done, choose Ok.

   D. On the Create Policy blade, click Create.

DEPLOY A POLICY

The newly created policy will not provide any functionality until it is deployed to a Group. Follow these steps to assign a device compliance policy to a group:

1. In Intune, choose the Device compliance blade.

2. In the Device compliance blade, select Policies and on the policy blade select the policy you want to assign.

3. The policy blade appears. Click Assignments to open the Assignments blade.

4. Select the groups to include or exclude.

5. In the Azure AD Groups, type the name of the group required.

6. Select the groups from the list and click Select.

7. Click Save, and close the blade.

8. On the Policies blade, notice that the policy now shows that it is assigned.

After assignment is complete, you can make changes to the policy configuration by selecting the policy, choosing properties, and then modifying the settings and actions.

Manage remote computers

You can use Microsoft Intune to manage several aspects of functionality for managed computers. The user interface for these actions is found where one or more devices is listed.

You can manage devices from Intune using these interfaces:

- Classic Intune Admin portal: Groups Workspace - Devices
- Intune Azure portal: All Devices Workspace
- Microsoft 365 Business home page

Not all of the following actions are available on all device types or platforms. These actions are determined by the device platform, and the configuration of the device, and also by the MDM and vendor.

- **Remote Lock**   Lock supported devices, even if you do not have the device in your possession.

- **Reset passcode**   Force the end user to reset the passcode on supported devices.

- **Sync**   Force the selected device to immediately check in with Intune and receive any pending actions or policies that have been assigned to it.

- **Retire/Wipe**   When you choose this option, you are given two options:

  - **Selective Wipe / Remove Company Data**   This option removes only company data managed by Intune, leaving personal data intact. The type of company data removed varies by platform and includes profiles, applications, policies and the Intune Endpoint Protection software.

  - **Full Wipe/Factory Reset**   This option wipes the device and return it to its factory default settings by removing all data, including user personal data, from the device.

- **Delete** This command removes the device from Microsoft Intune, but does not modify device settings or software.

- **Run A Full Malware Scan** This command runs a full malware scan by using Microsoft Intune Endpoint Protection on the selected device.

- **Run A Quick Malware Scan** This command runs a quick malware scan by using Microsoft Intune Endpoint Protection on the selected device.

- **Restart Computer** This command restarts the remote device.

- **Fresh start** Removes any apps that were installed on a Windows 10 PC running the Creators Update (version 1703) or later, then updates the PC to the latest version of Windows. After Fresh start, devices are unenrolled from Intune.

- **Update Malware Definitions** This command initiates an update of malware definitions for the Microsoft Intune Endpoint Protection client.

- **Refresh Policies** This command requests a manual refresh of the client policies from the Microsoft Intune site.

- **Refresh Inventory** This command requests updated inventory information to be sent from the device to Microsoft Intune.

- **Remote Assistance Session** Use the TeamViewer software to give remote assistance to your users who are running the Intune software client.

> **_MORE INFO_ MICROSOFT INTUNE DEVICE POLICIES AND DEVICE ACTIONS**
>
> For more information about Microsoft Intune device management policies and available device actions, visit *https://docs.microsoft.com/intune/device-management*.

Skill 3.4: Configure information protection

Regardless of business size and industry, all companies have data that they consider sensitive. Microsoft aims to protect your corporate data from being lost, stolen, or getting into the wrong hands with their Information Protection solutions built into Office 365, Windows, Azure, and across the Microsoft Cloud.

Information protection is a huge issue for many enterprises, and some are bound by law and regulations, which stipulate how data should be protected and for how long it must be safeguarded before secure deletion. Let's examine new solutions from Microsoft and see how they can be configured and deployed to protect your data.

Manage and configure Office 365 Data Loss Prevention

Office 365 offers businesses an integrated solution with many popular features such as email, Office, SharePoint and OneDrive for Business. Yet hidden away is a full data protection suite which allows businesses to comply with industry regulations and laws that require organizations to protect sensitive information, such as personally identifiable information (PII), and prevent its inadvertent disclosure. Leaks of sensitive information can have huge negative impact on businesses. This can include sizable fines and lost goodwill.

Following the Health Insurance Portability and Accountability Act (HIPAA) in the USA, which aims to ensure protection for individually identifiable health data, officers in charge of running the business that lose PII can be jailed for not ensuring adequate safeguards are in place.

With a data loss prevention (DLP) policy in place using the Office 365 Security & Compliance Center, you can identify, monitor, and automatically protect sensitive information across the Office 365 suite of products. This includes Exchange Online, SharePoint Online, and OneDrive for Business.

A DLP policy can help in the following ways:

- Identify sensitive information in Exchange Online, SharePoint Online, and OneDrive for Business.
- Prevent the accidental sharing of sensitive information.
- Monitor and protect sensitive information in Office 2016 – Word, Excel, and PowerPoint.
- Help train users to stay compliant with their work.
- View DLP compliant reports.

With Office 365, you can create and manage DLP policies in the Security & Compliance Center.

A DLP policy can be configured on one of the Office 365 locations mentioned above, and then you need to establish rules that will protect the content. These are comprised of:

- Conditions   The content monitored by the DLP must match the conditions in place for the rule to be enforced.
- Actions   These are the actions that you want the rule to take when the conditions are met. For example, the action could block access to the document and send an email notification to the compliance team.

Office 365 includes over 40 ready-to-use templates containing rules that you can use or customize to meet your organization's compliance requirements.

There are DLP policy templates that can be used to help with the compliance requirements for the following industry regulations and legislations:

- Gramm-Leach-Bliley Act (GLBA)
- Payment Card Industry Data Security Standard (PCI-DSS)
- United States Personally Identifiable Information (U.S. PII)
- United States Health Insurance Act (HIPAA)

Create a DLP policy from a template

To create a DLP policy from a template follow these steps:

1. Sign in to Office 365 at *https://office.com* and click the Security & Compliance tile. (Alternatively sign in directly at *https://protection.office.com*.)

2. The homepage of the Office 365 Security & Compliance Center appears, as shown in Figure 3-20.

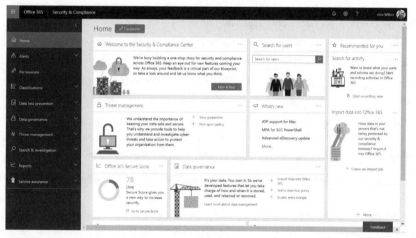

FIGURE 3-20 Office 365 Security & Compliance Center

3. On the Security & Compliance Center homepage, click Data loss prevention.

4. Click Policy and then click +Create a policy.

Choose one of the DLP policy templates—we will click Privacy template covering U.S. Personally Identifiable Information◻ (PII) ◻Data, as shown in Figure 3-21, and then click Next.

FIGURE 3-21 Creating a new DLP from a policy template

5.   Provide the policy a name and click Next.

6.   Choose the locations that you want the DLP policy to protect. We will choose Let Me Choose Specific Locations and click Next.

7.   On the Choose Locations page, you can fine tune the locations, accounts, and sites. Click Next.

8.   On the Policy settings page view the options to customize the type of content that the U.S. PII Data template looks for and then click Next. (You can modify the rule conditions and actions by clicking the Advanced option on the Policy settings page).

9.   On the What Do You Want To Do If We Detect Sensitive Info? Page, review the options and then click Next.

10. On the next page, there are three options. Choose whether to turn on the rule, test it out first, or leave the rules disabled and click Next.

11. Review your settings for this policy and then click Create.

12. Click Close.

Depending on the size of your organization, you should consider rolling your DLP policies out gradually to assess their impact and test their effectiveness. A DLP policy can unintentionally block access to documents that staff require for their daily work. It is therefore recommended that you initially pilot the deployment of DLP policies, and initially limit the location and scope.

Once the initial test deployment is successful, you can roll them out to a wider audience. Throughout the process you should monitor the DLP reports, the incident reports, and any notifications to make sure that the results are what you intend.

Windows Information Protection and BitLocker

Built into Windows 10, are tools that allow businesses to protect data, contain data, and prevent data leakage when it is both shared internally and externally outside of an organization. The key pillars of information protection are shown in Figure 3-22.

Information Protection Needs			
Device Protection	**Data Separation**	**Leak Protection**	**Sharing Protection**
Protect system and data when device is lost or stolen	Containment Data separation	Prevent unauthorized users and apps from accessing and leaking data	Protect data when shared with others, or shared outside of organizational devices and control

FIGURE 3-22 Key pillars of information protection needs

Windows Information Protection is the inclusion of many of the above needs, being incorporated directly into the information protection stack within Windows.

Windows 10 caters for Device Protection with BitLocker, which protects your data while it's at rest on the device, even if the device is lost or stolen. If the hard drive is removed from the device, all data is encrypted and unreadable.

The separation of data allows for administrators to identify personal vs. corporate data. As you've seen with Microsoft Intune, it is possible to contain data into these categories and securely wipe business data from a device remotely on demand. This is also possible within the operating system by having the Windows 10 Anniversary Update installed.

Next, Windows 10 contains capabilities to prevent business data from leaking out of the organization. For example, you can post data from a corporate Word document to a non-corporate location such as Facebook or Twitter. Make sure that only authorized apps have access to business data, employing copy and paste restrictions where needed.

The last pillar requirement is to help ensure that business data can be shared with others within and outside of their organization in a secure way. For example, corporate documents can be emailed to authorized colleagues, with controls on who can view or edit the document, with the ability to revoke permissions as needed.

If you use Microsoft 365, or Microsoft Intune, there are policies available within your MDM or System Center Configuration Manager to configure WIP remotely. An example of WIP in action using Intune is to enforce a Windows 10 device compliance policy to require that BitLocker is used, and reported through the Windows Health Attestation Service.

Create a WIP policy within Intune

If you use Intune in your organization, you can create a WIP-specific policy through the Azure portal. To create a WIP policy use these steps:

1. Sign into the Azure portal at *https://portal.azure.com* with an account that is a global administrator or a user account administrator.

2. Choose More Services > Monitoring + Management > Intune.

3. In Intune, choose Mobile Apps.

4. In the Mobile Apps blade, under manage, click the App protection policies.

5. Choose Add A Policy.

6. Enter the following values:

   - **Name**   Type a name for your new policy.

   - **Description**   Type an optional description.

   - **Platform**   From the drop down, select Windows 10.

   - **Enrollment state**   Choose without enrollment.

7. Click the Allowed apps, and then choose Add apps. The Add apps blade opens, showing you all apps that are currently available that are allowed to access your enterprise data.

> *NOTE* **ADD A DESKTOP APP**
>
> If you want to add a desktop app to your allowed apps list, use the drop down menu and select Desktop Apps. Enter the info into the fields, and choose OK to add the app to your Allowed apps list.

8. Select Microsoft Edge and click OK twice.

9. Click the Configure Required Settings. Here you will apply a protection mode as shown in Figure 3-23. Choose Silent or Allow Overrides if this is a pilot or test, because this setting will permit WIP breaches. If you want to enforce WIP, change the setting to Hide Overrides.

FIGURE 3-23 Configure WIP App protection policy in Microsoft Intune

10. Choose whether you want to pin to dashboard, and click OK.

11. Choose Create.

To deploy the policy to Windows 10 devices running the Creators Update and later, open the policy and assign it to AAD user groups.

BitLocker

BitLocker Drive Encryption has improved consistently since the version that shipped with Windows Vista, and it is now widely adopted and highly regarded in the marketplace. Businesses have usage rights to BitLocker with the Windows 10 Pro, Education, and Enterprise SKUs. For consumers running Windows 10 Home, their devices use Device Encryption, which offers the same level of encryption and data protection, but without access to the BitLocker Drive Encryption Tools and management tools.

BitLocker is simple to provision, with or without a Trusted Platform Module (TPM) chip, and most Microsoft own brand devices since Surface 3, includes device encryption as soon as a user signs into the device with administrative privileges right out of the box.

BitLocker has developed management tools including Microsoft BitLocker Administration and Monitoring (MBAM) for enterprises, which allows administrators to provision at scale, monitor and report on compliance, and provide user and help desk capabilities for helping recovery scenarios.

If devices contain a TPM chip, they can securely run BitLocker without the need for a PIN (password) or USB drive, which allows them to harness pre-boot authentication and SSO, making encryption more streamlined for users.

You will learn more about BitLocker in Chapter 5 covering configuring storage.

Azure Information Protection

Azure Information Protection continues the protection of information by helping classify, label, and protect documents and emails. Because this uses Azure, it is a cloud-based solution that requires no on premise infrastructure. The technology uses Azure Rights Management (Azure RMS), which allows administrators to define rules and conditions that then automatically add classification to the data, or users can manually add the classification to their files.

Organizations with one of the following Office 365 subscriptions include Azure RMS:

- Office 365 Enterprise E3, E4 or E5
- Office 365 Education A3, A4, or A5
- Office 365 Government G3 or G4

Administrators can track and control classified content and how it is used. This includes monitoring data flows, tracking access to documents, and preventing data leakage or misuse.

The labels in Azure Information Protection are not the same as the labels available in Office 365 Security & Compliance. AIP labels let you apply classification and protection policy for documents and emails. The Office 365 Security & Compliance labels are used to classify documents and emails for auditing and retention purposes within Office 365 services.

Documents and emails use labels to apply classification, which stays with the resources at all times, regardless of where the data is stored or if it is shared. The labels are visible to the user. Metadata embedded into the files and email headers is stored in clear text which ensures that other services, such as data loss prevention solutions, can view the classification and take appropriate action.

With the technology being cloud-based, it is integrated with Office 365 and Azure Active Directory. Developers and software vendors can use the Graph APIs to extend Azure RMS to work with 3rd party information protection solutions both on-premises, or in the cloud.

The Azure information protection solution keeps you in control of your data by using encryption, identity, and authorization policies. There are default templates within the Azure Rights Management service that you can use to restrict data access to users within your organization.

Configure Azure Information Protection

In order to use or evaluate Azure Information Protection, you need the following prerequisites:

- A subscription that includes Azure Information Protection.
- A global administrator account or security administrator account to sign in to the Azure portal and configure the Azure Information Protection policy.
- A computer running Windows (minimum of Windows 7 with Service Pack 1), with Office installed.

Activate the Azure Rights Management service

The first stage in configuring Azure Information Protection is to activate the Azure Rights Management service by using the following steps:

1. Sign in to the Azure portal as a global admin or security admin at *https://portal.azure. com.*

2. On the Azure hub menu, click +New, and then, from the Marketplace list, select Security + Identity and select Azure Information Protection from the list on the right side.

3. On the Azure Information Protection blade, click Create.

4. The information on the Quick start page appears.

5. On the Azure Information Protection blade, select Protection activation.

6. On the Protection activation select Activate.

Explore Azure Information Protection policies

Azure Information Protection comes with a default policy called Global Policy that you can use without modification, or you can customize. Let's take a look at the default policy.

1. On the Azure Information Protection blade, select the Global Policy item.

2. Review the information and expand the confidential label displayed on the Global Policy blade as shown in Figure 3-24.

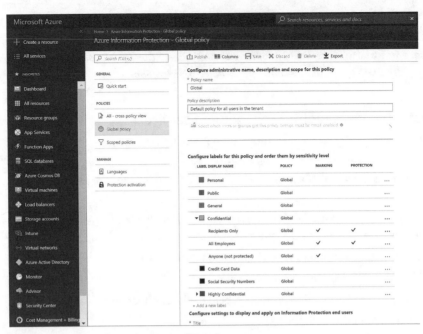

FIGURE 3-24 Azure Information Protection policy

3. To set the default label and prompt the user for justification when setting a lower classification label, select the General label and ensure that the label is enabled. .

4. Toggle the Users Must Provide Justification To Set A Lower Classification label, Remove A Label, Or Remove Protection option to On.

5. You should explore the policy further, creating a new label for protection, visual markers, and create a condition to prompt the user for classification.

6. If you have made any changes, click Save.

7. In order for the policy to be available to users, it needs to be published. Click Publish, and click Yes to confirm.

Install the Azure Information Protection client

Earlier in the Windows Information Protection and BitLocker section, we discovered that Windows 10 has the WIP framework built into the operating system. When you install the Azure Information Protection client, Windows will communicate to Azure and display the labels in Office applications.

To install the Azure Information Protection client, follows these steps:

1. On the client PC, ensure that Office has been installed, and that the user has signed into the Office application.

2. Quit all running Office apps and download the Azure Information Protection client (AzInfoProtection.exe), from the Microsoft download center at *https://www.microsoft.com/download/details.aspx?id=53018*.

3. Run the Azure Information Protection client and follow the prompts to install the client.

4. Open Word and create a new, blank document.

5. You should see a Congratulations page with basic instructions. Read the instructions and then click Close.

6. After the new document loads, you should see on the Home tab a new Protection group, a Protect button. , and a new bar under the ribbon. This is the Information Protection bar, which displays the labels that you saw in the Azure portal as shown in Figure 3-25.

FIGURE 3-25 Azure Information Protection policy

Create documents and protect them using Azure Information Protection to see how labeling works. Try other settings using Excel, PowerPoint, and Outlook, which support Azure Information Protection.

> ***MORE INFO* MOBILE DEVICE MANAGEMENT**
>
> For more information and a complete walkthrough using Azure Information Protection, consider the following tutorial: *https://docs.microsoft.com/information-protection/get-started/infoprotect-quick-start-tutorial*.

Microsoft Cloud App Security

You have seen how Microsoft provides information security for Windows 10 and your data through WIP and Azure RMS. This level of control and protection can also be provisioned for your cloud based apps, allowing you to protect critical data across cloud applications.

The Cloud App Security (CAS) framework consists of three layers that include:

- **Cloud Discovery**   This layer is concerned with the discovery of the cloud usage within your organization.

- **Data Protection**   This allows you to monitor and control your cloud data by establishing visibility, enforcing data loss prevention (DLP) policies, alerting and investigating data.

- **Threat Protection**   Once you have visibility, you need to look for and detect abnormal use and identify any security incidents. This layer uses behavioral analytics and advanced investigation tools to intelligently identify threats and mitigate risk. By tuning the threat protection, you can reduce the disruption caused by false positives and any performance burden over network cloud traffic.

Software vendors and developers can integrate their apps within the Cloud App Security framework by using ready-made app connectors and APIs. Administrators can sanction or deny access to apps in your cloud. At the time of writing this book, Microsoft has a catalog of over 15,000 cloud apps that can be integrated using the service.

You saw earlier how legislation and industry standards are involved in data protection. Cloud App Security is officially certified with Microsoft Compliance for ISO, HIPAA, CSA STAR, and EU model clauses. Additional certifications and compliance can be sought as they are developed.

An example of how to use Cloud App Security, even if your organization does not use cloud apps, is to upload your firewall traffic logs to the CAS service and allow CAS to scan and discover unapproved apps, and activity. Data passing through the Cloud App Security service is not retained or stored by Microsoft, although metadata, alerts and activity logs are retained for up to six months. All data is scanned using a sophisticated heuristic anomaly detection engine that corresponds to your security policy.

Explore Microsoft Cloud App Security

To access and explore the Cloud App Security service, use the following steps:

1.   If you have a license to use Cloud App Security, navigate to *https://portal.cloudappsecurity.com*.

2.   If you have a Microsoft 365 Enterprise or Office 365 Enterprise E5 subscription, you can access the portal by using the Office 365 Admin center at *https://office.com*, then click the Admin tile, and click the Cloud App Security within the list of Admin centers.

To set up Cloud Discovery, upload traffic logs from your firewall to Cloud App Security, as follows:

1.   Click the Settings Cog in the top right corner.

2.   Select Cloud Discovery settings.

3.   Choose Upload log automatically.

4.   On the Data sources tab, click Add data source and then upload your firewall traffic logs.

5.   On the Log collectors tab, configure the log collector.

The General dashboard will display activities being monitored, any discovered issues or actions taken, along with alerts that are under investigation. Review the information contained in the Cloud App Security general dashboard shown in Figure 3-26.

FIGURE 3-26 Cloud App Security General Dashboard

The alerts center gathers alerts from a wide variety of categories, including threat detection, privileged accounts and compliance violations.

The alerts center is displayed by clicking on the Alerts menu item. This center gathers all of the red flag items identified by Cloud App Security as shown in Figure 3-27. You can see that a user has triggered an anomaly alert by downloading a large amount of data. You can click on each alert and drill down to look at the activity log details for the activity. The alert can then be dismissed, marked as unread, or used to adjust the CAS policy.

FIGURE 3-27 Cloud App Security Alerts

Office 365 Cloud App Security

Office 365 Advanced Security Management has been renamed to Office 365 Cloud App Security and features a subset of the features available within the Microsoft Cloud App Security, which you saw in the previous section. The main differences between the Office 365 version of the Cloud App Security is scope and scale.

Microsoft Cloud App Security is available for organizations as a standalone subscription or as part of an enterprise Office 365 subscription.

The Office 365 Cloud App Security will provide insight into suspicious activity within your Office 365 subscription only and can help with all of the following areas:

- View how your organization's data stored in Office 365 is accessed and used.
- Create policies that trigger alerts for typical or suspicious activities.
- Suspend user accounts exhibiting suspicious activity.
- Require users to sign in to Office 365 apps after an alert has been triggered.

View the Office 365 Cloud App Security portal

If you have an Office 365 Enterprise E5 subscription, or E5 trial, you can perform the following steps to open the Office 365 Cloud App Security portal:

1. Open *https://protection.office.com* and sign in a global or security administrator.
2. The Security & Compliance Center is displayed.
3. Click Alerts in the navigation sidebar.
4. Click Manage advanced alerts to display the landing page, which allows you to turn on Office 365 Cloud App Security as shown in Figure 3-28.

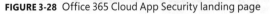

FIGURE 3-28 Office 365 Cloud App Security landing page

5. Select the checkbox to turn on Office 365 Cloud App Security, and then click the Go to Office 365 Cloud App Security button.

6. The Cloud App Security homepage now appears.

7. If your firewall logs or data source is supported and you have already connected them to Office 365 Cloud App Security, you can now view the analysis results.

8. Click the Discover menu item and select Cloud Discovery Dashboard, which shows information about cloud app usage within your organization, which is based on firewall logs that you upload. The cloud service analyzes the data and presents a dashboard view similar to the one shown in Figure 3-29. You can view information about apps, users, traffic, transactions, and more.

FIGURE 3-29 Office 365 Cloud App Security Cloud Discovery Dashboard

9. In addition to the Cloud Discovery Dashboard, you should review the Activity Logs and App permissions, by selecting the Investigate Menu item, followed by Activity log or App Permissions.

10. There are dozens of readymade cloud management policy templates that you can use that trigger alerts for specific activities that happen or happen too frequently. Click the Control menu item and then click Templates.

11. Finally, the Alerts dashboard allows you to react to anomaly detection policies and activity policies. To view alerts for your subscription, choose Alerts in the Navigation menu.

> **MORE INFO CONNECT YOUR DATA SOURCE TO OFFICE 365 CLOUD APP SECURITY**
>
> For more information about supported web traffic log files and data sources that you can use with Office 365 Cloud App Security, visit the following URL at *https://support.office. com/article/Web-traffic-logs-and-data-sources-for-Office-365-Cloud-App-Security-290b02bf-a988-4fb9-88b2-34e408216ac8?ui=en-US&rs=en-US&ad=US.*

Thought experiments

In these thought experiments, demonstrate your skills and knowledge of the topics covered in this chapter. You can find the answers to these thought experiments in the next section.

Scenario 1

Your organization has 500 employees and has implemented a bring your own device (BYOD) strategy that enables users to use their personal mobile phones and tablets for corporate purposes, as long as they comply with company policy regarding security and management features. After consulting an employee survey, you find that the users in your organization have either iOS, Android, or Windows Phone devices.

You have been asked to provide two aspects of functionality for the users in your organization: Ensure that devices can be managed and monitored centrally by IT staff, and provide a method for users to access files on company file servers.

1. What technology should you use to manage the devices?
2. What can you use to give the users access to their data on all of the platforms listed above?
3. What additional configuration or requirements are necessary for company file servers?

Scenario 2

You are responsible for managing software updates for remote clients at Contoso. All remote clients use the Windows 10 operating system and run the same suite of third-party applications. You want to ensure that any security and critical updates are deployed as soon as possible. You will review other updates before deciding to deploy them. With this information in mind, answer the following questions:

1. What subscription service would you recommend for remote management of the devices?
2. How can you ensure that Windows 10 security and critical updates are installed as soon as possible?
3. What steps must you take to deploy updates for the suite of third-party applications?

Scenario 3

You have been asked to provide a method for configuration of one hundred Windows 8.1 laptop computers in your organization. These laptops are used by travelling sales representatives who connect to the Internet and run a custom-developed sales web app. They are very rarely connected to the corporate intranet. You are required to ensure that the sales representatives' laptops have Windows Firewall enabled, and that future changes to the required policy happen as soon as possible.

1. What would be the most effective way to apply this policy?

2. What policy template should be used?

3. If the company wanted to subscribe to Microsoft 365 Business, what is the edition of Windows 10 required, and how could the company acquire it?

Scenario 4

You have recently started work at a healthcare enterprise that is regulated by the HIPPA. You need to ensure that all of the data is protected from data theft when at rest, and from data leakage when patient files are shared by staff. The enterprise uses Windows 10 for all employees and you understand that they are very trustworthy.

1. What versions of Windows 10 supports fully encrypting the hard drive?

2. What technology do you recommend to protect from data theft when at rest?

3. What cloud based subscription technology would you recommend to protect against data leakage relating to files being shared by staff?

Thought experiment answer

This section provides the solutions for the tasks included in the thought experiment.

Scenario 1

1. Microsoft Intune with Mobile Device Management enabled.

2. Work Folders. OneDrive for Business would not provide access to files on the company file servers.

3. File servers must be Windows Server 2012 R2 or later and have the Work Folders feature enabled.

Scenario 2

1. Microsoft Intune.

2. Create an automatic approval rule that approves all critical and security updates for computers running Windows 10.

3. Import third-party updates into Intune and then approve them for distribution.

Scenario 3

1. Microsoft Intune would work very well for deploying this policy. Microsoft Intune contains policy settings that enable control of Windows Firewall, and the policy settings will be applied whenever the clients are connected to the intranet, so policy changes will apply quickly.

2. You should use the General Configuration (Windows 8.1 and later) policy to enable this configuration.

3. For Microsoft 365 Business, you need to use Windows 10 Pro. A Microsoft 365 Business subscription provides licenses for Windows 10 Pro, version 1703 (Creators Update) therefore uses could perform an in-place upgrade to Windows 10.

Scenario 4

1. Windows 10 Pro, Education and Enterprise editions support BitLocker Drive Encryption. Windows 10 Home edition supports Device Encryption, but this is not licensed for business use and lacks management features.

2. BitLocker Drive Encryption

3. Azure Information Protection

Chapter summary

- You can use Work Folders and Sync Center to support mobile data access in Windows 10.

- Broadband Wi-Fi hotspots and tethered connections can be used to provide network access in Windows 10. These connections can be configured to support metered services and reduced data usage over a metered service.

- Mobile Device Management in Microsoft Intune can allow administrators to remotely manage devices on several different platforms without requiring corporate network connectivity.

- You can use the Microsoft Intune Updates page to view available and required updates. You can also generate reports to obtain more specific information about Microsoft Intune updates.

- You can use Microsoft Intune to approve or decline updates for groups of managed devices.

- You can configure automatic approval for updates through the Microsoft Intune console

- Microsoft Intune allows for deployment of third-party updates in MSI, MSP, or EXE format.

- You use user accounts in Microsoft Intune to deploy software, policies and group devices in the environment.

- When you enroll devices, they are manageable by Microsoft Intune.

- Microsoft Intune has several different views available to see and interact with the devices in your environment.

- Microsoft Intune subscriptions govern the functionality and the number of users that can be created in Microsoft Intune.

- The Microsoft Intune connector site is configured in System Center 2012 Configuration Manager to provide integration with Microsoft Intune and to enable management of Microsoft Intune devices with System Center 2012 Configuration Manager.

- User and computer groups are used to establish logical collections of users and devices.

- You can configure and view reports and alerts to obtain information about your Microsoft Intune environment.

- Microsoft Intune policies enable greater control and management of Microsoft Intune-managed devices.

- Data loss prevention policy can prevent the accidental loss or sharing of sensitive information and help users to stay compliant with their work.

- The Office 365 Security & Compliance Center provides ready to use DLP Policy templates that help your organization stay compliant with many industry and regulatory requirements.

- Windows Information Protection is built into Windows and allows applications and services including Microsoft Intune to enforce compliance policies such as requiring that devices are BitLocker encrypted.

- Azure Information Protection advances the protection of information by removing the complexity and requirement of on premises infrastructure. With Azure RMS and the Azure Information Protection client, organizations can classify, label, and protect sensitive documents and emails.

- Cloud App Security is offered in two variants, Microsoft Cloud App Security for large enterprises purchasing the service as a standalone subscription, and the Office 365 variant for businesses with an existing Office 365 Enterprise E5 subscription.

- Both versions of Cloud App Security provide insights into suspicious activity within your Office 365 subscription only and can help with all of the following areas:

  - View how your organization's data stored in Office 365 is accessed and used

  - Create policies that trigger alerts for atypical or suspicious activities

  - Suspend user accounts exhibiting suspicious activity

  - Require users to sign in to Office 365 apps after an alert has been triggered

  - You need connect or upload your web traffic log files and data sources to Office 365 Cloud App Security so that the service can provide analysis, alerts and warn you of atypical or suspicious activities.

CHAPTER 4

Configure networking

t is important to understand the fundamentals of networking in Windows 10 to pass the 70-697, Configuring Windows Devices exam. Network connectivity is an almost universal assumption in typical Windows 10 operation, so understanding how Windows networking works will help you in many areas of the exam. This chapter will cover the basics of main networking components of Windows 10, along with how to configure each of them.

Skills in this chapter:

- Skill 4.1: Configure IP settings
- Skill 4.2: Configure network settings
- Skill 4.3: Configure and maintain network security

Skill 4.1: Configure IP settings

The IP address is the most widely used point of contact for a Windows 10 computer that is connected to the network. A computer's IP address uniquely identifies it on the local network segment, and it serves as the functional component for most of the ways that computers communicate on a network, including name resolution and file transfer.

> **This section covers how to:**
> - Connect to a network
> - Configure name resolution
> - Configure network locations

Connect to a network

Networks are groups of computers and other resources. When connected, each resource that is connected (computer, network printer, server, or other host) must acquire, or have previously been assigned an exclusive address that will define it on that network. These addresses are unique, and you can't have two hosts on the same network with the same address. This makes addressing a very important part of configuring and connecting to networks.

Understanding IP address requirements

Each host on a network must have a unique Internet Protocol (IP) address. This address, when it's configured as an IPv4 address, is a 32-bit number that is styled as four sets of decimal numbers. For example: 192.168.4.20. Each host is also assigned a subnet mask, which determines which part of the IP address defines the network and which part defines the host. Together, the IP address and the subnet mask define the network within which a host can communicate. If the host requires communication outside of the local network segment, a gateway must be specified, which typically represents a network router that can provide network paths to other networks and the Internet. The IP address, subnet mask and default gateway together provide the full definition of IP connectivity for a network host. There are two ways to get an address to a resource: You can define it manually, or it can be assigned by a Dynamic Host Configuration Protocol (DHCP) server.

When an address can't be assigned this way, Windows will assign its own IP address using a technology called Automatic Private IP Addressing (APIPA). APIPA addresses fall in the 169.254.x.x address range.

EXAM TIP

Make sure to review the IP address ranges for Class A, B, and C to have an idea of how many networks and hosts each offers. Know their default subnet masks, too. Beyond that, know the private addresses available for local networks (192.x.x.x, 172.x.x.x, and 10.x.x.x for Class C, B, and A, respectively).

Understanding network terminology

Make sure that you are familiar with the following terms before continuing:

- **APIPA**   This is a link-local (IP) address that is assigned by Windows when no other addressing mechanism can be found. This enables the host to function on the local network segment. Routers do not forward packets from these kinds of addresses.

- **Default gateway**   This hardware or software device lets hosts connect to other networks. Often that network is the Internet, but it could also be another network segment in an enterprise domain.

- **DHCP**   This is a networking protocol that dynamically configures IP addresses for hosts on a network. A DHCP server assigns these addresses. These IP addresses are generally granted for a specified interval and must be renewed when the interval is up. If specific static addresses are required for clients, DHCP can be configured to allow reservations for those clients.

- **DHCP Scope**   A DHCP scope is a consecutive range of possible IP addresses that can be offered to hosts on a subnet (part of a network).

- **DNS**   Domain Name Service (DNS) is a service that enables users to type the name of the host to which they want to connect to instead of its IP address. A DNS server resolves the name.

- **IPv4**   This is an IP address that consists of 32 bits, notated by four 8-bit octets. It has two parts: the network ID and the host ID. The network ID describes the network, and the host ID defines the specific device on it. IPv4 addresses can be Unicast, Broadcast, or Multicast.

- **Subnet mask**   This 32-bit number, notated by four 8-bit octets that consist of a set of 1s followed by a set of 0s, is used to define which part of the IPv4 address is the network ID and which part is the host ID. The 1s denote the network; the 0s denote the host. The default subnet masks are in the form 255.0.0.0 for Class A addresses, 255.255.0.0 for Class B addresses, and 255.255.255.0 for Class C addresses. Translated to binary, 255.0.0.0 looks like this: 11111111 00000000 00000000 00000000.

- **IPv6**   The available IPv4 address combinations are dwindling, thus the need for a better option. IPv6 is that option. Instead of a 32-bit space, it's a 128-bit space with 16-bit boundaries. This allows for many more addresses. An IPv6 address typically looks like this: 21DA:D3:0:2F3B:2AA:FF:FE28:9C5A.

MORE INFO **IP ADDRESSING**

For more information on how IP addresses are defined and how they function, visit: *https://technet.microsoft.com/en-us/library/cc958829.aspx*.

Configuring IP settings

You can configure IP settings on a Windows 10 computer by accessing the Properties page for the network adapter. To open the Properties page, perform the following steps:

1. From the desktop, right-click the Start button, and then click Network Connections.

2. In Settings, click Change Adapter Options.

3. In the Network Connections window, shown in Figure 4-1, right-click the appropriate network adapter, and then click Properties.

FIGURE 4-1 Configuring network connections

4. In the Ethernet Properties dialog box shown in Figure 4-2, select Internet Protocol Version 4 (TCP/IP4), and then click Properties.

FIGURE 4-2 Configuring a network connection's properties

5. In the Internet Protocol Version 4 Properties dialog box shown in Figure 4-3, select the appropriate configuration options and specify addresses, if necessary. You can choose to either obtain the IP address and DNS server addresses automatically (from a DHCP server), or specify the addresses manually. You must, at a minimum, supply an IP address and a subnet mask.

FIGURE 4-3 Configuring the TCP/IPv4 properties for a network adapter

---

EXAM TIP

You might be asked how to configure IPv4 or IPv6 addresses from the command line. The command to do this is Netsh. Make sure you understand the options associated with this command. You might be asked to select the proper command to apply a static address for a host, among other things. That command would look like this: `netsh interface ipv4 set address 'Ethernet' static 192.168.5.12 255.255.255.0 192.168.1.10`. If you want the address to come from a DHCP server, the command would look more like this: `netsh interface ipv4 set address name="Ethernet" source=dhcp`.

Connecting to a network

The first time you connect to a local network, you are prompted to choose from one of these options:

- **No, Don't Turn On Sharing Or Connect To Devices**   This option is intended for public networks and hot spots (libraries, coffee shops). The user's computer can't be seen or accessed by others, and the user can't see other computers also accessing the network.

- **Yes, Turn On Sharing And Connect To Devices** This option is intended for private, trusted networks (home, work) and homegroups. Computers sit behind a trusted router and do not connect to the Internet directly.

These two options do not appear when you connect to an Active Directory Domain Services domain. However, when they do appear and when you choose an option, settings are configured automatically for network discovery, file and printer sharing, the state of the firewall, apps that can accept incoming connections, and so on. (Computers configured as Private or Domain have network discovery enabled; Public networks do not.)

Resolving connectivity issues

When a host can't reach a network, that host has connectivity issues. The issue might be isolated to only that device; perhaps the computer's Ethernet cable has come unplugged or the computer's wireless features have been disabled. Maybe there is an IP address conflict on the network and the user's IP address needs to be released and renewed. Often, using the troubleshooting tools in the Network And Sharing Center can expose the problem and offer a solution. If the issue isn't isolated though, you have larger problems. A network server, gateway, or other necessary resource might be down, a network segment or physical backbone might be damaged, or there could be an issue that is caused by the Internet service provider (ISP), cloud services, or other technologies that are out of your control.

> **NOTE VIEWING CONNECTION STATUS**
>
> To view the status of any connection, open the Network And Sharing Center, then click Change Adapter Settings. Double-click the icon that represents the connected network and click Details. In the dialog box that appears, you can view the physical address, DHCP information, and IP addresses. You can even see the IP address of the DNS server, default gateway, and DHCP server, along with when the DHCP lease was obtained and when it must be renewed. You can also run the ipconfig /all command from the command line.

NETWORK AND SHARING CENTER

The Network And Sharing Center enables you to view the status of your active networks. If there's a problem, you can click Troubleshoot Problems to see if the Network And Sharing Center can resolve it. It can be resolved by releasing and renewing the IP address, resetting adapter settings, or uncovering a simple problem such as a disconnected Ethernet cable (which you can then reconnect).

If a problem exists, but can't be resolved automatically, you can choose from a list of troubleshooting options that include: solving problems connecting to websites, accessing shared folders, finding computers or files in a homegroup, finding and fixing problems with wireless adapters, and troubleshooting incoming connections. When you select any option and start the troubleshooter, it generally finds the problem and performs the repair or prompts you to authorize the repair. It might also require you to do something first, like insert an ethernet cable into the ethernet port on the computer.

COMMAND-LINE TOOLS

When the Network And Sharing Center and the Action Center can't help resolve a connectivity problem, it's likely a more complex issue. Perhaps a domain's (or network segment's) gateway is offline or a router failed. Perhaps the DNS server isn't available or has been incorrectly configured on the host, or the unique, corporate, IP address of the computer has been changed to an APIPA address because of a currently unresolved network issue.

When these kinds of problems exist, you can use command-line tools to resolve them. Here are some of the tools you can use:

- **Ping**   This tool verifies IP-level connectivity to another TCP/IP computer. To do this, it sends Internet Control Message Protocol (ICMP) Echo Request messages to the recipient. The receipt of these messages is displayed, along with round-trip times, if the connection is successful. Ping is the primary command used to troubleshoot connectivity, reachability, and name resolution.

- **Ipconfig and Ipconfig /all**   This displays all current TCP/IP network configuration values. It can also refresh DHCP and DNS settings. Used without the /all parameter, Ipconfig displays IPv4 and IPv6 addresses, the subnet mask, and the default gateway for all adapters installed on the host. Common parameters are /release, /renew, and /flushdns.

- **Tracert**   This tool determines the path taken to a destination and shows information about each hop a packet takes to get to where it's going. A hop is a pass through a router. You can use this information to see where the transmission fails.

- **Netstat**   This displays a list of active TCP connections and the ports on which the computer is listening. It also displays Ethernet statistics, the IP routing table, and IPv4 and IPv6 statistics.

- **Netsh**   This enables you to make changes to the network configuration of the current computer at the command line.

- **Nslookup**   This tool displays information that you can use to diagnose problems with DNS.

Configure name resolution

Computers are represented by their unique IP address, and you can communicate with them using that address if you like. One way to communicate with an IP address is to do so at a command line. For instance, you can type something like **ping 192.168.4.5** to troubleshoot connectivity to another host on a local area network segment. Communicating this way however, is cumbersome.

DNS enables users to type names instead of numbers; this process is called *name resolution*. DNS servers store information about the names and addresses of Internet computers, and the lists they maintain are distributed among thousands of DNS servers available on the Internet, which are placed all over the world. The name resolution request is forwarded to one of these servers. If the name can't be resolved server, it's passed to another server and another, until it is resolved.

In many cases, your DHCP server will provide DNS server addresses for your client computers to use for name resolution. This occurs if Obtain DNS Server Address Automatically is selected. You can also manually configure a host to use a specific DNS server in the connection's Properties dialog box (shown in Figure 4-3). On a domain with a unique DNS server that the host is required to use, this is necessary. It might also be necessary in a virtual private network (VPN) or in a virtual machine.

Depending on the configuration, Windows 10 resolves host names by performing the following actions:

1. Checking whether the host name is the same as the local host name.

2. Searching the DNS resolver cache, which is populated from the local Hosts file.

3. Sending a DNS request to its configured DNS servers.

Troubleshooting name resolution

The primary tools for troubleshooting host name resolution are *IPConfig* and *NSLookup*, and their Windows PowerShell equivalents *Get-NetIPAddress*, *Get-NetIPv4Protocol*, and *Resolve-dnsname*.

If you cannot connect to a remote host, and if you suspect a name resolution problem, you can troubleshoot name resolution by using the following procedure:

1. Open an elevated command prompt, and then clear the DNS resolver cache by typing the following command:

   ```
   IPConfig /flushdns
   ```

   Or, you can use the Windows PowerShell cmdlet Clear-DnsClientCache.

2. Attempt to verify connectivity to a remote host by using its IP address. This helps you identify whether the issue is due to name resolution. You can use the Ping command or the Test-Connection Windows PowerShell cmdlet. If the Ping command succeeds with the IP address, but fails by the host name, the problem is with name resolution.

3. Attempt to verify connectivity to the remote host by its host name by using the fully-qualified domain name (FQDN) followed by a period. For example, type the following command at a Windows PowerShell command prompt:

   ```
   Test-connection LON-cl1.adatum.com
   ```

   You can also use the ping command.

4. If the test is successful, the problem is likely unrelated to name resolution.

5. If the test is unsuccessful, edit the C:\Windows\System32\Drivers\Etc\hosts.txt text file, and then add the appropriate entry to the end of the file. For example, add this line and then save the file:

   ```
   172.16.0.51        LON-cl1.adatum.com
   ```

6. Perform the test-by-host-name procedure again. The name resolution should now be successful.

7. Examine the DNS resolver cache to verify that the name resolved correctly. To examine the DNS resolver cache, type the following command at a command prompt:

```
IPConfig /displaydns
```

You can also use the Windows PowerShell cmdlet Get-DnsClientCache.

8. Remove the entry that you added to the hosts file, and then clear the resolver cache once more. At the command prompt, type the following command, and then examine the contents of the filename.txt file to identify the failed stage in name resolution:

```
NSLookup.exe –d2 LON-cl1.adatum.com > filename.txt
```

The Windows PowerShell equivalent command is:

```
Resolve-dnsname lon-cl1.adatum.com > filename.txt
```

Configure network locations

The first time that you connect a computer to a network, you must select whether you trust the network. This sets appropriate firewall and security settings automatically. When you connect to networks in different locations, you can ensure that your computer is set to an appropriate security level at all times by choosing a network location.

Windows 10 uses network location awareness to uniquely identify networks to which a computer is connected. Network location awareness collects information from networks, including IP address and media access control (MAC) address data from important network components, like routers and gateways, to identify a specific network.

There are three network location types:

- **Domain networks** These are workplace networks that attach to a domain. Use this option for any network that allows communication with a domain controller. Network discovery is on by default, and you cannot create or join a homegroup.

- **Private networks** These are networks at home or work where you know and trust the people and devices on the network. When you select home or work (private) networks, this turns on network discovery. Computers on a home network can belong to a home-group.

- **Guest or public networks** These are networks in public places. This location keeps the computer from being visible to other computers. When you select the Public place network location, homegroup is not available and network discovery is turned off.

The Public networks location blocks certain programs and services from running, which protects a computer from unauthorized access. If you connect to a Public network and Windows Firewall is on, some programs or services might ask you to allow them to communicate through the firewall so that they can work properly.

To make changes to the network location, if that location is a homegroup, you can run the Homegroup Troubleshooter. This might never happen in a homegroup, but it's worth noting that the Homegroup Troubleshooter is an option. If the location is a local network in a workgroup, you can make changes in the Settings app as follows:

1. In the Settings app, click Network & Internet.

2. On the Network & Internet page shown in Figure 4-4, click Ethernet, and then click the adapter for which you'd like to configure the network location (Ethernet, in this case).

FIGURE 4-4 Viewing network status

3. On the Network page, under Make this PC discoverable heading, shown in Figure 4-5, change the toggle switch to Off (do not find devices, which is recommended for a public network location) or On (find devices, which is recommended for a private network location). When you choose Off, the network location profile is Public, and when you choose On, the network location profile is changed to Private. You can verify this change by clicking Sharing options on the Status tab.

FIGURE 4-5 Changing the network location profile

Skill 4.2: Configure network settings

There are many networking settings that you can configure. You can connect to wireless and broadband networks, and manage the list of wireless networks to which you've previously connected. You can configure location-aware printing to enable users to print to the desired local printer automatically. You can configure network adapters to reconfigure default settings and tweak performance.

This section covers how to:

- Connect to a wireless network
- Manage preferred wireless networks
- Configure network adapters
- Configure location-aware printing

Connect to a wireless network

An increasing number of devices use wireless connections as the primary method for accessing corporate intranets and the Internet. Additionally, many users have come to expect a wireless infrastructure in a corporate workplace. As a result, a good working knowledge of wireless connectivity is a requirement for today's networking environment. In Windows 10, you can connect to a network from the network icon on the taskbar by following these steps:

1. From the Desktop, click the Network icon on the taskbar, as shown in Figure 4-6.

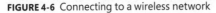

FIGURE 4-6 Connecting to a wireless network

2. Click the appropriate wireless network name in the list.

3. Optionally, select the Connect automatically check box. This option will save the network security key so you do not have to enter it each time you connect to the network.

4. Click Connect. If the network is secure, you will be asked to enter the network security key.

Manage preferred wireless networks

Windows 10 keeps track of all networks to which you connect and prioritizes them automatically. When you have more than one connection option, Windows 10 determines which type it will connect to in this order: Ethernet, Wi-Fi, and then mobile broadband. For example, if a Windows 10 computer has all three network types available, Ethernet will be its chosen first; otherwise, Wi-Fi is chosen. If both become unavailable, then broadband will be chosen (and will be chosen automatically if you've configured it to). When choosing from wireless networks to which you've connected in the past, when more than one of those is available at a given time, Windows 10 connects to the last one you used.

If you're connected to a network automatically, but want to choose another, click it from the list of networks. You can access this list by clicking the Network icon in the taskbar's system tray.

In Windows 10, you can manage preferred networks in one of two ways. First, you can use the Wi-Fi page in the Network Setting section of the Settings app:

1. Open the Settings app.

2. Click Network & Internet, and then click Wi-Fi.

3. On the Wi-Fi page, click Manage Known Networks.

4. At the bottom of the page, beneath Manage Known Networks, click the network you want to manage.

5. To configure the network, click Properties. You can configure the following properties:

   - Connect automatically when in range.

   - Make this PC discoverable.

   - Set as metered connection.

6. To remove the network, click Forget.

You can also manage wireless networks by using Netsh. To use Netsh to remove networks, perform the following steps:

1. From the command prompt, type the following:

   ```
   Netsh wlan show profiles
   ```

2. Locate the profile you want to remove, and use it in the following command:

   ```
   Netsh wlan delete profile name=<profile name>
   ```

Configure network adapters

When you right-click a network adapter in the Network Connections window, you can do any of the following:

- Enable or disable the adapter. (This can help you solve connection problems or keep wireless adapters from searching for networks when you don't need them to.)

- Connect to or disconnect from the associated network.

- See the status of the adapter or connection. (You can use this to view the number of bytes sent and received, to diagnose connection problems, to view signal quality and speed, and to view the service set identifier (SSID).)

- Diagnose problems with the adapter or connection. (You can use this to run an automated tool that can assist in diagnosing connection problems.)

- Bridge two or more connections. (You must select two connections that are LAN or High Speed Internet connections that are not being used by Internet Connection Sharing. A network bridge is a network device that connects to multiple network segments.)

- Create a shortcut to the adapter for easier access.

- Delete the entry, if the option is available.

- Rename the adapter.

- View the adapter's properties. (You'll see the Properties dialog box you learned about earlier in this chapter. From there, you can see the type of connection the adapter uses and install or uninstall protocols, Hyper-V Extensible Virtual Switch, Microsoft LLDP Protocol Driver, and more. When you select an option, you can view additional properties.)

Explore the options available from the adapters on a computer you have access to. Make sure to click Configure in any Wi-Fi Properties dialog box to view the advanced options. You can configure the computer to turn off that device to conserve power or to allow the device to wake up the computer (on the Power Management tab). You can also view events (Events tab), see adapter and driver details (Details, Driver, and General tabs), and view advanced configuration options (Advanced tab).

Configure location-aware printing

Users are not always working at the same desk, day after day. Instead, many people move around and work at different desks, and often in different offices. This means that they'll almost certainly need to access printers in various locations.

Printers can be available on any kind of network, including a network at home, at the office, or even at a company kiosk. Having to choose a printer every time they connect to a new network can annoy users, thus the need for location-aware printing. With location-aware printing, a default printer can be set for each location from which the user prints. This also keeps the user from accidentally printing to the wrong printer, which poses a potential security risk if the printed data is confidential.

EXAM TIP

Location-aware printing uses the Network Location Awareness service and the Network List service to determine the network location. The former collects and maintains network configuration information, and the latter identifies the network to which the computer is connected. If this feature doesn't work, be aware that you need to check to make sure these services are running.

To configure location-aware printing, follow these steps:

1. In Settings, click Devices and then click Printers & scanners.

2. Scroll down the list of printers, and as shown in Figure 4-7, select the Let Windows manage my default printer check box.

FIGURE 4-7 Enabling the Let Windows manage my default printer option

Skill 4.3: Configure and maintain network security

A computer that is running Windows 10 is more likely to face threats that originate from the network than from anywhere else. This is because attacks from the network can target a large number of computers and malicious users perform them remotely, whereas other forms of attacks require physical access to the computer. In this Skill, you will learn about common network-related security threats and the steps that you can take to mitigate them.

> **This section covers how to:**
> - Configure Windows Firewall
> - Configure Windows Firewall with Advanced Security
> - Configure connection security rules with IPsec
> - Configure authentication exceptions
> - Configure network discovery

Windows Defender Security Center

Windows 10 1703 introduces the Windows Defender Security Center. This Microsoft Store app consolidates a number of network-related security components:

- Virus & threat protection
- Device performance & health
- Firewall & network protection
- App & browser control
- Family options

To access Windows Firewall settings, open Windows Defender Security Center, and on the home tab, shown in Figure 4-8, click Firewall & network protection.

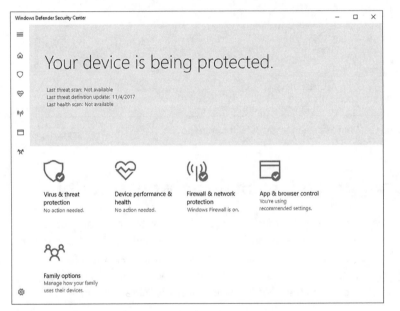

FIGURE 4-8 Windows Defender Security Center

On the Firewall & network protection page, shown in Figure 4-9, you can view the current Windows Firewall status and access links to enable you to configure firewall behavior.

FIGURE 4-9 Firewall settings

Configure Windows Firewall

Windows Firewall is a software solution that comes with Windows 10 that creates a virtual barrier between a computer and the network to which it is connected for the purpose of protecting the computer from unwanted incoming traffic and protecting the network from unwanted outgoing traffic. The firewall allows specific types of data to enter and exit the computer and blocks others; settings are configured by default (but they can be changed). This type of protection is called filtering. The filters are generally based on IP addresses, ports, and protocols.

- IP addresses are assigned to every computer and network resource connected directly to the network. The firewall can block or allow traffic based on an IP address of a resource (or a scope of addresses).

- Port numbers identify the application that is running on the computer. For example, port 21 is associated with the File Transfer Protocol (FTP), port 25 is associated with Simple Mail Transfer Protocol (SMTP), port 53 is associated with DNS, port 80 is associated with Hypertext Transfer Protocol (HTTP), and port 443 is associated with HTTPS (HTTP Secure).

- Protocol Protocols are used to define the type of packet being sent or received. Common protocols are TCP, Telnet, FTP, HTTP, Post Office Protocol 3 (POP3), Internet

Message Access Protocol (IMAP), HTTPS, and User Datagram Protocol (UDP). (You should be familiar with the most common protocols before taking the exam.)

Although there are many rules already configured for the firewall, you can create your own inbound and outbound rules based on ports, protocols, programs, and more to configure the firewall to suit your exact needs. You'll learn how later in this chapter.

Monitor the Windows Firewall

You can monitor the state of the Windows Firewall from Windows Defender Security Center. It's easy to tell from here if the firewall is on or off, and which is the active network. However, for more information, including how you are notified when the firewall takes action, open Control Panel, click System and Security, and then click Windows Firewall, as shown in Figure 4-10.

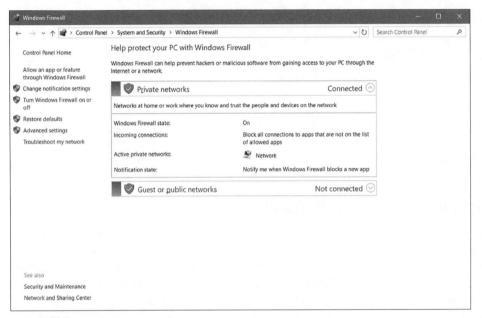

FIGURE 4-10 Viewing Windows Firewall settings

To make basic changes to the state of the firewall, in the left pane click Turn Windows Firewall On Or Off. From there you can change settings for both private and public networks. There are two options for each:

- Turn On Windows Firewall (this is selected by default).
    - Block All Incoming Connections, Including Those In The List Of Allowed Apps.
    - Notify Me When Windows Firewall Blocks A New App (This is selected by default).
- Turn Off Windows Firewall (not recommended).

What you'll be most interested in as a network administrator, are the options available in the left pane. Specifically, you'll use the Allow An App Or Feature Through Windows Firewall and Advanced Settings options. You'll learn about the Advanced Settings in the next section, but here we discuss allowing an app through the firewall that is blocked by default.

Allow an app through the Windows Firewall

Some data generated with and by specific apps is already allowed to pass through the Windows Firewall. You can see which apps are allowed by clicking Allow An App Or Feature Through Windows Firewall in the left pane of the Windows Firewall window in Control Panel. As you scroll through the list, you'll see many apps you recognize, including Bing Food & Drink, Games, Maps, Music, and Windows Media Player. See Figure 4-11. (Once you click Change Settings and give administrator approval, the Change Settings option will appear unavailable and the options in this list will be editable, as you see here.) You will also notice that some apps are not enabled by default, including Windows Media Player Network Sharing Service (Internet), Windows Remote Management, and Remote Shutdown.

FIGURE 4-11 Allowing an app through Windows Firewall

To allow an app through the firewall or stop one from getting through, select the check box under the appropriate network profile for which it should be configured. As shown in Figure 4-11, there are two options for each: Private and Public. If you don't see the app you want to allow or block, click Allow Another App. You can then select the desired app from the Add An App dialog box.

Configure Windows Firewall with Advanced Security

Although you can configure a few options in the main Windows Firewall window, most configuration tasks are performed within Windows Firewall With Advanced Security. You can open this window by clicking Advanced Settings in the Windows Firewall window as shown in Figure 4-12.

FIGURE 4-12 Windows Firewall with Advanced Security

Once opened, there are several options and terms with which you need to be familiar.

- In the left pane, your selection determines which items appear in the middle and right panes.
  - **Inbound Rules** Lists all configured inbound rules and enables you to double-click any item in the list and reconfigure it as desired. Some app rules are predefined and can't be modified, although they can be disabled. Explore the other nodes as time allows. You can also right-click Inbound Rules in the left pane and create your own custom rule. Rule types include Program, Port, Predefined, and Custom. They are detailed later in this section.
  - **Outbound Rules** Offers the same options as Inbound Rules, but these apply to outgoing data. You can also right-click Outbound Rules in the left pane and create your own custom rule.

- **Connection Security Rules**   Connection security rules establish how computers must authenticate before any data can be sent. IP Security (IPsec) standards define how data is secured while it is in transit over a TCP/IP network, and you can require a connection use this type of authentication before computers can send data. You'll learn more about connection security rules in the next section.

- **Monitoring**   Offers information about the active firewall status, state, and general settings for both the private and public profile types.

- In the right pane, you'll see the options that correspond to your selection in the left pane.

  - **Import/Export/Restore/Diagnose/Repair Policies**   Enables you to manage the settings you've configured for your firewall. Polices use the WFW extension.

  - **New Rules**   Enables you to start the applicable Rule Wizard to create a new rule. You can also do this from the Action menu.

  - **Filter By**   Enables you to filter rules by Domain Profile, Private Profile, or Public Profile. You can also filter by state: Enabled or Disabled. Use this to narrow the rules listed to only those you want to view.

  - **View**   Enables you to customize how and what you view in the middle pane of the Windows Firewall With Advanced Security window.

When you opt to create your own inbound or outbound rule, you can choose from four rule types. A wizard walks you through the process, and the process changes depending on the type of rule you want to create. The rules are as follows:

- **Program**   A program rule sets firewall behavior for a specific program you choose or for all programs that match the rule properties you set. You can't control apps, but you can configure traditional EXE. Once you've selected the program for which to create the rule, you can allow the connection, allow only if the connection is secure and has been authenticated using IPsec, or block the connection. You can also choose the profiles to which the rule will be applied (domain, private, public) and name the rule.

- **Port**   A port rule sets firewall behavior for TCP and UDP port types and specifies which ports are allowed or blocked. You can apply the rule to all ports or only ports you specify. As with other rules, you can allow the connection, allow only if the connection is secured with IPsec, or block the connection. You can also choose the profiles to which the rule will be applied (domain, private, public) and name the rule.

MORE INFO **CONNECTIVITY AND SECURITY**

When you create inbound and outbound rules, and when you opt to allow the connection only if the connection is secured by authenticating the connection with IPsec, the connection will be secured using the settings in the IPsec properties and applicable rules in the Connection Security Rules node. The next section covers how to create connection security rules.

- **Predefined** Sets firewall behavior for a program or service that you select from a list of rules that are already defined by Windows.

- **Custom** A rule you create from scratch, defining every aspect of the rule. Use this if the first three rule types don't offer the kind of rule you need.

EXAM TIP

You might encounter questions regarding how to create a rule on the exam. Therefore, you should spend a few minutes working through the wizard a few times, selecting different rule types each time to become familiar with the process.

With Windows Firewall With Advanced Security selected in the left pane and using the Overview section of the middle pane, click Windows Firewall Properties to see the dialog box shown in Figure 4-13. From there you can make changes to the firewall and the profiles, even if you aren't connected to the type of network you want to configure.

FIGURE 4-13 Viewing the Windows Firewall properties

In Figure 4-13, the Domain Profile tab is selected. If you want to, you can configure the firewall to be turned off when connected to a domain network. Additionally, you can strengthen the settings for the Public profile and customize settings for the Private profile. Finally, you can customize IPsec defaults, exemptions, and tunnel authorization on the IPsec Settings tab. Make sure to explore all areas of this dialog box and research any terms you are not familiar with.

Configure connection security rules with IPsec

You can use IPsec to ensure confidentiality, integrity, and authentication in data transport across channels that are not secure. Though its original purpose was to secure traffic across public networks, many organizations have chosen to implement IPsec to address perceived weaknesses in their own private networks that might be susceptible to exploitation.

If you implement IPsec properly, it provides a private channel for sending and exchanging potentially sensitive or vulnerable data, whether it is email, FTP traffic, news feeds, partner and supply-chain data, medical records, or any other type of TCP/IP-based data. IPsec provides the following functionality:

- Offers mutual authentication before and during communications.
- Forces both parties to identify themselves during the communication process.
- Enables confidentiality through IP traffic encryption and digital-packet authentication.

Exploring connection security rules

A connection security rule forces authentication between two peer computers before they can establish a connection and transmit secure information. Windows Firewall with Advanced Security uses IPsec to enforce the following configurable rules:

- **Isolation**   An isolation rule isolates computers by restricting connections based on credentials, such as domain membership or health status. Isolation rules allow you to implement an isolation strategy for servers or domains.
- **Authentication exemption**   You can use an authentication exemption to designate connections that do not require authentication. You can designate computers by a specific IP address, an IP address range, a subnet, or a predefined group such as a gateway.
- **Server-to-server**   This type of rule usually protects connections between servers. When you create the rule, you specify the network endpoints between which communications are protected. You then designate requirements and the authentication that you want to use.
- **Tunnel**   This rule allows you to protect connections between gateway computers. It is typically used when you are connecting across the Internet between two security gateways.
- **Custom**   There might be situations in which you cannot configure the authentication rules that you need by using the rules available in the New Connection Security Rule Wizard. However, you can use a custom rule to authenticate connections between two endpoints.

Firewall rules and connection security rules

Firewall rules allow traffic through a firewall, but do not secure that traffic. To secure traffic with IPsec, you can create connection security rules. However, when you create a connection security rule, this does not allow the traffic through the firewall. You must create a firewall rule to do this if the firewall's default behavior does not allow traffic. Connection security rules do not apply to programs and services. They apply only between the computers that are the two endpoints.

EXAM TIP

Connection security rules specify how and when authentication occurs, but they do not allow those connections. To allow a connection, you must create an inbound or outbound rule. During the inbound or outbound rule creation, you choose the required conditions for the connection, including requiring that the connections have been authenticated by using IPsec. When you do, connections will be secured using the settings in the IPsec properties and rules in the Connection Security Rule node.

Configure authentication exceptions

When you configure a rule to allow traffic only when the connection between the communicating computers is secured using IPsec, you are creating an authenticated exception. You configure this option from the application Action page of the Rule Wizard when creating an inbound or outbound rule. When you choose the Allow The Connection If It Is Secure option on the Action page, you are configuring the rule to allow the connection using the settings in IPsec properties and rules in the Connection Security Rule node.

To create an inbound rule that applies to a single TCP port (Telnet, port 23) and create an authenticated exception for it, follow these steps:

1. In Windows Firewall With Advanced Security, select and then right-click Inbound Rules.
2. Click New Rule.
3. For the rule type, click Port, and then click Next.
4. On the Protocol And Ports page, leave TCP selected and in the Specific Local Ports box, type 23. Click Next.
5. For the action to take, select Allow The Connection If It Is Secure, and click Next.
6. To configure authorized users or authorized exceptions, select the applicable check box, click Add, and use the Select Users Or Groups dialog box to add the applicable entries.
7. Repeat step 6 for authorized computers and exceptions. Click Next.
8. Choose the profiles to which the rules should apply. Click Next. Name the rule. Click Finish.

Configure network discovery

By default, Network Discovery is enabled for private and domain networks and disabled for public ones. Network Discovery enables a computer to locate other computers on a network and allows computers on the network to see it as well. This is fine when the network is trusted, but it isn't a good idea when the network is not. By having these settings and others already configured for the various network types, along with the applicable settings for ports and protocols, the network administrator does not have to configure every aspect of a connection manually. There is one caveat; even if Network Discovery is disabled, a Windows 10 computer can still access network resources if the user knows the names and locations of those resources (because they can't be discovered by browsing).

It's possible to make changes to how Network Discovery is configured. You do this from the Network And Sharing Center by following this procedure:

1. Open the Network And Sharing Center.

2. In the left pane, click Change Advanced Sharing Settings.

3. Click the down arrow, if applicable, beside the network type to change the settings: *Private* or *Guest Or Public*.

4. Make the desired change for Network Discovery Settings. Note the other options. See Figure 4-14.

5. Click Save Changes.

FIGURE 4-14 Advanced sharing settings

Thought experiments

In these thought experiments, demonstrate your skills and knowledge of the topics covered in this chapter. You can find the answers to these thought experiments in the next section.

Scenario 1

You are troubleshooting connectivity problems on a new laptop that has been added to a lo-cal, small business network that already includes eight other computers. Three of these eight are laptops that have always connected without issues. The new laptop can connect when plugged in directly to the router with an Ethernet cable, but it cannot connect wirelessly.

Answer the following questions related to how you would troubleshoot this issue:

1. What do suspect is causing this problem?

2. Do you think that the troubleshooter in the Network And Sharing Center can resolve this problem?

3. If the Internet Connection troubleshooter uncovers the issue but can't resolve it, where would you turn next and why?

Scenario 2

You support multiple mobile users who connect to a dozen wireless networks a month and print to the printers on those networks regularly. Users complain that they have to choose their printers manually when using those networks and that sometimes they choose the wrong ones. Not only is this annoying, but because they print sensitive documents, it's also a security issue for your company.

Beyond that, users have connected to wireless networks they'd rather have their laptops forget. The list of networks is quite long and they want you to remove entries for networks they'll never use again (or networks that offered poor connectivity, such as one they have connected to in the past at a hotel or conference center). In the case of networks with poor connections, they'd rather default to broadband.

Regarding this scenario, answer the following questions:

1. What feature do you enable on the users' Windows 10 laptops to enable the network connection to define the printer to which the users will print by default, and what two services does this feature rely on?

2. When a user is in a hotel where she's stayed before, and that user has also connected to the hotel's free Wi-Fi, what must you do to forget that network so that the user can default to broadband when she stays there next time?

Scenario 3

A client has a large library of media that contains thousands of music files. He wants to share that media in such a way as to be able to access it over the Internet from another computer he owns and keeps at his office. He's enabled the appropriate options in Media Player on both computers. However, he can't get sharing to work.

1. What do you need to do regarding the firewall so that this client can allow Media Player to share music files over the Internet?

2. Will you perform the required task in Windows Firewall or Windows Firewall with Advanced Security?

3. Will you need to be logged on as an Administrator to do this?

Thought experiment answers

This section provides the solutions for the tasks included in the thought experiment.

Scenario 1

1. There is probably something wrong with the wireless adapter. Maybe it isn't enabled or needs an updated driver to work.

2. Probably. The Network And Sharing Center Internet Connection troubleshooter can discover that the Wi-Fi adapter is disabled, although it might not know why. If the adapter is functional, it can enable it with administrator approval.

3. You can try the Action Center to see if a new driver is available for the Wi-Fi adapter. If not, you can try to locate one using Device Manager. You can also refer to the manufacturer's website to find out how to enable the Wi-Fi adapter, if that is the problem.

Scenario 2

1. Location-aware printing. This feature enables default printers to be configured based on the network the user is connected to. Location-aware printing uses the Network Location Awareness service and the Network List service to determine the network location.

2. Use the Netsh command to show the list of wireless profiles and then use this command to forget specific networks: Type **netsh wlan delete profile name=<profile name>**.

Scenario 3

1. You need to create an exception for the Media Player Network Sharing Server (Internet) in Windows Firewall.

2. You can perform this task in Windows Firewall. You will create an app exception.

3. Yes. You must be able to input Administrator credentials or be logged on as an Administrator to enable Change Settings in Windows Firewall.

Chapter summary

- After you connect to a network, your computer is given a unique IP address on that network segment. Every host connected to a network must have an IP address. You can use several troubleshooting tools to diagnose connection problems, if necessary.

- Name resolution enables network nodes to use friendly names to identify each other on the network rather than just an IP address.

- A network location determines the different types of network traffic that are enabled for a network adapter.

- There are several ways to connect to a wireless network including using Control Panel and the Network icon in the desktop's taskbar.

- There is a default priority for networks to which the user has previously connected: Ethernet, Wi-Fi, and mobile broadband. When there are two or more wireless connections available, Windows defaults to the last one used. You can manage networks by using the Settings app or the Netsh command.

- Each network adapter has options available for configuration. You can access these by right-clicking the network adapter in Network Connections and selecting an option from the shortcut menu.

- Location-aware printing lets users configure a default printer for each network they connect to.

- In Windows Firewall you can view the settings for private and public networks and make basic changes to the settings there. You can also disable the firewall there.

- In Windows Firewall, apps are either allowed through the firewall or not. You can create exceptions to configure specific apps to be able to get through the firewall.

- Windows Firewall with Advanced Security offers many more options for administrators, including configuring their own inbound, outbound, and connection security rules, configuring authenticated exceptions, and making changes to existing firewall settings.

- You can make changes to how Network Discovery is configured for the available public and private profiles using the Advanced Sharing Settings in the Network And Sharing Center.

CHAPTER 5

Configure storage

Configuring data storage requires the knowledge of both old and new technology. You need to be familiar with traditional local storage using hard drives, as well as newer cloud-based storage using services such as OneDrive for Business. You also need to consider distributed storage options such as using Distributed File System (DFS) to replicate data across WANs, as well as using Storage Spaces for local data resiliency.

Once you've decided how to store your data, you also need to consider how you can share data with others, safeguard it from theft, and protect it from unauthorized access.

Windows 10 provides extensive built-in support for both local and cloud-based storage. Windows 10 offers you a multitude of security-related choices for securing data while it is at rest either locally on OneDrive for Business, or when it is mobile on a removable drive. All storage must be both secure and accessible.

Skills in this chapter:

- Skill 5.1: Support data storage
- Skill 5.2: Support data security

Skill 5.1: Support data storage

In this section we focus on understanding how the recent storage technologies work, because solutions that are new or offer additional capability are typically found on the exams. (Local and traditional storage and data security are covered later in this chapter.) Storage Spaces was introduced in Windows 8 and continues to provide software-based fault tolerance to users requiring resiliency for their data storage without needing to purchase additional hardware or RAID controllers.

Distributed File System (DFS) is not new and has been very useful in situations where available bandwidth has been a limiting factor. Although high speed Internet is fast becoming commonplace, good bandwidth is essential for many cloud-based services such as OneDrive for Business and Office 365. With improvements in infrastructure comes additional functionality available in DFS to take advantage of increased bandwidth.

Distributed File System

Within a corporate environment, the traditional method of storing files is via a shared folder stored on a file server, which can then be accessed by multiple users with share access. Enabling accessible files across multiple geographic sites becomes challenging when using only shared folders. Therefore, you need to consider alternatives such as SharePoint Online, OneDrive for Business, or DFS. DFS has been available in various guises since Windows Server NT 4.0.

The replication aspect of DFS is referred to as DFS-R. DFS-R was first introduced in Windows Server 2003 R2 and offers the enterprise the ability to maintain file shares and keep them synchronized (or mirrored) across multiple geographic sites, such as across a WAN. The end users see a standard file share giving them a simplified logical shared folder; they do not need to be aware of the complex data replication and synchronization that operate as a service automatically in the background.

DFS, a server-based technology, is a role service installed by the server administrator. Although it is unlikely that you will be involved with the installation or configuration, you need to be aware of some benefits, features, and client-facing aspects of DFS. You are likely to come across DFS wherever there is a multi-site topology in place. It is quite common in large organizations for the underlying file server infrastructure to use DFS to share common files that might be required across the organization. For example, you might use DFS when using Windows Deployment Services (WDS) to share a set of common images that can be replicated across multiple sites. As an administrator, you can update any one of the files, and this update is pushed out using the DFS-R service.

DFS replication is optimized and uses differential compression and bandwidth controls to minimize the amount of data that is transmitted over a WAN link. This in turn minimizes the impact that the replication has on the network.

On smaller networks, administrators may opt to use alternatives such as OneDrive for Business, Windows PowerShell or scripting and scheduling Robust File Copy for Windows (Robocopy) to run their file sync and copying operations.

> **MORE INFO** **ROBOCOPY AS AN ALTERNATIVE TO DFS-R**
>
> Robocopy is a command-line tool built into Windows 10, which can be used in both a command window, or PowerShell, for copying files together with their permissions. To ensure that all NTFS permissions are replicated, use the /copy:s or /copyall switches. All of the available options can be seen by typing **Robocopy /?**. With a Robocopy scenario, you have a master file and this is mirrored (copied) to other sites.

You need to be aware of the key terminology and basic tools when discussing DFS and DFS-R such as:

- **DFS Namespaces (DFSN or DFS-N)**   A virtual view of the folder and subfolders that the administrator creates, which is presented to the user. The namespace server is a domain controller or member server that hosts a namespace.

- **DFS Replication (DFSR or DFS-R)**   The process that is running behind the scenes and that detects changes to files stored within the DFS-N as well as replicates the changes at a block level, which is more efficient than copying the entire file.

- **Remote Differential Compression (RDC)**   The compression algorithm that detects changes in the files that need to be replicated.

- **Link Target**   The destination object, usually a link to the resources. The format can be a Uniform Naming Convention (UNC) path, a shared folder, or another DFS path.

- **Referral**   This relates to the hidden list of targets that are sent from DFS to the DFS client whenever a client accesses the root or a link in the DFS namespace.

- **Link Referral**   Contains a list of link targets for a specific link.

- **Root Referral**   Contains a list of root targets for the DFS root selected.

- **Referral cache**   Entries are stored within the cache of the targets that are available. Each entry has a Time to Live (TTL), which specifies how long the record can be relied upon until it expires and a new referral becomes necessary.

There are over 60 new PowerShell cmdlets for managing DFS-N and DFS-R. To view all of the cmdlets that are available, on a Windows Server use:

```
Get-Command -Module DFSR
```

> **MORE INFO** **DFS NAMESPACE AND REPLICATION CMDLET REFERENCE**
>
> To view a reference of DFS Namespace and Replication cmdlet descriptions and syntax for all DFSN/DFSR cmdlets, for Windows 10 and Windows Server 2016, visit: *https://docs.micro-soft.com/powershell/module/dfsn/?view=win10-ps* and *https://docs.microsoft.com/power-shell/module/dfsr/?view=win10-ps*.

A helpful cmdlet to test whether DFS-R is behaving as expected is the Write-DfsrHealthReport cmdlet, which generates a DFS Replication health report.

Using Windows PowerShell is the recommended method of managing DFS-R. The built-in legacy DFS-R administration tools do not provide support for many of the features first introduced in Windows Server 2012 R2, including configuring database cloning or configuring debug logging.

To manage a Windows server providing DFS services, you need to connect remotely, using the Remote Server Administration Tools (RSAT). The Windows 10 RSAT can be downloaded in 18 languages at: *http://www.microsoft.com/download/details.aspx?id=45520*. When installed, all of the RSAT tools are enabled by default.

Once DFS has been installed on Windows Server 2016, Windows 10 can then access the DFS namespace by using Windows 10 and map the DFS share to a network drive, or access the DFS share through the Universal Naming Convention (UNC) path in Windows Explorer.

If you prefer to use a command-line tool rather than PowerShell, you can use a range of tools such as Dfsradmin.exe, Dfscmd.exe, Dfsdiag.exe, or Dfsutil.exe after you have installed the RSAT DFS Management Tools to help you manage DFS.

Dfsutil.exe is the most popular DFS command-line tool. Additional switches available with Dfsutil.exe include:

- **/Root**   Displays, creates, removes, imports, or exports namespace roots
- **/Link**   Displays, creates, removes, or moves folders (links)
- **/Target**   Displays, creates, or modifies folder targets (link targets)
- **/Property**   Displays or modifies a folder target or namespace server
- **/Client**   Displays or modifies client information or registry keys
- **/Server**   Displays or modifies namespace configuration on the server
- **/Diag**   Enables you to perform diagnostics or view dfsdirs/dfspath
- **/Domain**   Displays all domain-based namespaces in a domain
- **/Cache**   Enables you to view or flush the Domain, Referral, or Provider cache

Sometimes if the DFS Namespace service (Dfssvc.exe) or DFS Replication (DFSRs.exe) service stops, it prevents replication from taking place. Often this happens during cycling of the server because the DFS service on initialization attempted to perform a complete check to verify the availability of all replicated folders. If that wasn't possible due to bandwidth or WAN issues, the service might halt. Restarting the service or configuring the service to have a delayed start often solves the problem.

For the exam it might be wise to know what the client-side components are and how to change the amount of time that clients cache namespace root referrals. The DFS device driver is:

```
Dfsc.sys (%SystemRoot%\System32\Drivers\Dfsc.sys)
```

The DFS client provider uses:

```
Ntlanman.dll. (\%SystemRoot%\System32\Ntlanman.dll)
```

To change the amount of time that clients cache namespace root referrals use these steps:

1. Click Start, then Administrative Tools, and then click DFS Management.
2. In the console tree, under the Namespaces node, right-click a namespace, and then click Properties.
3. On the Referrals tab, in the Cache duration text box, type the amount of time that clients cache namespace root referrals. The default setting is 300 seconds (five minutes).

To modify this setting by using Windows PowerShell, use:

```
Set-DfsnRoot TimeToLiveSec
```

The DFS service was significantly overhauled with the release of Windows Server 2012 R2 and the processes have been optimized to take advantage of the increased performance of networks, increased bandwidth capacity and speed as well as general server performance. DFRS is now able to process file-level replication in most cases without the need to stage the files. This is done by making a special temporary copy to a staging area, thus effectively processing replication tasks live. Windows client and server operating systems often share the same kernel and work well together. For the benefit of performance, reliability, security, and interoperability, it is better to match servers and client operating systems when possible.

Support Storage Spaces

First introduced in Windows 8 and Windows Server 2012, Storage Spaces provides a popular method of enabling you to add storage to your system and to pool existing drives without needing to purchase traditionally expensive Storage Area Network (SAN) devices. This is a great alternative to using RAID, SANs, and iSCSI at a fraction of the cost.

EXAM TIP

If a question refers to the least expensive means of adding storage, remember that Storage Spaces is often the most economical option.

Within a Storage Space, you create a storage pool by adding disks. A storage pool can span multiple physical disks. Being able to add and remove disks from a pool as your capacity demand changes offers a great deal of flexibility. Once you create a Storage Space, the storage is represented as a number of virtual disks within the pool, which behave exactly like physical disks. The virtual disk is sometimes referred to as a Logical Unit Number (LUN), which is a term taken from the more expensive world of Storage Area Network protocols, which encapsulate SCSI, such as Fibre Channel or iSCSI.

To configure Storage Spaces, you need to first attach your storage, which can be a mix and match of type, size, and interface. And it can have internal and external drives, USB drives, Serial ATA (SATA), Serial Attached SCSI (SAS), and so forth. If you are looking for the best performance with a Storage Space, in terms of higher IOPS and IO throughput, you can also use SSD or NVMe (Non-Volatile Memory Express) drives. If you already have RAID technology enabled, you will need to de-activate RAID in order to be able to use Storage Spaces. While each new storage device added doesn't necessarily need to be empty, the disk will be erased after it is added to the pool.

> **IMPORTANT** **ALL EXISTING DATA WILL BE DELETED WHEN ADDING DISKS TO A POOL**
>
> Each disk added to the pool will be first formatted and then configured to be part of the pool. Any existing data will be permanently lost unless you have backed up the data.

Storage Spaces enables users to configure volume-level resiliency, which helps to protect data while it's stored in the storage pool. Traditional single disk drives offer no resiliency; if the drive fails, all the data is lost. Depending on how many drives the storage pool contains, you can configure either volume mirroring or parity-volume levels of redundancy. Storage Spaces recommends using the Resilient File System (ReFS), which is a new file system developed by Microsoft and introduced with Windows Server 2012. The file system offers new functionality and scalability and is self-repairing with built-in resiliency. ReFS supports many NTFS features, but is not currently a replacement for NTFS. When formatting volumes created within Storage Spaces, you can choose either NTFS or REFS depending on your needs.

For the exam, you need to understand the four types of redundancy that are offered in Storage Spaces as shown in Table 5-1.

TABLE 5-1 Windows offers four types of redundancy with Storage Spaces

Type	Description
Simple (none)	No mirroring; data is lost if the drive fails.
Two-way mirror	Each volume in the pool is stored on at least two different physical drives, "mirroring" your data. You need to provide at least two drives to use a two-way mirror.
Three-way mirror	Each volume in the pool is stored on at least three different physical drives. This allows you to lose two drives. You need to provide at least five drives to use a three-way mirror.
Parity	At least three drives are required for parity. Data is stored on at least two different physical drives and the parity information is saved on another disk. This method uses less disk space but can be higher on disk I/O overhead when writing to disk as the parity information needs to be calculated. You need to provide at least three drives to use a parity storage space.

After your drives are connected, follow these steps to configure Storage Spaces:

1. Click the Start button, select Settings, search for Storage Spaces in the search box, and then in Settings open Manage Storage Spaces.

2. Select Create A New Pool And Storage Space, as shown in Figure 5-1.

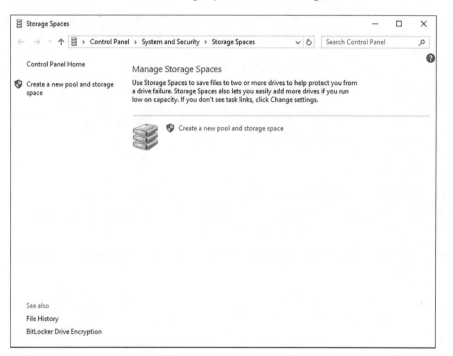

FIGURE 5-1 Creating a new storage pool and storage space

3. If requested, accept the UAC prompt.

4. Storage Spaces identifies available drives to create the storage pool. Select the drive you want to add, as shown in Figure 5-2 (all drives that are not formatted are automatically selected).

FIGURE 5-2 Select the drive to create a storage pool

5. Click Create Pool.

6. Name the Storage Space and select the drive letter you want to use.

7. Depending on the type of resiliency you require, you might be able to format the Storage Space using either NTFS or REFS file system.

8. Use the drop-down list, as shown in Figure 5-3, to select the level of resiliency that you require.

FIGURE 5-3 Selecting the storage space resiliency type

9. Set the Size of the Storage Space. Note that a suggested size is provided, but you can amend this to be larger than the current capacity of the storage pool. I have amended this to 500 GB.

10. Click Create Storage Space.

Your storage pool is now created and is ready to use.

EXAM TIP

ReFS can only be selected when using mirrored drives and cannot be used for simple or parity resiliency types.

Setting the size of the Storage Space is often misunderstood. Storage Spaces allows you to specify a maximum size larger than the total amount of available physical drive space. This is known as *thin provisioning*, which enables you to provision space and then add drives as they are required at a later date. The system prompts you once the physical limit is reached to add more drives to the pool. You can also increase the maximum size of an existing storage space at a later stage. Alternatively, you can use fixed provisioning, which enables you to specify a hard limit for the size of the storage pool.

> **REAL WORLD** **KEEP DISK DRIVES TOGETHER WHEN MOVING THEM TO A NEW PC**
>
> Drives configured as part of a storage pool must be kept together if the pool is moved to a different Windows 10 PC. If a disk is removed permanently from the pool, it needs to be reformatted before it can be reused in another PC. It is good practice to place a label that is visible on the outer case of the drive so that you can identify it without having to remove the drive when it is installed in the computer.

After you create a storage pool, it can be managed using the Manage Storage Spaces console. With the console you can create additional storage spaces, add drives, and delete or rename both the storage space and the name of each physical drive.

If one or more of the physical disks fails, Windows will alert the user and suggest that the failed drive be replaced so that resiliency can be restored.

As an example, if the computer that is hosting storage space in a two-way mirror configuration fails, it is entirely possible to take one of the physical disks and attach it to another computer, and that computer will be able to access the files.

In practice, the Storage Spaces mirrored resiliency can be quick, especially for write performance, quicker than motherboard RAID-1, whereas storage space parity is significantly slower than the hardware RAID-5 equivalent.

To view disk usage, go to Settings, select Storage, and then select a Drive to see available disk space, as shown in Figure 5-4.

FIGURE 5-4 Viewing storage usage within Settings

If you click the drive icon, the operating system will analyze and categorize the contents of the drive and display a summary as shown in Figure 5-5. You are further able to drill down to the actual files, which will ultimately be viewed within File Explorer.

Settings — □ ×

⚙ This PC (C:)

Storage usage

↻ Last refreshed on 11/11/2017 10:15 PM
Total: 75.0 GB

■ Used: 21.2 GB
░ Remaining: 53.8 GB

💻	System & reserved	13.5 GB
🖥	Apps & games	6.53 GB
🗑	Temporary files	898 MB
👥	Other people	334 MB
📖	Other	29.2 MB
	Documents	60.0 KB

FIGURE 5-5 Windows categorizes storage usage for each drive within Settings

In addition to the Windows 10 Graphical User Interface (GUI), you can also manage Storage Spaces using the following methods:

- Windows PowerShell
- Windows Management Instrumentation (WMI)

For server based operations, you can manage Storage Spaces using the following methods:

- Server Manager
- System Center Virtual Machine Manager
- Failover Cluster Manager

Windows 10 includes several enhancements to the Storage Spaces feature, since it was first introduced in Windows 8. Using PowerShell, you can now force the optimization of drives in a storage pool to accommodate removed or additional drives and re-distribute data across the drives. The rebalancing process only works on simple and mirrored spaces.

Manage Storage Spaces using PowerShell

You can script the creation, repair and administration of Storage Spaces using built-in Power-Shell cmdlets. Some of the Storage Spaces' specific cmdlets that can be used are shown in Table 5-2.

TABLE 5-2 Storage Cmdlets in Windows PowerShell

Storage Cmdlets	Description
New-StoragePool	Creates a new storage pool using a group of physical disks
Add-PhysicalDisk	Adds a physical disk to a storage pool for the creation of one or more VirtualDisk objects
Get-StoragePool	Gets a specific storage pool, or a set of StoragePool objects that are available
Set-StoragePool	Modifies the properties of the specified storage pool.
Set-PhysicalDisk	Sets the attributes on a specific physical disk.
Get-VirtualDisk	Returns a list of VirtualDisk objects that are available
New-VirtualDisk	Creates a new virtual disk in the specified storage pool.
Repair-VirtualDisk	Deletes an existing virtual disk and reclaims the used space for use by other virtual disks in the same storage pool.
Optimize-StoragePool	Rebalances a Storage Space configured as simple or mirrored, optimizing files based on disk space, disk size and file size.
Update-StoragePool	Used on pre Windows 10 storage pools to upgrade the storage pool metadata to enable new features and functionality.
Remove-PhysicalDisk	Removes a physical disk from a specified storage pool.
Remove-StoragePool	Deletes a storage pool and associated VirtualDisk objects

To list all of the Storage cmdlets that are available, use the Get-Command –Module Storage cmdlet.

Support OneDrive

Windows 10 users can use OneDrive by signing into OneDrive with their Microsoft account. OneDrive provides users with reliable and robust cloud services that are used by millions of users across the world. What users see on their desktop or via the browser is just the client-facing presentation layer. Beneath the hood, OneDrive has several layers of complexity to ensure efficient file synchronization takes place that you will never see.

Microsoft has improved the level of security and encryption to protect customer data held on OneDrive. This upgrade has enabled Perfect Forward Secrecy (PFS) encryption support when accessing OneDrive through *onedrive.live.com*, the OneDrive mobile app, and the sync clients.

Find Help

For many users, the concept of cloud-based applications (and you could use the analogy that OneDrive is a cloud-based version of File Explorer, to your users) is still very new. They may need some help and training to become competent users of OneDrive. Microsoft provides comprehensive intelligent online help for OneDrive, as shown in Figure 5-6. You can search the help repository by typing a keyword, or question into the search box and then clicking the bulb icon.

FIGURE 5-6 OneDrive online help

Service availability

Microsoft Online Services runs on thousands of inter-connected servers in many datacenters across the globe. This is presented to you as the cloud. Since these are not local instances of a web app or service, running on your corporate servers, there is little or no maintenance for you to perform.

Although rare, there might be instances of service failure, even in the cloud, and this can lead to OneDrive not offering 100 percent uptime. You need to remember that cloud services offer excellent service availability, but the OneDrive service might be unavailable from time to time, a situation that could vary depending on your region.

Microsoft states in the Service Availability section of their Services Agreement that "they strive to keep the Services up and running; however, all online services suffer occasional disruptions and outages, and Microsoft is not liable for any disruption or loss you may suffer as a result. In the event of an outage, you may not be able to retrieve Your Content or Data that you've stored. We recommend that you regularly backup Your Content that you store on the Services or store using Third-Party Apps and Services."

> **MORE INFO** **MICROSOFT SERVICES AGREEMENT**
>
> The Microsoft Services Agreement can be found at: *https://www.microsoft.com/servicesagreement*.

If you are experiencing connection issues and you do not experience them for other online services, check the Microsoft service status provided at *https://portal.office.com/servicestatus*, which will outline any issues with the availability of the end user services as shown in Figure 5-7.

FIGURE 5-7 Service status

If you have an Office 365 subscription, you can click the link at the bottom left of the Service status screen shown in Figure 5-7, or sign into the Office 365 and view the Service Health from the Admin Center. You will notice in Figure 5-8 that the Office 365 Service Health shows that all services are running, with the Office 365 Portal showing one advisory.

FIGURE 5-8 Service status

Recover files from OneDrive

When you delete a file within File Explorer, you are able to use the Recycle Bin to recover the file. OneDrive offers two methods of recovering files. These are:

- Undo
- Recycle Bin

The Undo feature works as it does on an Office document. If you delete an object within OneDrive by selecting Delete on the context menu, the message shown in Figure 5-9 is displayed. The message includes the Undo button. Click the Undo button to cancel the deletion and the files will be restored. If you click anywhere else within OneDrive while the deletion progress bar is displayed, or if you do nothing for approximately 10 seconds, the message automatically closes. So, if you want to use the Undo button, you need to promptly click it!

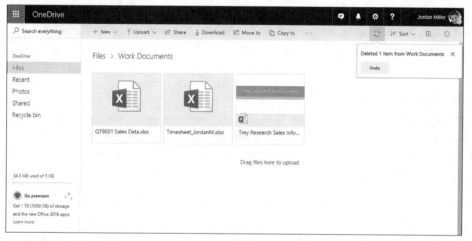

FIGURE 5-9 OneDrive Undo feature

When the file has been deleted, the item is moved to the Recycle Bin folder. The Recycle Bin offers functionality similar to what File Explorer offers. Click the Recycle Bin within OneDrive and all the files that have been deleted will be listed. With no files selected, the Restore item at the top offers you the option to Restore All Items.

Once you locate the files that need to be restored, you can then click the Restore menu item and the files will be recovered, as shown in Figure 5-10. If you click Delete within the Recycle Bin, you'll be warned that the items will be permanently deleted.

FIGURE 5-10 OneDrive Recycle Bin

The Recycle Bin in OneDrive stores items for a minimum of three days and up to a maximum of 30 days, with the capacity of the Recycle Bin set to 10 percent of the total storage limit. If the Recycle Bin is full, old files that are less than 30 days old will also be deleted in order to make room for new items.

For work or school accounts, OneDrive is known as OneDrive for Business and is hosted on SharePoint Online servers. Items in the OneDrive for Business Recycle Bin are permanently deleted after 93 days on these accounts by default. OneDrive for Business is included as part of Microsoft 365 and Office 365 subscriptions and includes a much larger default storage capacity of 1 TB.

Skill 5.2: Support data security

You have stored your data and now you need to consider how to ensure it remains secure. This skill covers the security options available and reviews share permissions, NTFS file permissions and Dynamic Access Control (DAC), and the encryption options within NTFS using Encrypting File System (EFS).

With removable storage prevalent within many organizations, you'll also review how to secure this type of storage media by using technologies such as BitLocker and BitLocker To Go, together with methods for enterprises to manage encryption.

This section covers many topics and gives more prominence to newer technologies such as DAC and BitLocker. You'll need to ensure that your understanding of the basic Share and NTFS permissions is robust because this will be assumed within the exam.

> **This section covers how to:**
> - Manage permissions including Sharing, NTFS and Dynamic Access Control (DAC)
> - Support Encrypting File System (EFS), including Data Recovery Agent
> - Control access to removable media
> - Support BitLocker and BitLocker To Go, including Data Recovery Agent, and Microsoft BitLocker Administration and Monitoring (MBAM)

Manage permissions including Sharing, NTFS and Dynamic Access Control

Only volumes that are formatted with NTFS or REFS are able to apply NTFS file and folder permissions in Windows 10. Thankfully, NTFS is the default file system used, the vast majority of businesses use NTFS on their Windows systems. Since NTFS was introduced there have been subtle improvements to NTFS technology, which has maintained its status as robust, reliable, and effective.

Whenever you are in an exam environment, you need to read the scenario very carefully to establish what role you have because this is crucial when determining what you can modify. As a system administrator you often make changes using administrative rights, which effectively means you have a "master-key" to all the NTFS locks in the organization. Whenever you are setting permissions, you need to always test to ensure that the outcome of your actions does not result in unexpected increases of privilege for another user.

Resolve NTFS permission issues

The type of security that can be configured on Windows 10 is determined by the file system in place. NTFS is the default underlying file system and it offers several security options, but you may also encounter removable drives or legacy systems that use FAT16, FAT32, or exFAT, which offer less security.

It has been several years since NTFS was established as the default file system of choice for all recent Windows client and server operating systems. NTFS file permissions offer administrators a very powerful tool for granting, controlling, auditing, and denying access to resources. Unlike share-level permissions, NTFS operates at the file level, which means NTFS permissions are applicable to resources shared over a network or accessed locally.

When troubleshooting resource access issues, you need to determine the following:

- Is the file system in NTFS?
- Are the files and folders being accessed locally or over the network?

It is easy to test if the file system is using NTFS by checking to see if there is a security tab on the volume on which the resource resides, as shown in Figure 5-11. The Security tab relates to NTFS permissions.

FIGURE 5-11 An NTFS formatted volume will display a Security tab

NTFS permissions can be complex and sometimes difficult to manage, especially for a junior or inexperienced administrator. Often the most challenging environment is one in which a newly hired administrator has to adopt an enterprise, which has an existing problematic NTFS permission infrastructure in place that has very little documentation. Small changes required can sometimes have unintended consequences, which pose security risks. The role of the system administrator is to optimize data security, and also to make sure that data is accessible to the right users. If users are denied access to files to which they have rights or given access to privileged files, it is a major problem that needs immediate remediation.

NTFS permissions are cumulative, which means a user may have been given various group memberships as well as explicit permissions to resources that they are able to access. If a user has not been given any implicit or explicit permissions, they will not have access. If a combination of permissions for a resource has been set, you'll need to calculate the cumulative effect of all permissions.

Faced with an issue resulting from lack of access or over privilege, you need to start troubleshooting the problem by determining the effective permissions for the files or folders in question. Establish the scope; for example, who does this problem affect, and is it confined to a single user or a group of users? Establishing the effective permissions will allow you to quickly determine permissions that apply and provide you with a starting point.

User-effective permissions are based on the total of all permissions that they have been granted or denied. Take special care to look for any Deny permissions because these are infrequently set, but when they are, they are very powerful because any explicit Deny permission will have precedence over Allow entries.

To view the effective permissions for a user or a group that has been set on a file or folder, follow these steps:

1. Open File Explorer, right-click the file or folder that is under review.
2. Click Properties, click the Security tab, and then click Advanced.
3. In the Advanced Security Settings For dialog box, click the Effective Access tab.
4. Click the Select A User link, and choose the appropriate user, group, or device that you want to view the effective permissions for.
5. Click OK.
6. Click View Effective Access, as shown in Figure 5-12. The effective permissions are displayed as required.
7. Click OK twice to close the dialog boxes.

FIGURE 5-12 NTFS object access effective permissions for a user displayed

EXAM TIP

The Share tab shown in Figure 5-12 will only be visible if you are viewing the effective permissions for a shared folder.

The Effective Access tool is very useful in resolving many access issues. However, there are a small number of special cases where the tool is limited. For example, where a user is also the original creator of the resource, they have the Creator Owner special identity, which is not reported by the Effective Access tool.

REAL WORLD DOCUMENT ALL CHANGES

The best practice when configuring NTFS permissions is to document a plan of how the NTFS permissions will be applied to the predefined users, groups, and folders. Ensure that all new users, groups, and folders are created according to the plan. Then apply NTFS permissions to this structure. Once the NTFS plan has been created, repeat for the Share permissions. Once permissions have been configured, continue to the testing phase where you perform tests for selected users to establish whether their effective access to resources matches the intended objectives of the plan. Over time, your NTFS change log will extremely-ly useful when troubleshooting NTFS access issues.

TroubleshootShare permission issues

Share permissions can cause many problems when troubleshooting access to files and folders. You need to remember that Share permissions work together with NTFS permissions and that the most restrictive permission will apply. Another common cause of confusion is that Share permissions only affect shared resources over the network.

If your file system is configured with FAT or FAT32, there is no option to configure NTFS permissions. If no Security tab is available in the resource Properties dialog box, we know that it cannot be formatted with NTFS, and the file system is likely to be FAT/FAT32, as shown in Figure 5-13.

FIGURE 5-13 A FAT32 formatted volume will not display a Security tab

If you need to confirm the file system in use, you can view the properties of the drive by following these steps:

1. Open File Explorer, right click the drive that is under review.
2. Click On the General tab view the File System.
3. Click OK to close the dialog box.

Combine NTFS and Share permissions

Within a corporate environment, administrators share files over the network, using Share permissions. If the volume is formatted with NTFS, there are likely to be NTFS permissions configured on the shared file as well. In order to fully understand the effects of these two sets of permissions, you will need to combine them.

When troubleshooting access, always look for the most restrictive permission that has been set and evaluate whether this is being applied. You can view the effective permissions if necessary. If the most restrictive permission is not being applied when the resource is being accessed, you need to determine the problem. Some other permission must be overlapping and affecting the resource—perhaps the user is a member of the administrators group, or another group that has full control permissions? You can also test what permissions are effective both at the local access level and also when accessing the resource over the network share.

Often the cause of many permission-based issues when troubleshooting file and folder access is that the Share permissions being applied on the share are too restrictive. It is preferable to use the more powerful NTFS permissions because these will be effective at all times, regardless of how they are accessed (over the network share or locally).

Dynamic Access Control

Dynamic Access Control (DAC) was first introduced in Windows Server 2012 and Windows 8. DAC enables Active Directory administrators to deploy a robust method of applying data governance across their file servers. The key improvement over NTFS permissions is that with DAC you can control and audit data access by providing the ability to set controls on files and folders based on conditions that you could pre-configure within your Active Directory. These conditions can be dynamic. An example of a condition is the physical location of the user. For instance, you may want to restrict access to confidential company data when a user is using a VPN connection, but allow them full access when they are using their computer in the office.

Additional options are available to you when configuring DAC such as the following:

- **Central access policies and rules**   Rules can be created for groups, user claims, device claims, and resource properties. Rules protect resources and can be tightly controlled with conditional expressions, Access Control Entries (ACEs), and expressions.

- **Claims**   This is a single piece of information about an object, such as an Active Directory Domain Services (AD DS) attribute associated with a user, a computer, a device, or a resource. Multiple claims can be used to protect resources.

- **Expressions**   You can set conditions to control access management. These conditions include the state of the device, its location, and any groups that the object belongs to.

- **Proposed permissions**   These permissions enable you to create a what-if scenario to test permissions before applying them.

The process is not enabled by default on the client side and you'll need to turn on the feature by enabling Group Policy Objects, which are located at Computer Configuration\Administrative Templates\System\Kerberos. In particular, you will need to use the Kerberos Client Support For Claims, Compound Authentication And Kerberos Armoring.

Support Encrypting File System

The built-in Encrypting File System (EFS) is a very powerful method of restricting access to files within a NTFS environment. Although EFS has been available since Windows 2000, very few organizations actually implement file and folder level encryption. Most organizations requiring encryption will use BitLocker Drive Encryption which encrypts complete drives Where EFS is utilized , most issues reported to the helpdesk relating to EFS often result from an over enthusiastic member of staff encrypting some of their own files. By default, they have permission to encrypt their own files because they have the Creator Owner special identity.

The best way to ensure that EFS is not inadvertently used, potentially causing problems later, is to implement some or all of the following measures:

- Stand-alone computers that are not domain-joined should backup their encryption keys to ensure they can be used for recovery later.

- Explain the usage criteria of EFS in the staff handbook / policy.

- IT staff training relating to the use of EFS and potential implications of unauthorized usage.

- Planning and documenting of where and by whom EFS will be applied.

- Sufficient restrictions placed across the domain to prevent unauthorized use of EFS.

- Implementation of an EFS Data Recovery Agent (DRA) so that if EFS is misused then an Administrator can recover any encrypted files.

- Implement employee-leaving procedures and scan for encrypted files to ensure all encrypted files are decrypted or ownership transferred.

- Disable rather than delete user accounts for a fixed time period in case the user account needs to be reactivated in order to remove EFS from corporate resources.

It's necessary to ensure that selected users and members of IT departments appreciate that EFS is an extremely secure method of protecting files and often this level of protection is not necessary. Only the original file owner who applied the encryption is able to access the file and remove the encryption.

If an organization does not have a DRA in place, this needs to be created as soon as possible because this will enable subsequent files encrypted with EFS to be decrypted by the DRA should this be necessary.

The process for creating a DRA certificate in Windows 10 for a device that is not domain joined, is as follows:

1. Open a PowerShell windows, or a command prompt window (this does not require administrative privilege).

2. Navigate to the location where you want to store your DRA certificate.

3. Type **cipher /r:** *file name* and press Enter.

4. Provide a password to protect the DRA certificate (this can be null).

To install the DRA so that a user can use the DRA, follow these steps:

1. Sign in with the user credentials of the user for whom you want to create access to the DRA.

2. In the search box, type **secpol.msc** and press Enter.

3. In the left pane of Local Security Policy, double-click Public Key Policies, right-click Encrypting File System, and then click Add Data Recovery Agent.

4. In the Add Recovery Agent Wizard, click Next.

5. Browse to the location of the DRA recovery certificate (it will have a .cer file extension).

6. Select the certificate, and then click Open.

7. When you are asked if you want to install the certificate, click Yes, Next, and then click Finish.

8. In the right pane of Local Security Policy, scroll across and note that the Intended Purposes for the certificate is File Recovery.

9. Open a Command Prompt window and type **gpupdate**, and press Enter to update Group Policy.

Once the DRA has been created, all EFS encrypted files can be recovered by the DRA.

The encrypted files that are already encrypted are not automatically updated and cannot be recovered by the DRA unless they are opened and closed by the resource owner so that the DRA can update the file, or by using cipher.exe /u.

Troubleshoot Encrypting File System

When users report that they are unable to use EFS to encrypt files, you need to verify that all of the four statements are correct:

- A recovery agent policy has been defined, which prevents the use of EFS unless a DRA has been created.

- The file volume is NTFS; EFS is only supported on NTFS.

- The file is not compressed. NTFS allows files to be encrypted or compressed, not both.

- You have Write access to the file. You need to be able to save the encrypted file.

Other examples of helpdesk EFS issues include the following scenarios and possible answers:

- **I can't open files I have encrypted** Only users with the correct EFS certificate and private key for the file can open EFS-protected files. Has the user account been deleted/

recreated since the file was created? Use a DRA to recover the file and have the user encrypt the file again.

- **Will I get a warning that I will lose the EFS protection on my file when I copy my file a FAT32 USB drive?** There is no warning if the user has the necessary NTFS permissions to move or copy the file, then Windows will carry out the operation without error or warning.

- **I saved a file which is protected using Windows Information Protection (WIP) to a FAT32 USB drive. The file looks like it is encrypted using EFS. Is this correct?** WIP is supported in Windows 10 to protect files. Protected files look and behave like EFS files, but they do not use EFS. The file is an encrypted PFILE which stores the Enterprise Data Protection metadata, which can be stored on a FAT32 drive.

- **I can't open an EFS file after upgrading from a previous version of Windows** You can still recover the files by importing the EFS certificate and key from your old computer into your new computer.

- **My anti-virus check program runs but I get "Access Denied" error messages** An anti-virus check program can only read your encrypted files. If the device is a shared computer and other users have encrypted files on the hard disk, the anti-virus tool will not be able to access these files. Other users need to perform a virus check for files by signing in on the device.

Controlling access to removable media

USB flash drives are very popular and versatile. Rapid technological improvements have resulted in increases in USB drive capacity, enabling users to carry a huge amount of information in their pockets. While having easy access to this data can be very convenient to the user, it is also a major worry for IT Managers and Data Controllers, because of the risk of corporate data loss. For example, leaving a USB flash drive on a train or plugged into a guest PC can result in significant data leakage.

In addition to USB drives, users can also copy corporate (or private) data to CDs, DVDs, external hard drives, and memory cards. While these media may be smaller in capacity when compared to a USB drive, a DVD can still contain millions of records from a database. Managers will need to decide on policies that determine which users within an organization may use these kinds of devices. Some employees need to use portable drives, but most don't.

You can restrict the use of devices in several ways by using Group Policy. One way is to block all removable data drives. Another is to restrict the use of removable drives to a specific make and model (hardware ID), and another option is to ensure that all removable drives are encrypted. Windows 10 provides a feature called BitLocker To Go which can encrypt removable drives.

For the exam, you should review the available policies with the following section of Group Policy: Computer Configuration\Administrative Templates\System\Removable Storage Access.

To access Removable Storage Access policies, follow these steps:

1. Launch Group Policy Editor (gpedit.msc).

2. Navigate to Computer Configuration\Administrative Templates\System\Removable Storage Access.

3. Review the available GPOs, paying particular attention to the All Removable Storage classes: Deny all access policy.

Another popular method is to restrict writing to devices that have a specific hardware ID by preventing Windows from installing the device driver whenever a USB flash drive is inserted. GPO settings that restrict devices can be located in the following section of Group Policy: Computer Configuration\Administrative Templates\System\Device Installation\Device Installation Restrictions.

Conversely, a company might purchase a specific type of USB flash drive and issue them to executives. You can use a GPO setting that enables Device Installation for these users, based on the hardware ID of the device. Review the GPO setting Allow Installation Of Devices That Match Any Of These Device IDs, which enables you to specify the hardware ID of a removable drive, and can be found by using Device Manager on a machine that already has the hardware items installed. Within Device Manager, locate the device, right-click the particular item, select Properties, and then select Details. On the Details tab, choose Hardware Ids from the Property drop-down list. Right-click the specific value and select Copy. This value needs to be pasted in the GPO setting.

To require that users write data to BitLocker-protected storage (covered later in this chapter), you enable the GPO Deny Write Access To Drives Not Protected By BitLocker, which is located in Computer Configuration\Administrative Templates\Windows Components \BitLocker Drive Encryption\Removable Data Drives. When applying a GPO to your local machine, you can either restart the device or run gpupdate /force to apply the updated GPOs to your system.

Support BitLocker and BitLocker To Go

BitLocker Drive Encryption enables you to encrypt an entire hard disk, which can be the Windows operating system drive or a data drive. The Windows 10 Pro, Enterprise, and Education editions support BitLocker in both x86 and x64-bit varieties.

Many modern computers now ship with a Trusted Platform Module (TPM), which a microchip that is used to securely store cryptographic information, such as the encryption keys that BitLocker uses. BitLocker supports versions 1.2 and 2.0 of the TPM specification and information contained on the TPM is more secure from external software attacks and physical theft. If a device has been tampered with, such as a hard drive removed from the original computer, BitLocker will prevent the drive from being unlocked. BitLocker will seek remediation from the user by entering BitLocker recovery mode and requiring the user to enter a 48-digit recovery key. While a TPM is the most secure option, BitLocker technology can also be used on devices without a TPM, by configuring a GPO to require that BitLocker obtains the required cryptographic information from a USB flash drive. This information must be presented to unlock the volume.

A portable version of BitLocker, BitLocker To Go, aimed at protecting removable USB devices, uses the same technology as BitLocker Drive Encryption, but does not require use of a TPM. BitLocker To Go can protect flash drives, Secure Digital (SD) cards, removable hard disks formatted with NTFS, Fat16, FAT32, or exFat file systems. To unlock a protected drive, the user must input a password or a smart card with a PIN to unlock the drive. For frequent users of BitLocker To Go, encrypted drives can be configured to be unlocked automatically when inserted on specific computers.

To assist with the management of BitLocker for corporate clients, Microsoft provides a management tool called Microsoft BitLocker Administration And Monitoring (MBAM), which is available as part of the Microsoft Desktop Optimization Pack (MDOP), a suite of utilities for customers with an active Microsoft Software Assurance license agreement.

Using BitLocker

BitLocker offers users several protection options. Administrators can choose which type of protection users should adopt to unlock a BitLocker encrypted drive. BitLocker supports multi-factor authentication for operating system drives, allowing you to require additional authentication such as adding a smart card or a USB drive with a startup key on it, or requiring a PIN on start up. These are called key protectors.

BitLocker offers multiple key protectors that can be used to unlock a protected system. The BitLocker authentication methods are as follows:

- **TPM + startup PIN + startup key** This is the most secure combination. The encryption key is stored on the TPM chip. The user might find this option cumbersome because this requires multiple authentication tasks.

- **TPM + startup key** The encryption key is stored on the TPM chip. The user needs to insert a USB flash drive that contains a startup key.

- **TPM + startup PIN** The encryption key is stored on the TPM chip. The user needs to enter a PIN to unlock the device.

- **Startup key only** The user needs to insert a USB flash drive with the startup key on it. The device doesn't need to have a TPM chip. The BIOS must support access to the USB flash drive before the operating system loads.

- **TPM only** The encryption key is stored on the TPM chip, and no user action is required.

When the BitLocker encrypted drive is in recovery mode, you can also unlock the drive by using either the recovery password or recovery key.

- **Recovery password** This is a 48-digit number typed on a regular keyboard, or by using the function keys (F1-F10) to input the numbers.

- **Recovery key**   This is an encryption key created when the BitLocker is first employed and is for recovering data encrypted on a BitLocker volume. Often the encryption key is stored on removable media.

Because the TPM chip together with BitLocker protects the hard drive, administrators can also configure BitLocker to operate without additional unlock steps, so long as the device (and TPM) recognize the drive then it will be unlocked.

With BitLocker enabled, the drive is no longer susceptible to data theft. On an unprotected system, simply removing the drive from the PC and attaching it as a slave to another PC allows the data to be read, bypassing all NTFS security.

EXAM TIP

Administrators can fine-tune within Group Policy the settings for BitLocker and you would do well to review the available GPOs in detail because they are likely to appear on the exam. Review the GPOs located in Computer Configuration\Policies\Administrative Templates\ Windows Components\BitLocker Drive Encryption.

You need to also learn which versions of Windows 10 support BitLocker, the supported TPM versions, and how to tell whether your computer has a TPM.

> **NOTE USED DISK SPACE ONLY**
>
> An improvement to BitLocker enables administrators to choose whether to encrypt only the used disk space or encrypt the entire drive during the initial deployment of Windows. Choosing the first option significantly reduces the time to deploy and requires less administrative effort, though purists will tell you this is slightly less secure.

To configure BitLocker on Windows 10 with a TPM, follow these steps:

1. Type BitLocker into the Start menu and then select Manage BitLocker.
2. On the BitLocker Drive Encryption page, click Turn On BitLocker on the operating system volume. Accept UAC if prompted.
3. The BitLocker Drive Encryption Wizard then requires you to take a backup of the BitLocker recovery key. This can be saved to your Microsoft account, to a USB flash drive, to a file, or in printed form.
4. On the Encrypt The Selected Disk Volume page, confirm that the Run BitLocker System Check check box is selected, and then click Continue.
5. Click Restart Now. The computer restarts and BitLocker verifies whether the computer is BitLocker-compatible and ready for encryption.

   The drive will now be encrypted. Although the drive is immediately protected, the individual files will need to be encrypted and this can take a while, depending on the capacity of the drive

To discover whether your device has a TPM, type **TPM.msc** in the search bar and review the TPM Microsoft Management Console (MMC), as shown in Figure 5-14. If you believe you have a TPM chip, you may want to ensure that it is enabled in either the BIOS or Unified Extensible Firmware Interface (UEFI) settings.

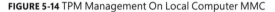

FIGURE 5-14 TPM Management On Local Computer MMC

By default, a modern Windows device such as a Surface Pro will contain a TPM, and Bit-Locker Drive Encryption will be already enabled when shipped. When the user signs onto the device for the first time with a Microsoft account, the recovery key is saved to their Microsoft account. A user viewing the TPM Management On local Computer MMC, shown in Figure 5-14, might be confused by the TPM owner password, what it is, and where it is stored. You need to know that BitLocker is able to initialize the TPM and create a TPM owner password, which will be automatically saved in the same location as the BitLocker recovery password. In a corporate environment, administrators need to ensure that the TPM owner password, which can be saved to a file, is set and stored safely away from the local computer. The TPM owner password is useful if you are locked out of the TPM, or if you need to reset or disable the TPM.

If a TPM isn't found, click Cancel on the BitLocker Drive Encryption, and follow the displayed instructions to configure the Require Additional Authentication At Startup GPO located in Computer Configuration\Administrative Templates\Windows Components\BitLocker Drive Encryption\Operating System Drives. Enable this GPO and select the Allow BitLocker Without A Compatible TPM check box, as shown in Figure 5-15.

FIGURE 5-15 Configuring BitLocker to work without a TPM

Within Control Panel, BitLocker administrators can manage, encrypt, and decrypt fixed data drives and backup recovery keys. Standard users can change the PIN or password on operating system drives.

A new GPO called Computer Configuration\Policies\Administrative Templates\Windows Components\BitLocker Drive Encryption\Operating System Drives\Configure Pre-boot Recovery Message And URL, included with Windows 10, enables an administrator to configure a custom recovery message and to replace the existing URL that is displayed on the pre-boot recovery screen when the operating system drive is locked.

Upgrade a BitLocker-enabled computer

BitLocker is designed to protect your computer from pre-boot changes, such as updating the BIOS. If you upgrade your computer, for example, with a BIOS firmware upgrade, this can cause the TPM to perceive it is under attack. In order to prevent Windows 10 from entering BitLocker recovery mode, it's recommended that some precautions are taken while upgrading a BitLocker-enabled computer. Prior to updating the BIOS, you should carry out the following steps:

1. Temporarily suspend BitLocker by opening the BitLocker Drive Encryption in Control Panel and select Suspend Protection on the operating system drive, placing it in disabled mode.

2. Upgrade the system or the BIOS.

3. Turn BitLocker on again by opening BitLocker Drive Encryption in Control Panel and select Resume Protection on the operating system drive.

Forcing BitLocker into disabled mode keeps the data encrypted, and the volume master key is now encrypted with a clear key. The availability of this unencrypted key disables the data protection that BitLocker offers, but it ensures that subsequent computer startups succeed without further user input. After the BIOS upgrade, you need to re-enable BitLocker so that the unencrypted key is erased from the disk and BitLocker protection is functional again. The encryption key will be resealed with the new key that has been regenerated to incorporate new values of the measured components that changed as a part of the upgrade.

> **NOTE** **THROUGHOUT SUSPENSION DATA IS ENCRYPTED**
>
> Although BitLocker is suspended, the drive is still encrypted and all new data written to the disk is still encrypted. Suspension prevents BitLocker from validating system integrity at startup and is a security risk; therefore, the protection status should be resumed at the earliest opportunity.

Move a BitLocker-encrypted drive to another computer

Moving a BitLocker-encrypted drive to another BitLocker-enabled computer requires that you turn off BitLocker temporarily (by using the Suspend Protection option). After the move is complete you need to re-enable BitLocker, which will then resume BitLocker protection.

The PowerShell command for suspending BitLocker encryption is:

```
Suspend-BitLocker -MountPoint "C:"
```

Sometimes a system change can cause the BitLocker system integrity check on the operating system drive to fail. This prevents the TPM from releasing the BitLocker key to decrypt the protected operating system drive and requires the user to enter into recovery mode.

- Moving the BitLocker-protected drive to a new computer.
- Installing a new motherboard with a new TPM.
- Turning off, disabling, or clearing the TPM.
- Making changes to any boot configuration settings.
- Making changes to the BIOS, UEFI firmware, master boot record, boot sector, boot manager, option ROM, or other early boot components or boot configuration data.

Configure BitLocker using command-line tools

Administrators can also manage BitLocker Drive Encryption using the command-line tool Manage-bde.exe or by using the Command Prompt, PowerShell and WMI. Managing recovery keys is discussed later.

There are 20 parameters that can be used with Manage-bde to turn on or turn off BitLocker, specify how drives are unlocked, and to update recovery methods. Table 5-3 displays the most used parameters.

TABLE 5-3 Manage bde parameters

Parameter	Description
Manage-bde -status	Provides information about all drives on the computer, whether or not they are BitLocker-protected.
Manage-bde on	This encrypts the drive and turns on BitLocker. Use the UsedSpaceOnly switch to set the encryption mode to Used Space Only encryption.
Manage-bde -off	This decrypts the drive and turns off BitLocker. All key protectors are removed when decryption is complete.
Manage-bde -pause & Manage-bde -resume	Use with a drive letter to pause or resume encryption or decryption.
Manage-bde -lock & manage-bde -unlock	Use with a drive letter to lock and unlock access to BitLocker-protected data.
Manage-bde -autounlock	Manages automatic unlocking of a data drive
Manage-bde -protectors	Manages protection methods for the encryption key.
Manage-bde -changepassword	Modifies the password for a data drive.
Manage-bde -changepin	Modifies the PIN for an operating system drive.
Manage-bde - forcerecovery	Forces a BitLocker-protected drive into recovery mode on restart.
Manage-bde -changekey	Modifies the startup key for an operating system drive.
Manage-bde WipeFreeSpace	Wipes the free space on a drive.
Manage-bde -help or -h	Displays complete Help at the command prompt.

> **MORE INFO** **MANAGE-BDE COMMAND-LINE TOOL**
>
> More information on using the manage-bde command-line tool is available in this article at: *https://docs.microsoft.com/windows-server/administration/windows-commands/manage-bde*.

Windows 10 offers built-in support for 13 BitLocker PowerShell cmdlets, as listed in Table 5-4. You can also use Get-help <BitLocker cmdlet>, such as Get-Help Enable BitLocker examples.

TABLE 5-4 BitLocker PowerShell cmdlets

Cmdlet	Description
Add-BitLockerKeyProtector	Adds a key protector for a BitLocker volume
Backup-BitLockerKeyProtector	Saves a key protector for a BitLocker volume in AD DS
Clear-BitLockerAutoUnlock	Removes BitLocker automatic unlocking keys
Disable-BitLocker	Disables BitLocker encryption for a volume
Disable-BitLockerAutoUnlock	Disables automatic unlocking for a BitLocker volume
Enable-BitLocker	Enables encryption for a BitLocker volume
Enable-BitLockerAutoUnlock	Enables automatic unlocking for a BitLocker volume
Get-BitLockerVolume	Gets information about volumes that BitLocker can protect
Lock-BitLocker	Prevents access to encrypted data on a BitLocker volume
Remove-BitLockerKeyProtector	Removes a key protector for a BitLocker volume
Resume-BitLocker	Restores BitLocker encryption for the specified volume
Suspend-BitLocker	Suspends BitLocker encryption for the specified volume
Unlock-BitLocker	Restores access to data on a BitLocker volume

MORE INFO **CONFIGURE BITLOCKER USING POWERSHELL CMDLETS**

For more information about how to configure BitLocker using PowerShell cmdlets, visit this reference article at: *https://docs.microsoft.com/powershell/module/bitlocker/?view=win10-ps*.

Using PowerShell, you can obtain very detailed information from systems, including status, key protectors used, encryption method, and type. If you run the Get-BitLockerVolume > fl cmdlet to provide information about an encrypted drive without first unlocking the drive, the amount of information obtained will be restricted. To compare the information obtained when the command is run on the same drive, when unlocked and locked drive, see Figure 5-16.

FIGURE 5-16 Detailed BitLocker information using PowerShell

Configure BitLocker To Go

For users of Windows 10 Pro, Windows 10 Enterprise, and Windows 10 Education, BitLocker To Go enables the encryption of removable USB devices, using BitLocker technology. These devices can be flash drives, Secure Digital (SD) cards, or removable hard disks formatted with NTFS, Fat16, FAT32, or exFat. All users can protect their removable drive by using the same BitLocker Drive Encryption Control Panel used before.

To create a BitLocker To Go drive, insert a removable drive and select Turn BitLocker On. If the option to encrypt the drive is not available, you need to check to ensure you are using a supported version of Windows, and that the feature has not been disabled by Group Policy.

Just as when you encrypt a fixed drive, when you select the Turn On BitLocker menu option for a removable drive, you need to also specify how you want to unlock the removable drive. You can select one of the following methods:

- A recovery password or passphrase (this complexity can be set within Group Policy)
- A smart card
- Always auto-unlock this device on this PC

The last option is very useful for users who frequently use removable drives because it reduces the likelihood of frustration from entering the password every time they use their removable drives. If the removable drive is used on other devices once the user unlocks the removable drive, it can also be configured to auto-unlock if required.

Standard users can turn on, turn off, or change configurations of BitLocker on removable data drives. They are also able to change their own password for encrypted drives via BitLocker Drive Encryption in Control Panel. However, if a user loses or forgets the password for the data or removable drive, you need to have access to the BitLocker recovery key to recover the data and unlock the drive.

The following GPOs are available within the BitLocker To Go settings found at Computer Configuration\Policies\Administrative Templates\Windows Components\BitLocker Drive Encryption\Removable Data Drives:

- Control use of BitLocker on removable drives
- Configure use of smart cards on removable data drives
- Deny Write access to removable drives not protected by BitLocker
- Configure use of hardware-based encryption for removable data drives
- Enforce drive-encryption type on removable data drives
- Allow access to BitLocker-protected removable data drives from earlier versions of Windows
- Configure use of passwords for removable data drives
- Choose how BitLocker-protected removable data drives can be recovered

Users of Windows 10 Home cannot encrypt removable data drives, but they can access BitLocker To Go enabled data drives if they provide the correct recovery password, passphrase, or smart card.

Configure startup key storage and recovery options

You know that without access to the encryption key contained in the TPM or stored in the startup key, you are unable to unlock a BitLocker-encrypted drive.

You need to ensure that you're familiar with BitLocker-related terminology:

- **Recovery password and recovery key**   When you first configure BitLocker it will create a recovery key and prompt you to store it safely. You'll need to provide this recovery key if the TPM is unable to validate that the drive hasn't been tampered with or if the startup key, password, or pin have not been supplied during boot time.
- **Password**   A password or passphrase is created to protect fixed, removable, and operating system drives with or without a TPM. The password length can be set in Group Policy and can consist of eight to 255 characters.
- **PIN**   When you use a TPM you can configure BitLocker with a PIN that the user must type during the initial startup of the device to allow Windows 10 to start. The PIN can consist of between four to 20 digits and the length can be set in the Configure Minimum PIN Length For Startup Group Policy setting.
- **Enhanced PIN**   Enables administrators to force the use of a complex PIN, just like a password or passphrase (including spaces), by configuring the Allow Enhanced PINs For Startup GPO setting. This policy is applied when you turn on BitLocker and is configurable only for operating system drives.

- **Startup key**   This is stored on a USB flash drive and can be used with or without a TPM. To use this method of unlock, the USB flash drive must be inserted every time the computer starts. The USB flash drive can be formatted by using NTFS, FAT, or FAT32.
- **TPM Lockout**   By default, TPM 2.0 will lock the user out for two hours whenever the TPM is under attack (TPM 1.2 lockout duration varied by manufacturer).

Within an enterprise environment, workstations are often required to be patched during non-working hours. One of the automated methods of doing this would be to use System Center Configuration Manager by using a process such as Wake-on-LAN (WoL). However, if BitLocker was configured, the system would wait until a startup key or PIN was entered, and would potentially miss the update.

To overcome this shortcoming, the process of validating and unlocking a drive can be made automatic by enabling a server feature called BitLocker Network Unlock. By verifying the existence of a trusted key that's provided to the workstation by a Windows Deployment Services server on the network, the machine will continue to boot while it is connected to the corporate network.

There are several requirements for this functionality:

- The computer must have UEFI firmware and UEFI DHCP capability.
- Any UEFI Compatibility Support Modules (CSM)/Legacy modes must be disabled.
- The BitLocker Network Unlock feature must be installed on a Windows Deployment Server.
- A separate DHCP server needs to be available to provide an IP address.
- The client computer must be running Windows 8 or newer.
- Certificates for the public/private key pairing must be configured.
- Group Policy settings to configure Network Unlock as a secondary authentication method on the client need to be configured.

MORE INFO **BITLOCKER NETWORK UNLOCK**

The following article provides more information on how BitLocker Network Unlock works and how to configure it: *https://docs.microsoft.com/windows/device-security/bitlocker/bitlocker-how-to-enable-network-unlock*.

Understand BitLocker and BitLocker To Go data recovery

You need to support users who have devices that will not boot into Windows due to BitLocker issues during boot time. There are several situations where BitLocker, BitLocker To Go or Device Encryption will immediately reboot and enter into BitLocker recovery mode due to a perceived threat to the system such as one of the following:

- Repeatedly failing to provide the startup password
- Changing the startup boot order to boot another drive in advance of the hard drive

- Changing the NTFS partition table such as creating, deleting, or resizing a primary partition

- Entering the PIN incorrectly too many times so that the anti-hammering logic of the TPM is activated

- Turning off, disabling, deactivating, or clearing the TPM

- Upgrading critical early startup components, such as a BIOS or UEFI firmware upgrade, causing the related boot measurements to change

- Adding or removing hardware; for example, inserting a new motherboard or video card into the computer

You can also force a BitLocker-protected device into recovery mode by pressing the F8 or F10 key during the boot process.

> **MORE INFO** **BITLOCKER RECOVERY GUIDE**
>
> The following article provides a useful list of examples of specific events that will cause BitLocker to enter recovery mode when attempting to start the operating system drive at: *https://docs.microsoft.com/windows/device-security/bitlocker/bitlocker-recovery-guide-plan*.

When the device has entered the BitLocker recovery mode, you need to recover the drive by using one of these methods:

- Supply the 48-digit recovery password.

- Use a DRA to unlock the drive.

- Allow a domain administrator to obtain the recovery password from AD DS.

- Run a script to reset the password, using PowerShell or VBScript, which can extract the key package from AD DS.

For home and small-business users, the BitLocker recovery key is stored in their Microsoft account at *https://onedrive.live.com/recoverykey*. You will need to use the keyboard number or function keys to enter the number to unlock the drive. Once the operating system has started, users can then recreate a new startup key, otherwise the BitLocker recovery mode will remain in place.

For corporate users, there are several settings that can be configured in Group Policy that will define the recovery methods that require Windows to save BitLocker recovery information to AD DS. These GPOs found in the subfolders of Computer Configuration\Administrative Templates\Windows Components\BitLocker Drive Encryption are as follows:

- Choose how BitLocker-protected operating system drives can be recovered

- Choose how BitLocker-protected fixed drives can be recovered

- Choose how BitLocker-protected removable drives can be recovered

For each of these GPOs, you can also enable the Do Not Enable BitLocker Until Recovery Information Is Stored In AD DS check box to keep users from enabling BitLocker unless the device is connected to the domain and the backup of BitLocker recovery information to AD DS has succeeded.

Once BitLocker recovery information has been saved in AD DS, this can be used to restore access to a BitLocker-protected drive by using the Manage-bde command-line tool introduced earlier.

You may be familiar with the Remote Server Administration Tools (RSAT) that you can install onto your client PC to remotely manage your servers. If you are a domain administrator, or have been delegated permissions by a domain administrator, you can use the BitLocker Recovery Password Viewer that is included in the RSAT. This tool allows you to locate and view BitLocker Drive Encryption recovery passwords which are stored in AD DS. Once the tool has connected to AD DS, you can view the computer object's properties to view the BitLocker recovery password and then use it to recover the PC.

> **NOTE BITLOCKER FAQ**
>
> You need to take some time to review BitLocker. It is an important feature that protects against data loss. Read the BitLocker FAQ at: *https://docs.microsoft.com/en-gb/windows/device-security/bitlocker/bitlocker-frequently-asked-questions*.

Understand Microsoft BitLocker Administration and Monitoring

You have seen how in small and medium-sized organizations, Windows 10 Pro, Windows 10 Enterprise and Windows 10 Education editions can be managed by using Group Policy to force the centralization of BitLocker recovery keys in AD DS. In a large enterprise environment where there may be tens of thousands of devices that are required to be managed, Microsoft provides a tool called Microsoft BitLocker Administration and Monitoring 2.5 SP1 (MBAM), which performs the following management tasks:

- Deployment and recovery of encryption keys
- Centralized compliance monitoring and reporting of individual computers or even of the enterprise itself
- Automates the provisioning of encrypting volumes on client computers across the enterprise
- Reduces the workload on the Help Desk to assist end users with BitLocker PIN and recovery key requests
- Support for encrypted drives, including a self-service portal for users to recover encrypted devices independently
- Audit access to recover key information
- Enforcement of organizational BitLocker policies

MBAM is available as part of the Microsoft Desktop Optimization Pack (MDOP), which is included as a benefit to Microsoft Software Assurance customers as part of Microsoft Volume Licensing. MBAM offers helpdesk operators and administrators a GUI to manage BitLocker for domain joined devices and offers many features including reporting on the encryption status of computers within the whole enterprise, and easy access to recovery key information when users are locked out of their devices.

MBAM is composed of the following components:

- **Administration and Monitoring Server**   Hosts the management console and monitors web services; enables the audit of activities, compliance, and status; enables the management of hardware capability and access to the BitLocker recovery keys.
- **Compliance and Audit Database**   Holds compliance information for MBAM clients, which can be parsed for reporting functions.
- **Recovery and Hardware Database**   MBAM clients provide recovery and hardware information that is obtained from the centralized database.
- **Compliance and Audit Reports**   Enables the generation of different reports to monitor BitLocker usage and compliance activities, and MBAM reports that can be viewed from the Management console or from SQL Server Services (SSRS).
- **Group Policy Template**   Enables administrators to deploy MBAM GPO settings for configuring BitLocker drive encryption.
- **MBAM Client Agent**   This uses Group Policy to enforce encryption settings; collects recovery keys, recovery, and hardware information from MBAM clients, and passes compliance data to the reporting system. The MBAM client software can be installed on Windows 7 (Enterprise/Ultimate Editions), Windows 8 (Professional/Enterprise Editions), and Windows 10 (Pro/Enterprise Editions). Clients must have a TPM v 1.2 or higher chip, which must be enabled in the BIOS.

MBAM 2.5 SP1 is the current version and offers administrators the following features:

- Support is available for managing Windows 7, Windows 8, Windows 10, Windows To Go, and removable storage devices.
- Integration with Microsoft System Center Configuration Manager.
- Support for Microsoft SQL Server 2014.
- BitLocker pre-provisioning with Windows PE includes the use of Used Disk Space Only (Manage-bde on <drive letter>).
- Ability to enforce encryption policies on operating system and fixed data drives.
- Ability to provide a URL in the BitLocker Drive Encryption Wizard to point to your security policy.
- Support for Federal Information Processing Standard (FIPS)-compliant recovery keys on devices with Windows 8.1 and Windows 10 operating systems.
- Support for high-availability deployments.

- Additional Windows PowerShell cmdlets for configuring MBAM server features.
- MBAM can take ownership of the TPM and initialize it without requiring a restart.
- Devices left in Protection Suspended mode automatically resume protection after restart.
- Windows 10 operating system drives can be protected with the Password Protector.
- You can deploy MBAM with less infrastructure, but with the ability to scale 200,000 managed devices with just two servers.

MBAM 2.5 SP1 offers the following improvements for image deployment over previous versions, as listed in Table 5-5.

TABLE 5-5 New functionality to enable BitLocker during imaging

Image Deployment	New functionality
Process	Completely written in PowerShell, compatible with PowerShell v2 Easy to use with MDT, SCCM, or standalone
Volume Support	Supports OS volumes with TPM Protector Fixed data drive support Support for pre-provisioned drives Immediate prompt for PIN after imaging
Reporting	Immediate compliance reporting TPM OwnerAuth parameter escrowed TPM OwnerAuth available outside of WinPE
Error Handling	Robust error handling Improved logging

An example of a suggested stand-alone topology infrastructure utilizing MBAM without SCCM is shown in Figure 5-17.

FIGURE 5-17 Stand-alone topology infrastructure utilizing MBAM

MORE INFO DEPLOYING MBAM 2.5

This article offers some good foundational learning on deploying MBAM 2.5 at: *https://docs. microsoft.com/microsoft-desktop-optimization-pack/mbam-v25/deploying-mbam-25*.

Thought experiments

In these thought experiments, demonstrate your skills and knowledge of the topics covered in this chapter. You can find the answers to these thought experiments in the next section.

Scenario 1

You want to re-use some hard drives that you have and create a Storage Space with them. You have four disks, each disk is 500 GB in capacity, but two of them have 200 GB of data that you want to keep. You want to configure them to offer fault tolerance so that if any one disk fails, you do not lose any data. You do not need to use all of the available disks as part of the Storage Spaces solution. Answer the following questions about how you should set up Storage Spaces.

1. Which types of resiliency could you choose: simple, mirrored, three-way mirror, or parity?
2. How many of the four disks would you use?
3. How will you ensure that the data on the two drives will not be lost?

Scenario 2

You are the new IT Manager for your organization and you cannot find any documentation relating to the current file structure or Share & NTFS permissions on the File Server. A manager has also asked you to create a new shared folder, which needs to be shared to only him and his secretary.

Answer the following questions regarding how you would set this up.

1. Discuss how you will undertake the documentation deficit.
2. What types of issues could result that relate to the current level of NTFS security?
3. After provisioning the new share, how can you test the access before advising the manager that the new share is ready for deployment?

Thought experiment answers

This section provides the solutions for the tasks included in the thought experiment.

Scenario 1

1. You could create a Storage Pool and choose to use either a two-way mirror or a parity Storage Pool with the four drives.

2. Answers may vary but you can add additional drives to increase the size of a Storage Pool, therefore you can utilize all four drives.

3. You should label the disks carefully to ensure you do not accidentally use the incorrect disk because all drives that are added to the Storage Pool will be formatted, and the data will be deleted. You should use the two blank disks to create a new Storage Pool and provision a new Storage Disk, which is a two-way mirror with the two blank disk drives, and then back up the 200 GB data onto this new Storage Pool. You can add the remaining drives to the Storage Pool once the data transfer has completed.

Scenario 2

1. You should undertake a thorough audit of the users, groups, and shares available and document the file structure in place. During the audit you will get to know the system and better understand the logical structure that has been deployed. Make a note of any anomalies that you come across and review these with management.

2. You need to immediately inform senior management that there is no documentation in place and explain that this is a security concern and could result in data leakage and unauthorized data access.

3. You need to test the robustness of the new share to ensure that NTFS and Share permissions produce the desired outcome. This can be achieved by auditing the users and groups using the NTFS Effective Access feature so that you are able to view and evaluate effective permissions on selected resources without the physical requirement to sign on as each user.

Chapter summary

- DFS is a powerful server feature that distributes shared folders within a domain environment to ensure that users are able to access and save files on shared resources that are efficiently replicated to chosen geographic locations while conserving bandwidth and providing reliable data availability.

- Storage Spaces lets you use unused storage disk drives, including SATA, SAS, and USB drives, and combine the drive capacity to create a virtual disk for storing data. It's used on Windows 10 clients and servers, and enables users to benefit from an "easy to expand storage" facility and optional data redundancy with fault tolerance without the typical high cost of ownership that a traditional SAN facility would incur.

■ Storage Spaces can be forcibly optimized using the Optimize-StoragePool PowerShell cmdlet, which is useful following disks being added or removed.

■ By using a Microsoft account, users can access their private "always available" cloud storage facility called OneDrive in which they can store files, folders, pictures, and other content. OneDrive is integrated and synchronized with Windows 10. Users' control which files and folders are made available locally and can also share them externally. Users can take advantage of 5 GB free storage and easy-to-use file recovery and online help.

■ NTFS Permissions work at the file and folder level, offering robust file security and enable files and folders to be either compressed or encrypted.

■ The Effective Access tool enables you to view and evaluate permissions given to users and groups on a specific resource stored on a NTFS-formatted volume.

■ Share permissions only apply for file access to shares over the network. The three Share permissions are: Read, Change, and Full Control.

■ DAC provides administrators the ability to apply permissions and restrictions based conditionally on rules and policies, such as whether the user is accessing the network via a VPN, or using a laptop.

■ Encryption File System (EFS) is a very strong method of protecting data from unauthorized access should a device or data drive be compromised. Prior to using EFS in a domain environment, it is recommended that a DRA is created. CertMgr and Cipher.exe are two tools you can use to back up and recover your EFS-encrypted files.

■ BitLocker Drive Encryption enables full disk volume encryption and uses a TPM to store the startup key. BitLocker will enter a recovery mode if the drive or TPM have been compromised, forcing the user to enter a 48-digit recovery key.

■ Group Policy enables you to configure settings for controlling how removable storage is to be used within an organization, such as enforcing BitLocker To Go on all removable data drives.

■ The BitLocker Recovery Password Viewer included in the Remote Server Administration Tools (RSAT) allows you to search for and find BitLocker recovery keys for devices.

■ MBAM is an enterprise tool, available with the Microsoft Desktop Optimization Pack for Software Assurance customers, which provides useful key management, deployment, and recovery features for administrators and users using BitLocker Drive Encryption.

CHAPTER 6

Manage data access and protection

Networking revolutionized computing for organizations. Most modern devices no longer have DVDs, CDs, or floppy disk storage capabilities for data storage and retrieval. Nearly all of the resources needed at work or at home are shared via the Internet to the cloud or across a business network to file servers.

Like previous versions of Windows, Windows 10 offers the capability to share files and folders, and also access files that have been shared across the network. At home, you don't require a server to share files, though in a corporate environment, sharing of files internally is normally provided and managed by Windows Server 2016 with the File Services role installed.

If you work in IT, you are often put in a position of significant trust by your employer. Your role might require you to provision shares and make files available to other users. This can be achieved by using share permissions and NTFS permissions. As an administrator, you are often entrusted with safeguarding the business data and preventing unauthorized access or data leakage. To perform your role effectively, you need to fully understand your options and learn the skills necessary to implement mechanisms to make files and folders accessible.

Skills in this chapter:

- Skill 6.1: Configure shared resources
- Skill 6.2: Configure file and folder access

Skill 6.1: Configure shared resources

Windows 10 offers several methods of sharing, or giving access to others, including public folder sharing, HomeGroup sharing, and the traditional Any folder sharing. Each method of sharing will appeal to the specific audience, for example home users and small networks typically use HomeGroup or Public sharing, whereas in a Windows domain environment found in larger organizations, traditional folder sharing is more appropriate.

Sharing is not restricted to files and folders. This skill includes a review of file libraries and OneDrive, which enables your resources to be accessed over the Internet, and optionally synchronized between devices.

Configure HomeGroup settings

A HomeGroup enables home users to easily share content such as documents, printers, and video with others on their home local network. A home network will normally be configured as a single read-only function, enabling individual users to share content that they want other members of the household to access.

To keep HomeGroups relatively simple to set up, they are limited in what they can offer, especially when compared to the permissions and restrictions that can be configured using Any folder sharing. Despite their simplicity, HomeGroups are password protected and are aimed at enabling sharing within a family home across multiple devices.

If the read-only limitation is too restrictive, this can be modified and family members can be granted write access.

EXAM TIP

THERE CAN BE ONLY ONE HOMEGROUP PER NETWORK AND IPV6 IS REQUIRED, SO CHECK TO ENSURE THAT THIS HAS NOT BEEN DISABLED.

To create a HomeGroup, perform the following steps:

1. Sign on to your device with administrative privileges.
2. Click the Start button on your non-domain joined computer.
3. Type **HomeGroup** in the search box.
4. In the search results, click HomeGroup (Control Panel).
5. If a warning message appears indicating that you need to change the network location to Private, you should click the Change Network Location link, and then in the Networks charm, click Yes.
6. Click Create A HomeGroup.
7. In the Create A HomeGroup Wizard, click Next.
8. On the Share With Other HomeGroup Members page, as shown in Figure 6-1, click the libraries, folders, and devices that you want to share with the HomeGroup, and click Next. The wizard creates the HomeGroup, and creates a random password.
9. Make a note of the password provided, and then click Finish.

FIGURE 6-1 Using the Create A HomeGroup Wizard to create a HomeGroup, and share files and devices

NOTE HOMEGROUPS AND DOMAINS

If your computer belongs to a domain, you are not able to create your own HomeGroup, but you can join to one that someone has already created.

To join a HomeGroup that has already been created, you can follow these steps:

1. Sign on to your device with administrative privileges.

2. Click the Start button on your non-domain joined computer.

3. Type **HomeGroup** in the search box.

4. Click Join Now, then follow the HomeGroup Wizard, and then enter the HomeGroup password.

If you encounter any issues relating to the HomeGroup, you can start the HomeGroup troubleshooter, which will try to find and fix problems relating to viewing computers or shared files in a HomeGroup.

If you're not familiar with HomeGroups, you need to create a HomeGroup in your lab environment, so that you can see how simple it is and how other computers can join it. You need to also explore the HomeGroup options offered in the Network And Sharing Center. As you will see, the HomeGroup is displayed as Joined within the Network And Sharing Center. To amend what is being shared, view the password, start the HomeGroup troubleshooter, or leave a HomeGroup, you can open HomeGroup in Control Panel or type **HomeGroup** in the search box and press Enter. Links to each of these actions can be found on the Change HomeGroup Settings page.

If you want to share files or folders that are not included in the libraries, you can share folders with the HomeGroup directly from File Explorer.

One method is to select the folder that you want to share, right-click, and select Give Access To, and choose the appropriate share option to View or View And Edit the HomeGroup, as shown in Figure 6-2. Notice that with the File Explorer Share menu displayed, the Give Access To options are visible.

FIGURE 6-2 Sharing folders with the HomeGroup, using the context menu in File Explorer

Although HomeGroups are mostly used to share resources with all members of a Home-Group, you can fine-tune this and select the Specific People option, which enables you to make available the shared resources to certain people only, as shown in Figure 6-2, with either Read or Read and Write permissions.

Configure libraries

Libraries are visible in File Explorer in Windows 10 (they were removed in Windows 8.1 File Explorer), and by default, you are provided with four default libraries: Documents, Music, Pictures, and Videos. You may also see Camera Roll and Saved Picture libraries if you have connected a camera or phone to your device.

Libraries represent a "collection" of files and folders, and are a special type of folder. Libraries enable users to aggregate files that are stored in multiple locations (and even on multiple computers), and pull them together to make them appear as though they are all stored in a library. They are designed to help you organize your files, which are scattered across your PC or network. Even though libraries show files and folders from multiple locations, the actual files are not moved or copied to the library, only a link (like a shortcut) is placed in the library.

In addition to the default libraries, you are able to add your own. Right-click Library in the left pane of File Explorer, and click New Library. Give your library a name and then open the library. To include folders, click folders in the right pane and then select the folders that you want.

To add additional locations in your library, follow these steps:

1. Open File Explorer.

2. If you don't see libraries, click the View tab on the File Explorer ribbon, the click the Navigation Pane button and tick Show Libraries.

3. Click the Libraries icon on in the Navigation Pane.

4. Select the Documents library.

5. At the top of File Explorer, click Library Tools, and click Manage Library to open the Documents Library Locations dialog box.

6. Click Add to add another location to the library.

7. Navigate to the location of the files and folders you want to include and then click Include Folder.

8. If you want to change which folder is the default location for saving files, highlight the folder, and right-click Set As Default Save Location, as shown in Figure 6-3.

9. Click OK.

FIGURE 6-3 Modifying the library Default Save Location in File Explorer

Windows 10 has a new File Explorer feature called Quick Access. On first glance, it might appear that Favorites has been replaced by Quick Access, but it actually combines the scope and functionality of the Favorites feature and Libraries, enabling you to pin folders and libraries to the Quick Access area.

Quick Access is the default view that appears whenever you open File Explorer whether directly or through another application, perhaps to open or save a file. In practice, this can offer significant productivity enhancements, if users are often opening and saving files regularly. If Quick Access is not required, File Explorer can be configured to open directly to This PC view instead of selecting the option within Folder Options, as shown in Figure 6-4.

FIGURE 6-4 Modifying the default File Explorer view

Look closely at the Quick Access area in the left pane in File Explorer, as shown in Figure 6-4. You will notice that the Desktop and Pictures folders are pinned to the Quick Access area. The Work Folders (Local) folder does not have a small push pin next to the folder icon, and therefore it is shown in the Quick Access area because it has been recently accessed. To pin a new folder to the Quick Access area, you need to navigate to the folder anywhere in File Explorer, and then right-click the folder. In the context menu, select Pin To Quick Access. To remove a pinned folder from the Quick Access area, right-click the folder, and select Unpin From Quick Access.

At the bottom of the Folder Options dialog box, shown in Figure 6-4, are some new privacy settings, which enable users to remove the option to show recently used files and folders in Quick Access, and also an option to clear File Explorer History.

Configure shared folder permissions

When data is stored on a network server, you need to have access to the data over the network. You'll see that NTFS permissions will protect the actual files and folders from unauthorized access, but it is Share permissions that are responsible for making data resources available to users over a corporate network.

Shares are managed by Server Message Block (SMB), and Share permissions and NTFS permissions are totally independent of each other. However, the effective access permissions on a shared folder are determined by taking into consideration both the Share permissions and the NTFS permissions. When you create a shared folder, there will be SMB Share permissions in place, which can be more restrictive than any existing NTFS permissions. For example a user accessing files through a share with read permission configured, which is providing network access to files protected by NTFS Full Control permission will be given only Read permission on the files.

> **NOTE SMB SHARE PERMISSIONS**
> SMB Share permissions are ignored if the user accesses the resource locally or via Remote Desktop.

Windows 10 supports SMB version 3.1.1 (Windows 8.1 supports SMB version 3.02). To establish the SMB version (dialect), which you are using, type the following two PowerShell cmdlets into an elevated PowerShell window:

```
PS C:\> dir \\localhost\c$
```

```
PS C:\> Get-SmbConnection -ServerName localhost
```

Windows will automatically negotiate between the connecting parties to ensure that the same (and latest) SMB version is used.

Sharing is not enabled by default, which minimizes the risk of a network attack, and each Windows machine must explicitly enable the ability to permit sharing, which can be controlled within the Network And Sharing Center by following these steps:

1. Open Control Panel, select Network And Internet.

2. Choose Network And Sharing Center.

3. On the left, choose Change Advanced Sharing Settings.

4. Windows will expand the network profiles in use (Private, Guest, or Public). For the network profiles that you want to enable file and printer sharing, select Turn On File And Printer Sharing.

5. Click Save Changes.

These settings are configurable by using Group Policy, as are the Network Discovery settings, which use the new Link Layer Topology Discovery (LLTD) protocol, enabling Windows to identify with other devices within the local subnet. Enabling network discovery on your devices modifies the Windows Firewall security settings so that your computer will become "discoverable" on the network by other Windows clients, and your computer can also see other computers and devices on the network.

The Network Discovery status is disabled by default, but an organization can manage the status of the LLTD Mapper (LLTDIO) and Responder (RSPNDR) via two Group Policy settings, which are located at: Computer Configuration\Policies\Administrative Templates\Network\Link Layer Topology Discovery.

Sharing by using Public Folders

As you might presume, Public folder sharing involves the sharing of Public Folders, which are found in the %systemdrive%\Users\Public folder within File Explorer. There are several default Public Folders, including Public Documents, Public Music, Public Pictures, and Public Videos. Installed applications may also add new folders in this location, and you can also create your own. To use this method of sharing, you need to move any data to be shared to the appropriate Public folder. You could also copy the data, but this would then create potential issues with storing multiple documents as well as subsequent versioning issues.

Public Folders offer users an easy method of sharing data with anyone who has access to the device. By default, all local users have access to Public Folders, and users can configure network access to Public Folders within the Network And Sharing Center. Within a small business, this "open box" functionality can be a useful method of sharing files without the complexity of other methods of sharing. The disadvantage of using Public Folders is the limited ability to implement access control at a fine-grained level.

To turn on Public folder sharing over the network, open the Network And Sharing Center, click the Change Advanced Sharing Settings link and, in the All Networks profile, configure the Turn Public Folder Sharing on or off.

The default permissions for Public Folders enable local users to read, write, change, and delete any public files.

Configuring Any folder sharing

When you are using Any folder sharing, you can share files and folders using one of the following tools:

- Sharing Folders using File Explorer
- Sharing Folders using Computer Management Microsoft Management Console (MMC) snap-in
- Sharing Folders from the command line, using the Net Share and PowerShell commands

Windows 10 permits a maximum of 20 concurrent users to access a shared resource when shared within a workgroup environment. In comparison, a Windows Server 2016 File Server has no limitation.

When sharing folders, using File Explorer, you are presented with two choices:

- **Share** Basic sharing, which is accomplished by using a wizard to share the folder
- **Advanced Sharing** Traditional fine-grained folder sharing, which enables you to:
  - Create the share name, which can be different from the actual folder name
  - Enable the fine-grained setting of Share permissions
  - Set the caching of the folder if you want to use Offline Files

The list of permissions set on each object is called an Access Control List (ACL). The default permissions settings for a newly created share will create an Access Control Entry (ACE) giving Everyone: Allow Read.

You can (and need to) edit the default Share permissions by adding users and groups to whom you want to give access, and by removing the built-in Everyone group. When the NTFS permissions (covered later) and Share permissions are evaluated together, the most restrictive of the permissions on either side is effective. Where a user is a member of several groups and has different permissions based on his membership, his overall Share permissions are cumulative.

To stop sharing a folder, you need to right-click the shared folder, click the Give Access To option, and then click Remove Access.

You gain more functionality when creating shares using the Computer Management MMC snap-in, but you also need to have administrative privileges to create them. The Computer Management MMC snap-in also enables administrators to create shared folders on remote computers.

To create a shared folder using Computer Management MMC, you should carry out the following steps:

1. Right click the Start button and select Computer Management (you can also type **compmgmt.msc** in the Search bar).
2. Expand System Tools\Shared Folders and select Shares.
3. To create a new share, right-click the Shares icon and select New Share.

4. The Create A Shared Folder Wizard will launch, click Next.

5. Enter the Folder path or click Browse to find the folder you want to share.

6. Click Next.

7. Provide a share name and a description (optional).

8. You can modify the Offline settings, if required.

9. Click Next to display the Shared Folder Permissions options.

10. Choose the permissions that you require, and click Finish twice.

> **_NOTE_ RENAMED FOLDERS ARE NO LONGER SHARED**
>
> If you rename a folder that is shared, the folder will stop being shared once it is renamed.

Sharing folders from the command line

If you have more than a few shares to create, it is more efficient using either PowerShell or the command prompt to create them. Net Share is a command-line tool, which has been used for many years and is very popular within logon scripts to establish mapped drives at logon.

The syntax is Net Share name=*drive:path*, which will create a simple share using the share name that you specify, and will grant all users the Read permission.

Additional parameters when creating a share include the following:

- **/Grant:user permission**   Enables you to specify Read, Change, or Full Share permissions for the specified user.

- **/Users:number**   Enables you to limit the number of users who can connect to the share.

- **/Remark:"text"**   Enables you to add a description to the share.

- **/Cache:option**   Enables you to specify the offline caching options.

- **sharename /Delete**   Deletes an existing share.

For more information, type **net share /?** at the command prompt for the syntax and available switches. To view all shared folders on a device, you can run the **net share** command.

Sharing folders by using Windows PowerShell

A topic that is more likely to appear on the exam is the role of PowerShell, which can be used in scripts and offers additional capabilities for configuring and managing SMB shares locally and remotely.

An example SmbShare PowerShell command to create a new SMB share called Review, which shares the C:\Work Files (Local)\New York Launch - Highlights folder, can be created by typing:

```
New-SmbShare -Name Review -Path "C:\Work Files (Local)\New York Launch - Highlights"
```

To view all shared folders on a device, you can run the Get-SmbShare cmdlet. The cmdlets available within the SmbShare module are:

- Block-SmbShareAccess
- Get-SmbShare
- Get-SmbShareAccess
- Grant-SmbShareAccess
- New-SmbShare
- Remove-SmbShare
- Revoke-SmbShareAccess
- Set-SmbShare
- Unblock-SmbShareAccess

For more information, you can type **Get-Help SmbShare** in a PowerShell prompt.

The Universal Naming Convention (UNC) address is sometimes used to access a shared folder over the network. UNC addresses contain the name of the host computer, preceded by two backward slashes (\\), and the shared folder name, separated by a backward slash (\). For example, the UNC name for the shared Review folder, shared on the computer named Server, would be: \\Server\Review.

Access-based enumeration

Dynamic Access Control (DAC), which was covered in Chapter 5,"Configure storage," offers administrators a robust method of controlling data access by using filters and claims. Nestled in between NTFS and DAC is access-based enumeration (ABE), a little known feature, which can be enabled as a feature within the File Server role on Windows Server 2008 or newer server operating systems.

ABE forces Windows to evaluate each and every shared object to ensure that resources are effectively hidden from users (for example, when viewing shared resources using File Explorer) unless they have at least the Read permission on the resource. When you provision a new shared folder from a file server, you will have the option to enable ABE on the share, as shown in Figure 6-5.

FIGURE 6-5 Configuring ABE on a Windows Server 2016 shared folder

> **NOTE ABE WORKS FOR SHARED RESOURCES ONLY**
>
> ABE is effective only when users access resources via shared folders over the network, and is not effective if a user accesses resources locally or via Remote Desktop.

Although ABE is a server technology, you are able to configure advanced share properties such as ABE in Windows 10 by using Windows PowerShell. To enable ABE for a share named Work in Progress, you would use the cmdlet:

```
Set-SmbShare -Name "Work in Progress" -FolderEnumerationMode AccessBased
```

And then type Y to confirm.

> **NOTE FILE EXPLORER SHARING INDICATOR**
>
> In the current version of Windows 10 there is no indicator icon shown within File Explorer that a folder is being shared.

Configure shared printers

Users who have experience of installing, sharing, and troubleshooting printing on Windows 7 or newer versions of Windows is familiar with the printing capabilities in Windows 10. This section includes a review of the key areas and also highlights the few additional features offered in Windows 10, which include Near Field Communication (NFC) support and Type 4 printer drivers.

It is useful to define the key terms used when dealing with printers:

- **Printer and printing device** This refers to a physical device, which is connected to the PC locally or via the network (can include wired, wireless, or Bluetooth), or available on a print server. On a single print device, you can configure multiple instances of the same printer within Windows. This is useful if you want to configure a printer to have different settings, such as user security; feature restrictions, such as color or monochrome printing, and available times or print priority for different users or groups.

- **Printer port** This is typically used for older ports, which allow printers to be connected directly to the device, such as serial, parallel ports, and network printers. Unlike printers connected via a modern connection, such as USB, these types of printers will not be detected automatically by Windows 10 and will require manual configuration.

- **Printer driver** Each printer must have a printer driver, which is used to enable Windows 10 to communicate with the device and render print jobs. Printer drivers are responsible for converting the print job into page description language (PDL), a format that is understood by the printer. The most common types of PDL are PostScript, Printer Control Language, and XML Paper Specification (XPS). Printer drivers are included with Windows 10, or they can be supplied by the printer manufacturer, or are available through Windows Update.

> **NOTE USING PNPUTIL.EXE**
>
> The command-line tool Pnputil.exe will enable administrators to manually install printer drivers directly in the driver store, which enables them to appear in the Add Printer Wizard.

Type 4 print drivers

Traditionally, each printer manufacturer produces customized print drivers for each of their devices, which enables Windows to use the printer features. These print drivers must be shared with all clients on the network that use the printer. These are known as Type 3 print drivers and require administrative effort to ensure that both 32-bit and 64-bit drivers are up to date and available when required.

In Windows Server 2012 and Windows 8, Microsoft introduced a new type of print driver, which enabled the printer manufacturer to write a single Print Class Driver that offers support for common printing features and languages, such as PostScript, PCL, XML, and XPS, across many printer models. These print drivers are known as Type 4 (or V4) print drivers and are typically obtained through Windows Update or Windows Software Update Services (WSUS), and are not distributed across the network or maintained by the print server.

The Type 4 printer driver model provides the following benefits:

- No need for architecture-specific printer drivers
- Type 4 drivers can support multiple printer models
- Driver files are isolated on a per-driver basis, thereby reducing conflicts
- Driver packages can be smaller and can install faster
- Enables separation of the printer driver and the printer software

> **MORE INFO** **PRINT AND DOCUMENT SERVICES ARCHITECTURE**
>
> You can find more information regarding Type4 print drivers at: *https://docs.microsoft.com/windows-hardware/drivers/print/v4-printer-driver*.

Print management

Within an organization, most printing is centralized by using print servers to provide access to network printing devices. Windows 10 offers several tools to manage printing, including Devices And Printers, Print Management, and Windows PowerShell cmdlets. Table 6-1 describes various print management tasks that you can carry out with these tools.

TABLE 6-1 Print management tasks

Task	Description
Change printer properties, modify security, advanced properties	You can configure printer properties, including printer common name, location, ports used, printer availability, which users can use the printer, and how print jobs are rendered, as shown in Figure 6-6.
Configure sharing	You can share a printer, appoint a friendly name, and make available additional drivers.
Select the default printer	In Windows 10, only one printer can be set as the default printer, and it will be marked with a green check mark in Devices And Printers.
View and manage the print queue	For any print job, you can view, pause, or cancel it through the print queue, which can be opened from Devices And Printers by right-clicking a printer and selecting the See What's Printing option, or by double-clicking the printer icon. The print queue shows what is printing or is waiting to print, information such as job status, who is printing, and how many unprinted pages remain. You can also use the Window PowerShell Get-PrintJob cmdlet: Get-PrintJob -PrinterName Printer.
Pause or resume printer	If a printer is paused, all pending and new print jobs will be accepted, but they will wait in print queue. If the printer is resumed, paused print jobs will be sent to the printing device and printing will continue.

Pause, resume, restart, or cancel print jobs	All print jobs can be paused or resumed by right-clicking the print job in the print queue window, and then clicking Pause or Resume. To pause all print jobs, you need to pause the printer. Restarting a print job will enable the print job to be re-sent to the print device. To cancel a print job, right-click the print job you want to remove, and then click Cancel. To cancel all current print jobs, click the Printer menu, and then click Cancel All Jobs.
Reorder print jobs in a print queue	Where there are multiple print jobs, you can force a print job in the queue to be printed before others by increasing the priority number of the print job. Print jobs with higher priority print first.
Restarting the Print Spooler Service	This is used when troubleshooting printing. It's very effective if other methods don't work. Data loss can occur because the current print job might be lost.

Review the Security tab on the printer Properties dialog box, shown in Figure 6-6. You will notice that printers behave just like other system objects, and you can choose the groups or users that are allowed or denied access to the printer.

FIGURE 6-6 Advanced printer properties

There are three permissions that can be configured for printers:

- **Print**   Connect to a printer; print; control the user's own print jobs.
- **Manage this printer**   Cancel documents; share and delete printers; change printer properties; change printer permissions.
- **Manage documents**   Pause, resume, restart, and cancel all documents; control job settings for all documents.

By default, the Everyone group can print to any printer, administrators can manage all printers and documents, and the Creator Owner special identity is the permission that allows users to manage their own print jobs.

Managing print server properties

Windows 10 clients can share printers that they are connected to and can also act as a print server. The Print Management MMC console, as shown in Figure 6-7, is included in the Administrative Tools of Windows 10 Pro and Enterprise editions, and enables you to connect to other print servers and manage them remotely. You can also launch the Print Management console by typing **Printmanagement.msc** in the Run or Search box on the taskbar.

The Print Management console enables the following printer-related management tasks:

- View printers and print servers
- Add and remove print servers
- Add and delete printers
- Add and manage drivers
- Deploy printers using Group Policy
- Open and manage printer queues
- Initiate printer test pages
- View and modify status of printers
- Create custom filters to view printers based on filters

FIGURE 6-7 Print Management console

Although Windows 10 displays the option to deploy printers with a Group Policy object (GPO), this functionality will only work if you are connected to a domain environment. If connected to AD DS, the Deploy With Group Policy Wizard enables you to set the GPO name and control to which users or computers the printers can be deployed. This feature is outdated and most printers that are deployed within a domain environment will use Group Policy preferences, rather than the Print Management console.

Understanding NFC

Windows 10 has built-in support for near field communication (NFC), which is still an emerging technology based on short-range wireless radio technologies using radio frequency identification (RFID). NFC-enabled printing enables users to "tap" a device (such as a tablet or phone) onto a printer to connect to it. Where the components cannot be tapped together, NFC should still work if the devices are brought close together, within a maximum distance of 4 inches (10 centimeters).

NFC is similar to Bluetooth, but without the requirement to manually pair each component. NFC communication is triggered due to mutual physical proximity. NFC uses short-range radio waves for discovery and for transmitting data, and requires some form of NFC-enabled hardware, such as a smart tag, sticker, key fob, or wallet card, which may also be located inside a laptop or tablet. Many new mobile phones have NFC capabilities built into the devices, which enables NFC sharing of photos between NFC-connected devices.

Once an enterprise has made available NFC-enabled devices, administrators can perform the following management tasks:

- Add a NFC smart tag to their printer, or purchase printers with NFC built in.
- Enable the following connection types to be used: Universal Naming Convention (UNC), Web Services on Devices (WSD), and Wi-Fi Direct.
- Optionally, use the PowerShell cmdlet Write-PrinterNfcTag to provision an NFC tag with information about a printer.

Although NFC built-in support is provided by Windows 10, this is available for OEMs and ISVs to produce NFC-enabled hardware.

NFC offers mobile devices significant opportunities to access resources by using proximity alone. Other emerging technologies include Windows 10 support for the Windows Sensor and Location platform, and support for the Windows Biometric Framework (WBF). These frameworks enable developers to utilize support for sensors, which can be attached or embedded within modern Windows devices (phone, tablets, Internet of Things, PCs), and includes capabilities such as:

- Speed, motion, acceleration, gyrometer
- GPS location, elevation, inclinometer, compass orientation
- Humidity, temperature, light, atmospheric pressure
- Biometric human proximity, human presence

Configure OneDrive

OneDrive is a cloud storage service provided by Microsoft that offers users the ability to store their data in the cloud (in their private OneDrive), and to optionally enable a trusted computer to hold and synchronize local copies of files and folders. In order to store data in OneDrive the user needs to use a Microsoft account. To share an item, you would select the file or files, and then click the Share option, as shown in Figure 6-8, and configure the sharing options. Notice that the web page is unavailable (dimmed) during the Share operation.

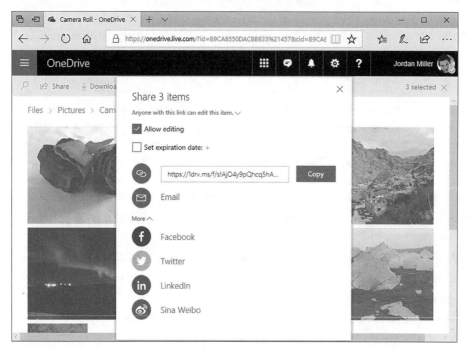

FIGURE 6-8 Sharing a file with others, using the OneDrive web interface

The OneDrive sharing option that allows you to set an expiration date for shares, is part of Premium OneDrive. This is a monthly subscription offer, and can be purchased standalone, or included with Office 365.

Items can be shared with someone as read-only or editable. With OneDrive, you can use the *https://onedrive.live.com/* website to access your files from any browser, or work with the files directly via the OneDrive folder in File Explorer, as shown in Figure 6-9.

FIGURE 6-9 Accessing OneDrive files via File Explorer

Microsoft provides all new users with a free 5 GB storage quota, and users can purchase additional storage, as shown in Table 6-2.

TABLE 6-2 Pricing plans for additional storage

OneDrive Plan	Storage Amount	Price*
OneDrive Basic 5 GB	5 GB	Free
OneDrive 50 GB	50 GB	$1.99/month*
Office 365 Personal with Premium OneDrive Features	1 TB	$6.99/month**
Office 365 Home with Premium OneDrive Features	5 TB	$9.99/month**

Prices correct as of April 2018

* From early 2016 OneDrive discontinued the 100 GB and 200 GB paid plans for new users, but they are retained for existing customers.

** Includes Office 365

Because OneDrive is a cloud-based service, the features can be improved or deprecated easily. When supporting OneDrive for users you need to understand some of the limitations of OneDrive and some of the changes implemented since previous versions, including the following:

- **Recycle Bin**   By default, items are stored for a minimum of 3 days and up to a maximum of 30 days. The capacity of the Recycle Bin is set to 10 percent of the total storage limit by default. This may have an impact on the 30-day retention period if the Recycle Bin is full old items will be deleted to make room for new items as they are added. You can access deleted files stored in the OneDrive Recycle Bin from within the OneDrive web portal and also in the File Explorer on a synchronized PC. Take care should you choose to use the Restore All Items or Empty Recycle Bin options as these tasks are irreversible.

- **Folders and Files**   Using the OneDrive web portal both folders and files can be uploaded, copied, moved, or downloaded. Entire folders can be uploaded or downloaded with a limit of 4 GB or 65,000 individual files. Additionally you can upload folders and files to OneDrive by copying or moving them to your OneDrive desktop app, and these will be synchronized and appear in the OneDrive web portal. If you use a browser such as Google Chrome or Microsoft Edge which supports folder dragging/dropping you can drag folders directly into OneDrive.com.

- **Privacy**   Similar to other cloud storage services, files stored within OneDrive are subject to the usage policy that authorizes Microsoft to suspend or block any account that stores content that breaches its code of conduct. Prohibited content includes inappropriate images, such as nudity or pornography, and using the service to engage in activities that are false, misleading, illegal, and exploitative, and that generate spam, among several other actions. Full details of the code of conduct can be found here: *https:// www.microsoft.com/servicesagreement*.

- **Synchronization**   In Windows 10, the synchronization engine employed to sync File Explorer and the OneDrive cloud storage service has been improved from earlier versions and uses the same engine as employed by OneDrive for Business. In Windows 10, users will only see the files and folders that have been explicitly chosen to be kept in sync. Any files that are not marked as requiring synchronization will not be visible within the OneDrive desktop app in File Explorer. Future planned improvements to the OneDrive service will include a new feature called "Files-On-Demand", which will offer the ability to select, download and synchronize files held in OneDrive to the desktop app.

- **File size and quantity**   Microsoft has increased the maximum size for files uploaded to OneDrive from 2 GB to 10 GB when using the website, and still limits the number of items (files and folders) stored in a single OneDrive account to 20,000.

Because OneDrive is fully integrated within Windows 10, you can access your OneDrive files seamlessly via your applications, such as Microsoft Office, if you configure the application to use your Microsoft account as the identity.

OneDrive options

From the OneDrive web portal, users can fine-tune several settings to customize their user experience. Select the Options setting by clicking the cog icon, as shown in Figure 6-10.

FIGURE 6-10 Configuring OneDrive options

Within the Options screen you have a dashboard with the following settings that relate to your OneDrive:

- **Manage Storage**   This enables users to view their current storage plan and buy additional storage by upgrading, redeeming a OneDrive code or earning Referral Bonuses.
- **Plans and upgrades**   This enables users to upgrading their current plan.
- **Office file formats**   This enables users to choose a default format for Office documents, such as Microsoft Office Open XML Format (.docx, .pptx, .xlsx), or OpenDocumentFormat (.odt, .odp, ods).

- **Photos**   This allows just users to let OneDrive to create albums you're your uploaded photos automatically.

- **Tagging**   This allows just users to select to allow OneDrive to automatically tag your photos by theme.

- **Notifications**   This enables OneDrive to send an email when people make changes to files that are being shared from their OneDrive account, or OneDrive recaps their photos.

- **Device backups**   This lets you see and optionally delete your device backups. Devices include PCs, phones, and tablets. The list will show the date of the device backup.

- **Search**   This allows just users to turn off allowing OneDrive to automatically show previous searches as suggested search terms, and delete all cached searches.

Administrators can block the use of OneDrive within Group Policy by navigating to Computer Configuration\Administrative Templates\Windows Components\OneDrive\ and enabling the Prevent The Usage Of OneDrive For File Storage setting. This is will prevent File Explorer and apps from displaying OneDrive files and prevent synchronization of files with the cloud.

Sync settings

Within Windows 10, you can configure the built-in OneDrive client, as shown in Figure 6-11, to maintain the automatic synchronization of your files between Windows 10 and the cloud storage service. Launch the OneDrive client by right-clicking the OneDrive tray icon and selecting Settings. Alternatively, you can launch the OneDrive client by clicking the OneDrive tray icon and then selecting the icon with three vertical dots to the right of the folder icon.

FIGURE 6-11 Configuring the OneDrive client to synchronize your files

During the out-of-box experience (OOBE), you may have given permission to Windows 10 to use your Microsoft account. Windows 10 will use this account to automatically configure the connection to OneDrive. If you change your Microsoft account, or want to access a different OneDrive, you will need to unlink the existing Microsoft account.

From the Account tab, you are able to disable OneDrive synchronization by selecting the Unlink this PC link. Once you have unlinked your account, you need to log out and sign back in to Windows 10. The files that were synchronized to your device will still be present, however, they will no longer be synchronized.

After unlinking your account, the OneDrive client service will still be running, but it will be dimmed in the notification area. You will be presented with the Welcome To OneDrive Get Started window each time you click the notification icon or click the OneDrive icon within File Explorer. Within Windows 10, you are able to link only one Microsoft account to OneDrive; this can be a different Microsoft account from the one used to sign in to the operating system.

Co-existence of OneDrive and OneDrive for Business

If you have an Office 365 work account, you can also add an OneDrive for Business. Windows 10 differentiates them by using a different color for each app.

To add an OneDrive for Business account follow these steps:

1. On the Account tab, click Add an Account.
2. On the Set Up OneDrive page, click Enter Your Business Email Account/
3. Follow the initial configuration wizard and click Next.
4. On the Sync your OneDrive files to this PC select files and folders that you want to synchronize to this device, and click Next.
5. Once the wizard is complete, click Open my OneDrive folder.
6. In the notification area, as shown in Figure 6-12, you can now see two OneDrive icons, one white, and one blue.
7. The blue one is the OneDrive for Business account.
8. In File Explorer you now see two OneDrive folder locations, with the name of the account shown.

FIGURE 6-12 OneDrive and OneDrive for Business client

When a OneDrive account is removed, but unlinking the account in the OneDrive settings, the synchronization is immediately stopped, but the files are not deleted and you should manually remove the local copy of the files if they are no longer required.

Fetch files on your PC by using OneDrive

With OneDrive configured on Windows 10, you can use the Let Me Use OneDrive To Fetch Any Of My Files On This PC feature to access all your files on that PC from another computer over the Internet. You must first enable the setting on the PC, within the OneDrive Settings as shown in Figure 6-11. Then sign in to the OneDrive website and browse to the PCs listed in the left pane. Once connected to a PC, you are also able to access network locations, mapped drives, and local drives on the PC, as shown in Figure 6-13. Files opened using this feature will be opened on the local PC, and not on the remote PC.

Although the feature is heavily dependent on your Internet connection, the option to fetch and open any of your files on your PC is a useful feature of OneDrive, which may be covered in the exam.

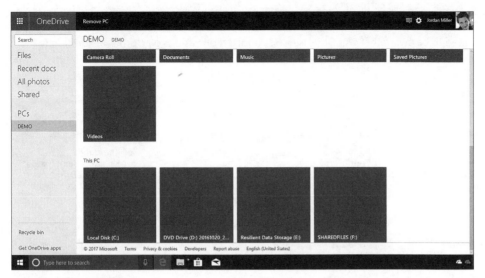

FIGURE 6-13 Using the OneDrive Fetch files feature to remotely access files on your PC over the Internet

NOTE **ONEDRIVE FETCH IS NOT AVAILABLE TO ONEDRIVE FOR BUSINESS**

The OneDrive Fetch files feature is only available to personal customers with a Microsoft account. It is not licensed for business use and the option to enable the Fetch feature does not appear within the OneDrive for business app.

Before you can connect to the PC, the following prerequisites must be in place on the PC that you want to access by using the Fetch files feature. You need to ensure that the PC that you want to access:

- Is turned on
- Is connected to the Internet
- Is running OneDrive Desktop app signed in using the same Microsoft account
- Has the Let Me Use OneDrive To Fetch Any Of My Files On This setting enabled

When you use the Fetch feature to fetch your files, you may be asked to enter a verification code to ensure that you have permission to access the PC.

MORE INFO **FETCH FILES ON YOUR WINDOWS 10 PC**

Only fetching files on a Windows 10 PC is supported. You can use a browser on a non-Windows 10 PC, such as a Mac to fetch files from a computer running Windows 10, but you can't fetch files that are on a Mac. For more information on the Fetch feature, go to: *https://support.office.com/article/Fetch-files-on-your-PC-70761550-519c-4d45-b780-5a613b2f8822*.

Using OneDrive on other devices

You need to be aware that OneDrive is also supported on various platforms, in addition to Microsoft devices, as shown in Table 6-3.

TABLE 6-3 OneDrive-supported device platforms

Desktop	Tablet	Phone	Xbox
Built-in:	**Built-in:**	**Built-in:**	**Built-in:**
Windows 10 Windows 8.1 (32- or 64-bit versions) Windows RT 8.1	Windows 10 Windows 8.1 (32- or 64-bit versions) Windows RT 8.1	Windows Phone 7.5 or later	Xbox One Say "Xbox, Bing" and then "OneDrive", or browse apps to install OneDrive from the Store.
Supported:	**Supported:**	**Supported:**	**Supported:**
Windows 7 Windows Vista Service Pack 2 and the Platform Update for Windows Vista* Download link http://go.microsoft.com/fwlink/p/?LinkId=248256	Windows 7 Windows Vista Service Pack 2 and the Platform Update for Windows Vista* Download link http://go.microsoft.com/fwlink/p/?LinkId=248256		Xbox 360 From Xbox Home, select Apps. Select Browse Apps, and then Social. Select OneDrive and install the app.
Non Windows Support:	**Non Windows Support:**	**Non Windows Support:**	**Non Windows Support:**
OneDrive app for Mac Download link: http://go.microsoft.com/fwlink/?LinkId=248255	OneDrive app for iOS 9.0 or later Download link: http://go.microsoft.com/fwlink/?LinkID=392251	OneDrive mobile app for iOS 9.0 or later Download link: http://go.microsoft.com/fwlink/?LinkID=392251	
	OneDrive app for Android Download link: http://go.microsoft.com/fwlink/?LinkID=392254	OneDrive mobile app for Android Download link: http://go.microsoft.com/fwlink/?LinkID=392254	

* After November 1st 2017, OneDrive will be phasing out support for Windows Vista SP2 (All versions), Windows Server 2008 and Mac OS X 10.9.

Skill 6.2: Configure file and folder access

Administrators who store data on file servers need to ensure that it is accessible, and remains secure. In this skill you will review how to protect data using NTFS file permissions and the encryption options offered by using Encrypting File System.

Administrators can prevent users from over-burdening file servers by implementing Disk Quotas and auditing access to resources to ensure compliance, and can prevent unauthorized access. The File Server Resource Manager (FSRM) role service on Windows Server 2016 allows server administrators to manage and classify data stored on file servers.

User Account Control (UAC) introduced with Windows Vista continues to protect systems by limiting system access for users and protecting against malware attacks. The refinements to UAC will be reviewed here.

You'll need to ensure that your understanding of NTFS permissions, inheritance, effective access, and taking ownership is robust because this knowledge will be assumed on the exam.

> **This section covers how to:**
> - Encrypt files and folders by using EFS
> - Configure NTFS permissions
> - Configure disk quotas
> - Configure file-access auditing
> - Configure authentication and authorization

Encrypt files and folders by using Encrypting File System

Encrypting File System (EFS) used with a Data Recovery Agent (DRA) is a very secure method to protect sensitive data by encrypting files and folders. Because EFS was first introduced in Windows 2000, EFS often suffers from being dismissed as being old or obsolete, and passed over in favor of BitLocker Drive Encryption or BitLocker To Go. Don't be fooled, though, EFS offers functionality that BitLocker does not, and despite EFS having been available for many years, it still offers an incredibly secure method of enterprise-grade encryption.

It is important to use EFS and a DRA together. Without a DRA available within your organization, you may never regain access to an EFS-encrypted resource. The DRA will help to recover data if the encryption key is deleted, or if the machine has been lost or compromised.

EFS offers encryption at a file and folder level it cannot be used to encrypt an entire hard disk for this you would use BitLocker (covered in Chapter 5). Users can encrypt any file or folder that they have created on an NTFS-formatted hard disk by right-clicking the resource, and selecting Properties from the context menu that appears. In the Advanced Attributes dialog box (shown in Figure 6-14) select the option to Encrypt Contents To Secure Data.

FIGURE 6-14 Enabling resource encryption

Encryption should not be used without prior planning and establishing some safeguards to secure the encryption keys that are used. EFS protects data from unauthorized access and it is especially effective as a last line of defense from attacks, such as physical theft.

EFS uses Windows Public Key Infrastructure (PKI) and a fast encryption algorithm to protect files. The public and private keys generated during encryption ensure that only the user account that encrypted the file is able to decrypt it. Encrypted data can be decrypted only if the user's personal encryption certificate is available, which is generated through the private key. Unless exported by the user, this key cannot be used by anyone else, and EFS prevents any access to the data. EFS will prevent attempts to copy or move encrypted data by anyone except users who have the proper credentials. If the user deletes his account or leaves the company, any encrypted resources will not be accessible, which could lead to data being lost. The only way to prevent data loss is to ensure that a DRA has previously been created, so that an administrator can use the DRA to decrypt the resource.

Here are some key points you need to learn about EFS:

- The process of encryption and decryption happens behind the scenes and is not visible to users.
- Encryption occurs when you close files; decryption occurs when you open them.
- EFS is available only on NTFS volumes.
- EFS keys aren't assigned to a computer; they are assigned to a specific user.
- If a hacker gains access to the user's PC while he is signed in, they will be able to access and open EFS protected files.
- The file owner can move or copy an EFS-protected file.
- You can't use EFS and compression together. It's one or the other.
- If the file owner moves an EFS-protected file to a volume that does not support EFS (such as FAT32), the file will be decrypted.
- Encrypted files and folders are no longer colored green in File Explorer, but now include a padlock icon on each file, as shown in Figure 6-15.
- EFS uses Advanced Encryption Standard (AES), which uses a 256-bit key algorithm, a very credible industry standard of encryption.
- EFS is only available on Windows 10 Pro, Enterprise, and Education editions.

By default, any user is able to use EFS to encrypt any file of which they have ownership. Unless company policy requires EFS, you need to consider disabling EFS within Group Policy, until a DRA is created.

It is very important that a DRA is in place before EFS is enabled, because without a DRA even an administrator is unable to recover EFS-protected files and folders. For the exam, you need to be able to configure a DRA using the command-line tool Cipher.exe. The process for creating a DRA certificate was outlined in Chapter 5, "Configure storage."

One you have created a DRA, you should update the encryption of each currently encrypted file to have the new DRA applied by using cipher /u. You can continue to encrypt your files and folders within File Explorer using the Encrypt Contents To Secure Data option, shown in Figure 6-14. Once you have encrypted the file or folder, the resource will be encrypted and no longer are they colored green in File Explorer, but now include a padlock icon on each file, as shown in Figure 6-15.

> **NOTE** **DRA AND EFS: THE SEQUENCE IS IMPORTANT**
>
> Only encrypted files that are created *after* the DRA has been created can be recovered using the DRA.

Performing backup and recovery of EFS-protected files

Built into Windows is a wizard for users who want to use EFS to create a file encryption certificate and key, and back up these files.

Use the following steps to start the wizard and complete the process to configure an EFS certificate.

1. Open Control Panel and select User Accounts.
2. Click Manage Your File Encryption Certificates to open the Encrypting File System Wizard.
3. Click Next. The wizard asks for your file encryption certificate; you can select your existing certificate or you can create a new certificate.
4. Click Create A New Certificate, and then click Next.
5. Select A Self-signed Certificate Stored On My Computer and click Next.
6. Provide a backup location and password, and click Next.
7. On the Update your previously encrypted files page, tick All Logical Drives and click Next.
8. On the Your encrypted files have been updated page, click Close.

In addition to the Cipher.exe command-line tool, you can also use the Certificates MMC (CertMgr.msc) to manage or backup your personal EFS certificate. You can also import your certificates to a new computer that doesn't already have your certificate. In the event of your certificate being lost, perhaps due to a failed computer or corrupted profile, you can import the DRA certificate onto a new computer, which would allow recovery of the encrypted files.

To import your EFS certificate into your personal certificate store via the Certificate Import Wizard, you should follow these steps:

1. Open Certificates MMC, by typing CertMgr.msc into the search box, and then press Enter.
2. Select the Personal folder.
3. Click Action, click All Tasks, and select Import.
4. Work through the Certificate Import Wizard to import the certificate.

Some of the most common parameters used with the Cipher.exe command include:

- **/c**   Displays information about an encrypted file
- **/d**   Decrypts specified files and directories
- **/s:<directory>**   Performs the specified operation on all subdirectories in the specified directory
- **/u**   Updates all encrypted files on the local drives (useful if you need to update previously encrypted files with a new recovery certificate)
- **/u /n**   Finds all encrypted files on a local drive
- **/?**   Displays help
- **/x**   Backs up the EFS certificate and keys to the specified file name
- **/r:<FileName>**   Generates an EFS recovery agent key and certificate, based on the user account, then writes them to a .pfx file (Personal Information Exchange file, which contains certificate and private key) and a .cer file (Security Certificate file, which contains only the certificate)

After you have encrypted your first file or folder, Windows 10 will prompt you to make a backup of the EFS certificate and key, as shown in Figure 6-15. This reminder will appear in the notification area and it will re-appear on a regular basis until you back up the EFS certificate and key, or choose to Never Back Up the files. You need to ensure you do take a backup and store this safely in a separate location from that of the files.

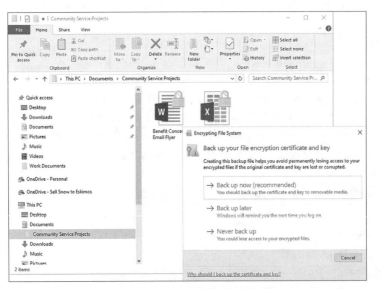

FIGURE 6-15 Backing up the file encryption certificate and key

Credential roaming

Credential roaming is a feature built into Windows 10 that can roam usernames and passwords, which are securely stored within the Windows Credential Manager in a protected area called Windows Vault. Credential Manager is only available on non-domain joined PCs.

EFS certificates used in a domain environment and that are signed by a Certificate Authority (CA) or are self-signed can be added manually to the Credential Manager. These credentials can then roam between multiple devices that share the same Microsoft account. On trusted devices, these credentials are automatically synchronized when you sign in to the device using your Microsoft account.

To view your Credential Manager and its contents, click Control Panel, click User Accounts and then click Manage Your Credentials in the left pane. Alternatively, search for Credential via the Search bar.

In most cases when you navigate to a network resource or to a web server that prompts you for credentials, once you enter the username and password, you may have the option to select Remember My Credentials. If you agree to this Windows stores the credentials in Credential Manager. There are some exceptions to which credentials can be stored with Credential Manager if devices are also protected with Windows Defender Credential Guard.

> **MORE INFO** **WINDOWS DEFENDER CREDENTIAL GUARD**
>
> More information can be found regarding how credentials are protected by Credential Manager and Windows Defender Credential Guard: *https://docs.microsoft.com/windows/access-protection/credential-guard/credential-guard*.

Configure NTFS permissions

An *object* is computer terminology for a physical or logical resource such as a file, a folder, or even a printer. NTFS enables us to set permissions on objects, enabling us to control access to that object. The Access Control List (ACL) for a file is shown in Figure 6-16. The Security tab is selected, and you can see that the Users group has Read & Execute (Allow), List Folder Contents (Allow), Read (Allow), permissions set for the Work Files (Local) folder object.

FIGURE 6-16 Reviewing permissions for the Work Files (Local) folder object

For the exam, you need to be comfortable with the definitions of NTFS-related acronyms, as defined in Table 6-4.

TABLE 6-4 Definitions of ACL, ACE, DACL, and SACL

Name	Acronym	Description
Access control list	ACL	A generic term that includes DACL and SACL displaying a list of users and groups who have permissions on the object
Access control entry	ACE	Identifies the specific permissions granted to a user or group, and used in SACL to define auditing
Discretionary access control list	DACL	List of ACEs that define users/groups that have permission to an object.
System access control list	SACL	This is used for auditing. It contains ACEs that define which users access to this object will be monitor/audited.

NTFS provides six basic (previously referred to as standard permissions) and fourteen advanced permissions (including Full Control) that can be configured. The six basic permissions that can be assigned to a file or a folder are listed in Table 6-5.

TABLE 6-5 Basic NTFS file and folder permissions

Basic Permission	Description: when applied to a Folder	Description: when applied to a File
Full Control	Permits the reading, writing, changing, and deletion of files and subfolders. Enables modification of permissions on folders	Permits reading, writing, changing, and deletion of the file. Enables modification of permissions on files
Modify	Permits the reading, writing, changing, and deletion of files and subfolders. Does not permit the modification of permissions on folders	Permits reading, writing, changing, and deletion of the file. Does not allow the modification of permissions on files
Read & Execute	Permits the content of the folder to be accessed and executed	Permits the file to be accessed and executed
List Folder Contents	Permits the contents of the folder to be viewed	N/A as cannot be applied to files
Read	Allows access to contents	Permits access to contents. Differs from Read & Execute in that it does not permit files to be executed
Write	Enables adding of files and subfolders	Enables a user to modify, but not delete, a file

Permissions are normally set at a top-level permission, and can then include other lower-level permissions. For example, if Full Control, Modify, or Read & Execute permissions are configured, you will find that several other permissions are included as well. This behavior is shown in Table 6-6.

TABLE 6-6 Additional permissions set when configuring basic permissions

Basic Permission	Additional permissions CONFIGURED
Full Control	Full Control, Modify, Read & Execute, List Folder Contents, Read, Write
Modify	Modify, Read & Execute, List Folder Contents, Read, Write
Read & Execute	Read & Execute, List Folder Contents, Read
List Folder Contents	List Folder Contents
Read	Read
Write	Write

Behind the basic permissions is a matrix of advanced permissions, which can also be applied to files and folders. It is worthwhile to take a look at how the basic permissions are actually collections of the thirteen advanced permissions (the fourteenth setting is Full Control which encompasses the other 13). The matrix in Table 6-7 shows the relationship between basic and advanced permissions.

TABLE 6-7 Basic and advanced permissions matrix

Advanced Permission	Full Control	Modify	Read & Execute	List Folder Contents	Read	Write
Traverse folder/execute file	X	X	X	X		
List folder/read data	X	X	X	X	X	
Read attributes	X	X	X	X	X	
Read extended attributes	X	X	X	X	X	
Create files/write data	X	X				X
Create folders/append data	X	X				X
Write attributes	X	X				X
Write extended attributes	X	X				X
Delete subfolders and files	X					
Delete	X	X				
Read permissions	X	X	X	X	X	X
Change permissions	X					
Take ownership	X					

Understand also what is meant when you see that some permissions are available while others unavailable, in the ACLs. This can be because some permissions have been explicitly set, while others are implied or inherited by virtue of their child relationship to a parent folder. Permissions can be one of 3 states: explicitly configured, not configured, or inherited, as shown in Table 6-8.

TABLE 6-8 NTFS permission states

Permission Type	Description	Check box status
Explicit Allow	The user is allowed the permission on the object	Selected
Explicit Deny	The user is denied the permission on the object	Selected
Not configured	Permissions that have not been assigned will have the effect of not allowing the user the permission on the object	Clear
Inherited Allow	Allow permission is applied to the object by virtue of permissions given to their parent object	Selected but dimmed
Inherited Deny	Deny permission is applied to the object by virtue of permissions given to their parent object	Selected but dimmed

Many advisers will state that a Deny permission will always take precedence over other permissions. This is normally true, as an Explicit Deny will always "win" when compared to other permissions. However, when you are troubleshooting permission-related issues, do not assume that Deny is always triumphant because an Explicit Allow will win over an Inherited Deny ACE.

Should you need to configure a lot of permissions or reset the system permissions back to default settings, the GUI is not always the most efficient option to use. In such cases, you need to consider using the command-line tool ICACLS.exe, which can be used to configure local NTFS permissions and can be used in scripts. PowerShell also enables you to script setting permissions on NTFS resources over the network.

You can use ICACLS to grant a permission, with the /grant switch. The most common use for ICACLS is to reset permissions. Using the reset command enables permission inheritance at the folder level and removes any custom permissions on all files, and subdirectories. The following example, which reset the permissions to the C:\Work Files (Local) folder:

```
Icacls.exe "C:\Work Files (Local)" /reset /T
```

> **NOTE** **ICACLSS**
>
> For more information about how to use ICACLS, go to: *https://docs.microsoft.com/windows-server/administration/windows-commands/icacls*.

PowerShell enables you to script the management of file and folder permissions using the two main cmdlets Get-Acl and Set-Acl. PowerShell enables an administrator to remotely configure settings across the network, using PowerShell Remoting.. For more information about the Get-Acl and Set-Acl cmdlets, type **Get-Help Get-Acl**, or type **Get-Help Set-Acl**.

Combining shared folders and NTFS file permissions

Using shared folders and NTFS permissions together requires some careful consideration because both the shared folder permissions and the file and folder permissions are combined when the user connects to the resource over the network. This situation only applies over the network because shared folder permissions are ineffective if a user accesses the resources locally or via Remote Desktop.

When you grant shared folder permissions to users accessing the resources over the network, the following rules apply:

- By default, the Everyone group is granted the Read shared folder permission.
- Users will also require sufficient NTFS permissions for each resource in a shared folder.
- You need to combine NTFS permissions and shared folder permissions, with the resulting permission being the most restrictive.
- Share permissions that are set on a folder apply to the folder and to all the files in the folder.
- Share permissions are applied to all child subfolders and their files when the resources are accessed through the share.

Even if Full Control NTFS file or folder permissions have been set for a folder, if the default shared folder permission is set (which is Read), the highest permission that any file or child object within that folder can have is the default Read permission, as the combined most restrictive permission is Read. Remember that NTFS file permissions always apply, but shared folder permissions only apply to shared folders and combine with NTFS to secure file resources when accessed over a network.

Understanding permissions inheritance

Permissions will "flow" from top to bottom and follow the folder hierarchy. By default, inheritance is enabled as this facilitates more efficient administration. NTFS enables you to disable inheritance from flowing from a parent folder to the child. To select the option to disable inheritance, click the Advanced option on the resource Security properties screen, and then click Disable Inheritance in the Advanced Security Settings For dialog box. You will then be offered the options shown in Figure 6-17.

FIGURE 6-17 Blocking Inheritance

In the Block Inheritance dialog box, there are two options, as follows:

- **Convert Inherited Permissions Into Explicit Permissions On This Object**   Prevents inherited permissions from being able to "flow" from top folders to the subfolders. Current inherited permissions are changed by the system from implicit permissions to explicit permissions. This can result in hundreds or thousands of inherited permissions being changed into explicit permissions.

- **Remove All Inherited Permissions From This Object**   Removes all permissions, and gives you a folder structure with no permissions set. Care needs to be taken with this option because option because it is very easy to remove all access, even system access, to the file structure.

Understanding Move, Copy, and permissions inheritance

When you need to move or copy a folder from one location to another, you need to understand how NTFS will perform the task with respect to how permissions on the resource are modified. Table 6-9 shows the behavior that NTFS adopts when copying files from one folder to another folder, and also between partitions.

TABLE 6-9 Resultant effect of moving or copying NTFS files

Action	Effect
Copy or Move a file or folder to a different volume	Inherits the permissions from the destination (new location) folder
Copy or Move a file or folder within the same NTFS volume	Inherits the permissions from the new parent folder, and explicitly assigned permissions are retained and merged with those inherited
Copy a file or folder to a non-NTFS volume	The copy of the folder or file loses all permissions

> *NOTE* **WHAT HAPPENS WHEN YOU MOVE A NTFS PROTECTED FILE TO A FAT VOLUME?**
>
> If you're moving a file or folder from NTFS to a non-NTFS partition, such as a FAT volume, all NTFS file and folder permissions will be lost since FAT does not support NTFS file and folder permissions. Only Creator Owners and users with the Modify permission (and administrators) are able to perform this task because they have permission to move files and folders.

When you copy a file or folder within the same volume or between volumes, the user must have Read permission for the source folder and Write permission for the destination folder.

When you move a file or folder within the same volume or between volumes, you need to have both Write permission for the destination folder as well as Modify permission for the source file or folder. This is because Windows 10 will move the resources (Write) and then delete (Modify) the resources from the source folder once it has completed the copy to the destination folder.

Effective Access

You might be required to calculate the access that a user has to a resource. Within the Advanced options of an object's Security settings, you will find the Effective Access tab (previously called Effective Permissions) as shown in Figure 6-18. If this action is performed on a domain joined device, you have the option to determine the effective permission a selected user, device, or group has on any object. When setting permissions in a corporate environment you should verify that NTFS permissions are applied correctly and use the Effective Access feature to ensure that the results are as expected.

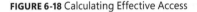

FIGURE 6-18 Calculating Effective Access

For example, for a resource, if you assign a user the Read permission and assign the Modify permission to a group that the same user is a member of, the effective access permissions are a combination of the Read permission and Modify permission, which is Modify permission.

When you combine permissions that include Deny permissions, NTFS will evaluate the Deny permissions before the Allow permissions that are set on the same resource with explicit Deny taking precedence over all Allow permissions.

If Deny and Allow permissions are set at different levels within a folder structure, for example, if Deny is set at the top-level folder and an Allow permission is set at its subfolder, Allow can take precedence and override Deny because the Allow permission is explicit and not implicit.

Be careful when using the Effective Access tool to review permissions on folders that you own the permissions given to the Creator Owner of the object are not taken into account.

Taking ownership of resources

It is possible to remove access to a particular user or group on an object, such as a folder. Sometimes, this happens accidentally when configuring permissions, but typically, it will happen when the user who originally created the resource leaves the organization and the resource is then said to be 'orphaned'.

In the Advanced Security Settings dialog box for an object, you will find the Effective Access tab and at the top of this screen, as shown in Figure 6-18, is an option to change the object owner. So long as you have administrative privileges, you can take ownership of the object and allocate it to another user or group. This operation can also be performed using the command-line tool **icacls <file name> /reset,** using an elevated command prompt.

Configure disk quotas

In addition to setting security permissions, compressing, and encrypting files and folders, NTFS also enables you to assign disk quotas for volumes. While disk space is inexpensive and restricting user storage space may seem unnecessary, some storage is more valuable than others. The increased availability of Storage Area Network (SAN) technology, with fast Non-Volatile Memory Express (NVMe) and Solid State Drive (SSD) drives and storage space being rented in the cloud, businesses are looking to reduce storage and the resultant backup costs. The NVMe and SSD drives are fast, but they also more expensive than traditional drives.

There is no business benefit in enabling users to store copious amounts of non-business data on company owned resources such as a laptop or desktop computer. This even more relevant when considering storage on the business cloud or file-server infrastructure, and therefore, its good practice to set modest limits on the amount of space that each user can use for cloud or server-based storage. Every administrator needs to have an appropriate size in mind, and if this was set, as an example, to 2 GB per user, then 95 percent of users would never exceed the limit. The few that do hit this limit are likely to be the type of user who may be storing their music or video collection on company space, and a disk quota would certainly prevent this type of behavior.

Disk quotas can be set for local storage on computers running Windows 10 by using the Graphical User Interface (GUI) of a local PC, or configured remotely via Group Policy. You can configure NTFS disk quotas on the disk volume using File Explorer, as follows:

1. In File Explorer, navigate to the volume to configure the disk quotas.
2. Right-click the volume, and click Properties.
3. Click the Quota tab.
4. If quotas have not been set before, click Show Quota Settings, and accept the UAC prompt.
5. Select the Enable Quota Management check box.
6. Once enabled, an administrator has several options, including:
    a. Deny Disk Space To Users Exceeding Quota Limit
    b. Limit Disk Space To (set the limit)
    c. Set Warning Level To (set the limit)
    d. Log Event When A User Exceeds Their Quota Limit
    e. Log Event When A User Exceeds Their Warning Level
7. To apply the settings, click OK, and then click OK again to apply.

The system will now scan the volume for disk usage, which may take several minutes, depending on the size of the disk. You can review the quota entries for the volume by clicking the Quota Entries button at the bottom of the dialog box as shown in Figure 6-19.

FIGURE 6-19 Setting a disk quota limit on a volume

EXAM TIP

Fsutil.exe is the command-line tool used to set quota limits. Review the options available using Fsutil, such as running Fsutil fsinfo statistics C: with administrative credentials.

Configuring disk quota policies

Rather than configure disk quotas on each system, you can configure and apply them using Group Policy. There are six GPO settings, which relate to disk quotas, in the Computer Configuration\Administrative Templates \System\Disk Quotas. These are summarized in Table 6-10.

TABLE 6-10 Disk Quota GPOs

Policy	Description
Enable disk quotas	Turns Disk Quotas Management On or Off for all NTFS volumes on the computer and prevents users from changing the setting
Enforce disk quota limit	This determines whether disk quota limits are enforced. If quotas are enforced, users are denied disk space if they exceed the quota. This setting overrides settings on the Quota tab for the NTFS volume.
Specify default quota limit and warning level	Sets a default disk quota limit and warning level for all new users of the volume
Log event when quota limit is exceeded	Determines whether the system records an event in the Application log when users reach their limit, and prevents users from changing the logging options in the GUI
Log event when quota warning level is exceeded	Determines whether the system records an event in the Application log when users reach the warning level on a volume
Apply policy to removable media	Determines whether to extend disk quota policies to NTFS volumes on removable media

The Disk Quota feature that is provided with Windows 10 is quite limited, and is only available on a per-volume basis. If you require more functionality to create quotas on your centralized file storage, the File Server Resource Manager (FSRM) that is available with Windows Server 2016, offers significant improvements in functionality over the Windows 10 Disk Quota feature. FSRM offers a set of features that enable you to manage and classify data, and report data that is stored on file servers by using the GUI or by using PowerShell.

EXAM TIP

The Resilient File System (ReFS), can be considered the next generation of NTFS does not support disk quotas.

Configure file access auditing

Several new corporate compliance regulations and laws, including the Sarbanes-Oxley Act (2002) in the USA, have created new requirements that CEOs of corporations are required to follow in order to ensure that all records and resources within a business are safeguarded, accounted for, and that access to sensitive or private data is tightly controlled.

Auditing of objects such as access to files and folders within NTFS, provides IT administrators with an in-depth tool that can monitor file and folder access in detail. Auditing complements the other measures implemented such as firewalls, and shared folder and NTFS permissions. This multilayered approach is an example of defense in depth, which should be taken to protect resources from unauthorized access and comply with the Sarbanes-Oxley Act requirements.

An example of defensive layering is as follows:

1. Inform all users about the current policies and security requirements on corporate resources and data
2. Set security on devices and servers using BitLocker Drive Encryption
3. Define and create groups; document and restrict membership to each group
4. Set permissions on the folders and files, and apply group access
5. Set auditing to monitor access to folders and file resources
6. Monitor log files and create alerts
7. Investigate security breaches and re-evaluate security measures if necessary

NTFS auditing is very detailed and can be used to record successful resource access and also attempted access that was prevented by NTFS permissions. NTFS auditing can record types of actions related to a file or folder, including file and folder access, or attempted access, modification and deletion.

The log file created will also record additional data including date, time, user account, location, and resource name.

To enable auditing, you need to enable it using one or more GPOs, which are found at Computer Configuration\Windows Settings\Security Settings\Local Policies\Audit Policy. The GPO Audit Object Access is the most commonly used because it enables us to audit all system-wide objects, including files and folders. The GPO can be configured to monitor and log successful access attempts, or to log failed access attempts, or both, as shown in Figure 6-20.

FIGURE 6-20 Configuring the Audit Object Access GPO

Once the GPO has been enabled, the last part of the configuration is to set the level of auditing required on the individual object, such as the folder and its contents. NTFS inheritance rules will also apply auditing to all child objects unless you disable this feature.

To configure auditing on files and folders, carry out the following steps:

1. Open File Explorer.

2. Select the file or folder that you want to audit, and click Properties from the File Explorer ribbon.

3. In the Properties dialog box, click the Security tab, and then click Advanced.

4. In the Advanced Security Settings dialog box, click the Auditing tab.

5. Click Continue, accept the UAC prompt.

6. Click Add to add an auditing action.

7. In the Auditing Entry For dialog box, click Select A Principal, type the name of the user, group, or computer that needs to be monitored, and click OK.

8. In the Auditing Entry For dialog box, select the type of auditing required, All, Fail, or Success.

9. Choose the Basic Permissions that you require, as shown in Figure 6-21.

10. Click OK three times to exit and complete the configuration.

FIGURE 6-21 Specifying the actions to audit for a user, group, or computer

Another option within the Auditing configuration is to Show Advanced Permissions, which shows the special permissions that allow for very granular auditing, should this be required.

If you have enabled DAC policies within the domain, you can further refine the scope of the auditing entry by adding claims-based conditions, which appears in the lower part of the Auditing Entry screen.

After you enable audit logging, you need to test that auditing is occurring as expected. Attempt to access the resources being monitored, and then open the Security log in the Event Viewer and view the audited events. Depending on the level of granularity that you have specified, you may have a few entries or several dozen log entries. If you review the log entries, you should be able to find a log entry that corresponds to the event that you are monitoring.

You can use the Attach Task To This Event option in Event Viewer, from the Action pane. This can be a screen popup or a PowerShell script that alerts you when the event occurs.

Within Windows 10, you can also configure advanced audit policy that enables an even greater level of auditing. This level of auditing is very specialized and unlikely to be required, except in the most specialized cases. To review the options available, open the GPOs shown in Figure 6-22, found at Computer Configuration\Windows Settings\Security Settings\Advanced Audit Policy Configuration, and then expand System Audit Policies. Some of the nodes are related to server-side functions. The Object Access node, highlighted in the Figure 6-22, is relevant to auditing the file system and registry access.

FIGURE 6-22 Advanced Audit Policy Configuration GPOs

Configure authentication and authorization

In Chapter 1, "Manage identity," you reviewed the options in Windows 10 relating to authentication and authorization situations that are available to users of Windows 10. Based on the sign-on credentials and group membership held, Windows 10 will determine the type and scope of access the user has to system resources and the ability to make system-wide changes. As a general rule, an administrator on a Windows device will have a very high level of control over the entire system, whereas a standard user will have limited abilities only.

Configuring User Account Control

Once a user has gained access to the operating system following successful sign-on, the Windows 10 feature called *User Account Control* (UAC) prevents unauthorized changes to the system.

For new users of Windows 10, especially if they have previously used a version of Windows prior to Windows Vista, such as Windows XP, it's important that they are introduced to the UAC feature and guided through the rationale for UAC. Older versions of Windows let users log on as administrators and enable them to retain full administrative authorization over all activities on the system until they log off.

Systems that suffer from malware attacks can easily be compromised because the malware can effectively use administrative access and wreak havoc on the system. This creates extra work for the helpdesk, increases support costs, and reduces productivity. UAC has been very successful in preventing users and malware from using administrative credentials to harm a system.

Administrators no longer have full access to the system. Rather than enabling administrators to implement system-wide changes, UAC presents a challenge pop-up prompt to the administrator to force them to confirm their actions. Similarly, a standard user who attempts to change system settings will receive a UAC prompt, which requires administrative credentials to be provided, or else denies them the ability to make the requested changes.

Since the introduction of UAC, Microsoft has fine-tuned the UAC process with the aim of making the use of UAC less frustrating for all users by reducing the number of application and system tasks that require elevation.

UAC offers various layers of protection, with the UAC prompt being the most visible to the user. The following features compliment UAC:

- File and Registry Redirection
- Installer Detection
- UAC prompt
- ActiveX Installer Service
- Secure Desktop
- Application Information Service

> **NOTE** **ACCESS DENIED**
>
> The Application Information Service component is required to be running, for UAC to function properly. If this service is stopped or disabled, applications that require administrative access will not be able to request UAC elevation and therefore will not launch, resulting in Access Denied errors.

Standard users

Except for administrators, all users are standard users with few privileges and limited ability to make changes to the system, such as installing software or modifying the date and time. Standard user accounts are described as "operating with least privilege." The list of system tasks that a standard user can perform include:

- Change the desktop background and modify display settings
- View firewall settings
- Change the time zone
- Add a printer
- Change their own user account password
- Configure accessibility options
- Configure power options
- Connect to a wireless or LAN connection
- Install drivers, either from Windows Update or those that are supplied with Windows 10

- Install updates from Windows Update

- Use Remote Desktop to connect to another computer

- Pair and configure a Bluetooth device with the device

- Perform other troubleshooting, network diagnostic, and repair tasks

- Play CD/DVD media

- Restore own files from File History

- Use Remote Desktop to connect to another PC

- View most settings, although they will require elevated permissions when attempting to change Windows settings

UAC prevents you from making unauthorized or hidden (possibly malware-initiated) changes to your system that require administrator-level permissions. A UAC elevation prompt is displayed to notify you, as follows:

- **Consent prompt**   This is displayed to administrators in Admin Approval Mode whenever an administrative task is requested. Click Yes to continue if you consent.

- **Credential prompt**   This is displayed if you are a standard user attempting to perform an administrative task. An administrator needs to enter their password into the UAC prompt to continue.

When an administrator provides permissions to a standard user using a UAC prompt, these are only temporarily operative and the permissions are returned back to a standard user level once the isolated task has finished.

Standard users can become frustrated when they are presented with the UAC prompt, and Microsoft has reduced the frequency and necessity for elevation. Listed are some common scenarios wherein a standard user would be prompted by UAC to provide administrative privileges. You will see that they are not necessarily daily tasks for most users:

- Add or remove a user account

- Browse to another user's directory

- Change user account types

- Change Windows Firewall settings

- Configure Automatic Updates

- Install a driver for a device unless it is supplied with Windows 10

- Install ActiveX controls

- Install or uninstall applications

- Modify UAC settings

- Move or copy files to the Program Files or Windows folders

- Restore system backup files

- Schedule Automated Tasks

Administrative users

Administrative users need to be limited to authorized personnel within the organization. In addition to the ability to perform all tasks that a standard user can, they also have the following far-reaching permissions:

- Read/Write/Change permissions for all resources
- All Windows permissions

From this, it looks like administrators have considerable power, which can potentially be hijacked by malware. Thankfully, administrators are still challenged with the UAC prompt, which pops up by default whenever they perform a task that requires administrative permissions, but they are not required to re-enter their administrative credentials. This is known as Admin Approval Mode.

A user who signs on to a system with administrative permissions will be granted two tokens one, which enables him or her to operate as a standard user, and another, which can be used when they perform a task that requires administrative permissions. Just as with the standard user, after the task is completed using elevated status, the account reverts to a standard-user privilege.

> **NOTE** **TURNING OFF UAC IS NOT SUPPORTED FOR WINDOWS 10 DEVICES**
>
> UAC helps prevent malware from damaging PCs and should not be turned off. If UAC is turned off all Universal Windows Platform apps will stop working.

Types of elevation prompts

UAC has four types of dialog boxes, as shown in Table 6-11, with a description on how users need to respond to the prompt.

TABLE 6-11 UAC elevation prompts

Type of elevation prompt	Description
A Windows 10 setting or feature needs your permission to start.	This item has a valid digital signature that verifies that Microsoft is the publisher of this item and it is usually safe to use the application.
A non-Windows 10 application needs your permission to start.	This application has a valid digital signature and it is usually safe to use the application.
An application with an unknown publisher needs your permission to start.	This application does not have a valid digital signature from its publisher. Use extra caution and verify that the application is safe before using. Search the Internet for the program's name to determine if it is a known trustworthy application or malware.
You have been blocked by your system administrator from running this application.	This application has been blocked because it is known to be untrusted. To run this application, you need to contact your system administrator to remove the restriction, if appropriate.

Within large organizations, nearly all users will be configured to sign in to their computer with a standard user account. On a managed system that has been provisioned and deployed by the IT department, standard user accounts should have little need to contact the helpdesk regarding UAC issues. They can browse the Internet, send email, and use applications without an administrator account. Home users and small businesses that lack a centralized IT resource to provision and manage their devices are often found to use administrative user accounts.

As with previous versions of Windows, an administrator can determine when the UAC feature will notify you if changes are attempted on your computer.

Search for **UAC**, and click Change User Account Control Settings to display the dialog box shown in Figure 6-23.

FIGURE 6-23 Changing User Account Control Settings

You need to review the information on this dialog box by moving the slider to each position in order to determine how the UAC feature will behave. The default is Notify Me Only When Applications Try To Make Changes To My Computer.

Table 6-12 shows the four settings that enable customization of the elevation prompt experience.

TABLE 6-12 User Account Control Settings

Prompt	Description
Never notify	UAC prompting is disabled.
Notify me only when applications try to make changes to my computer (do not dim my desktop)	When an application makes a change, a UAC prompt appears, but if the user makes a change to system settings, the UAC prompt is not displayed. The desktop does not dim.
Notify me only when applications try to make changes to my computer (default)	When an application makes a change, a UAC prompt appears, but if the user makes a change to system settings, the UAC prompt is not displayed. Secure desktop feature is active.
Always notify	The user is always prompted when changes are made to the computer by applications or by the user.

The settings enable changes to the UAC prompting behavior only, and do not elevate the status of the underlying user account.

In addition to the UAC settings within the Control Panel, there are many more UAC security settings that can be configured via Group Policy and can be found in Computer Configuration\Windows Settings\Security Settings\Local Policies\Security Options.

EXAM TIP

You need to take time to review the UAC settings configurable by Group Policy, with particular attention to the settings that feature Admin Approval Mode.

Secure Desktop

Whenever UAC prompts the user for consent or elevated credentials, it first switches to a feature called Secure Desktop, which focuses only on the UAC prompt. In addition, Secure Desktop prevents other applications (including malware) from interacting with the user or influencing the user response to the UAC prompt.

While it is possible for malware to generate a screen that imitates the look of Secure Desktop, and even re-create the visual UAC prompt, it is not possible for malware to actually provide UAC with the correct credentials. If a system was infected with malware, it could try to bypass the UAC security setting, using a bogus credential prompt to harvest usernames and passwords from unsuspecting users, and then use these credentials on genuine UAC prompts. It is important, therefore, that administrators are vigilant against potential malware attacks, and all devices are set to ensure that their malware protection is configured to automatically update.

NOTE UAC INTEGRATION WITH THE ANTIMALWARE SCAN INTERFACE

If the Antimalware Scan Interface (AMSI) detects malware behind the UAC elevation request the admin privilege is blocked.

Thought experiments

In these thought experiments, demonstrate your skills and knowledge of the topics covered in this chapter. You can find the answers to these thought experiments in the next section.

Scenario 1

You are the IT manager for your organization, which uses Server 2016 and Windows 10 computers in a domain-joined environment. The financial accountant has asked you to explain a recent sharp increase in printing costs for one of the shared network printers in the office. You investigate and find that the increased costs relate to one of the color printers on the first floor of the office. You need to understand why the usage of this printer has increased 400 percent over the past month,

Answer the following questions regarding the investigation.

1. How can you find out which user or group is responsible for the increase in printing?
2. How would you restrict access to the printer out of normal office hours?
3. Some users require color printing, others require only monochrome printing. How would you approach this requirement?

Scenario 2

You've been asked to help provide assistance to the team designing a new interactive exhibition for a learning center for children aged 7-14 years. The objective is to make the learning experience modern and exciting, but at the same time remove any moveable components, which could fail or be broken, such as levers and switches. Your team has been investigating whether NFC or other sensors could help. Visitors will be provided with a NFC-enabled Windows 10 device to use while they visit the facility.

Answer the following questions about NFC.

1. How could NFC be suitable for the learning center?
2. What types of NFC hardware could respond to the Windows 10 device?
3. What other hardware-based tracking feature(s) supported by Windows 10 could be explored by the team?

Thought experiment answers

This section provides the solutions for the tasks included in the thought experiment.

Scenario 1

1. You should immediately enable object auditing in Group Policy and configure auditing on the color printer. Since the printer is shared on the network, the auditing is performed on the server. After a couple of days review, the Security logs within Event Viewer on the server will identify all of the jobs that have been sent to the printer. The event log will also help you to identify the name of the user or group that has been sending print jobs to the printer. You may also be able to extract from the logs the filename of the files that have been printed.

2. Within the color printer advanced properties dialog box, you can configure the time when the printer is available. Enter the required office hours in this dialog box to restrict usage to office hours.

3. You could create two identical printers, and name one Color and the other Monochrome. Add permissions to allow the group that need to print in color to be able to use both printers. Add permissions to restrict the group that don't need to print in color to be able to use only the monochrome printer.

Scenario 2

1. You could use NFC smart tags within the learning center. Each exhibit could be given a prominent NFC smart tag, which visitors are invited to tap in order to activate the exhibit and/or the interactive audio-visual component on the device.

2. Answers may vary, but you can use a variety of NFC hardware, including smart tags, stickers, key fobs, or cards, or another Windows device with NFC hardware built in, such as a Windows phone or tablet.

3. Answers may vary, but you could use GPS location sensor tracking on the device to activate exhibits when the visitor carrying the device is located in a specific room or position.

Chapter summary

- Public Folders, HomeGroups, and Any folder sharing are useful for home-user and small networks, to enable easy file sharing. Folders can be shared with the default Share permission of Read on NTFS- formatted volumes.

- Access Based Enumeration prevents users who are not authorized to view files and folders from seeing them in NTFS.

- Libraries and Quick Access enable users to locate frequently used files and folders quickly within File Explorer and applications.

- Printers can be shared over the network and secured in a similar manner to files and folders using NTFS security.

- NFC technology enables the transfer of small amounts of data between a device and a NFC-enabled object that are in close proximity, such as a smart tag. When such devices are used with a NFC-enabled device, such as a printer, users can connect without having to physically connect to the device using the network.

- OneDrive offers users the ability to store, share, and synchronize files to a secure cloud-storage location linked to their Microsoft account, with 5 GB initial free storage capacity.

- Volumes formatted using NTFS enable users to configure file and folder security, EFS, disk quotas, and to enable auditing.

- Utilizing NTFS inheritance can increase the efficiency of deploying security to folders and files organized in a logical hierarchy.

- NTFS file permissions protect files and folders locally and over the network.

- Files copied or moved to a different volume will inherit the permissions from the new location, whereas if the destination volume is the same, the explicit permissions are retained.

- Explicit Deny permissions will always overrule Allow permissions, although explicit Allow permissions will overrule an implied Deny permission.

- EFS on Windows 10 Pro, Enterprise, and Education editions, uses AES, a 256-bit key algorithm, to securely encrypt files stored on NTFS volumes.

- Disk quotas are a simple method of restricting excess user-data usage on volumes.

- Auditing needs to be enabled in Group Policy, and then configured on the resource.

- User Account Control prevents unauthorized changes to Windows 10, and provides a safer environment for administrators to manage Windows 10.

- The Secure Desktop feature prevents malware from interfering with the user response to UAC prompts.

CHAPTER 7

Manage remote access

The trend of more and more people working remotely is clearly on the rise. Convenience and cost reduction are just two reasons for this trend. Providing employees with permanent office space, including desks, PCs, telephones, and ancillary support is very expensive, especially when located in a city center. In 2016, the Department of Labor in the USA reported that 22% of the workforce work away from the office or are willing to work from home on a regular basis. These users typically only require a secure and reliable Internet connection to access company resources, which are often stored in the cloud.

Advances in technology, including mobile device management, VPN Reconnect, mobile tethering, and cloud technologies are helping to create and maintain ever more reliable and secure connections for remote workers. Improvements in speed and the availability of fast WiFi, urban and rural broadband, and increased cellular carrier speeds, such as Long Term Evolution (LTE) or 4G, are accelerating the rate at which users are able to adopt the ability to work anywhere, and businesses are able to enjoy the potential cost and environmental savings.

Increased mobility trends are demanding better device security, portability, and management. You have seen how Microsoft Intune helps manage remote devices and how BitLocker Drive Encryption and BitLocker To Go ensure data stored on devices can be secured using encryption. You'll see in this chapter how using a Windows To Go workspace enables ultra-portability when working away from the office.

Skills in this chapter:

- Skill 7.1: Configure remote connections
- Skill 7.2: Configure mobility options

Skill 7.1: Configure remote connections

Windows 10 helps users to remain productive whether based in the office or at a remote location. In this section, you'll learn how to configure VPN connections in Windows 10, and understand the various encapsulation, authentication, and data encryption options available.

The Remote Desktop Protocol that has been available since Windows XP is used to connect to other desktops, and this protocol continues to evolve, offering increased speed and functionality within Windows 10 both on the PC and mobile device. You need to understand how to configure remote access and enable users to connect to other computers from their devices for remote management or for the purpose of telecommuting.

In a world that is becoming more mobile and connected, you also need to understand how to tether a Windows 10 device to personal cellular or other metered broadband connections. You'll need to also configure the devices so that data usage is controlled, both capabilities that are covered here.

> **This section covers the following topics:**
> - Configure remote authentication
> - Configure VPN connections and authentication
> - Configure Remote Desktop settings
> - Enable VPN Reconnect
> - Configure broadband tethering
> - Configure Remote Desktop client for Windows 10 Mobile, iOS, and Android
> - Protect remote desktop credentials with Remote Credential Guard
> - Enable restricted admin mode for RDP in Windows 8.1 and Windows 2012 R2

Configure remote authentication

When we refer to using Windows 10 to connect to a remote end point, such as connecting to an enterprise network, we usually use either dial-up or virtual private networking (VPN). Despite the ubiquity of high-speed Internet access today, there are still some users who regularly use dial-up for legacy services, such as synchronizing electronic point of sale (EPOS) and daily bulletin boards.

When discussing remote authentication, it is easy to become rather confused by the terminology and differences between the various VPN connection protocols, authentication methods, and encapsulation methods that can be used. The best advice relevant to the exam is to draw a picture, list the parts of a VPN connection, and ensure you know which technology is the most recent innovation, such as VPN Reconnect (covered later).

Configure VPN connections and authentication

In Windows 10, creating a VPN enables data to be transferred through a virtual private network via a secured connection (tunnel) over a public network, such as the Internet, as shown in Figure 7-1.

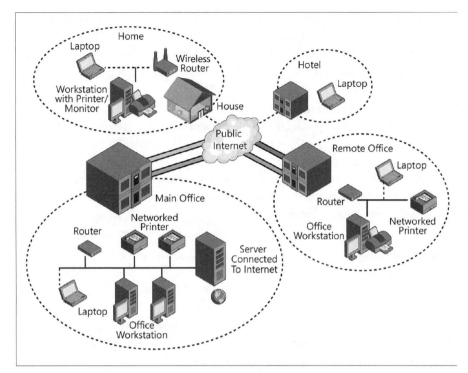

FIGURE 7-1 Using a VPN to connect locations securely over the Internet

Except in a few specialized scenarios, nearly all dial-up remote connections have been replaced by broadband-enabled VPN communications.

Windows 10 still supports Point-to-Point Protocol (PPP), which can be used with a dial-up connection. This is an old protocol, but because it creates a direct connection and maintains a dedicated link between the two points, it is used as the starting point for most dial-up and PPP connections.

For the exam, you will be required to understand the different types of VPN protocols that Windows 10 supports and when each protocol should be used.

VPN protocols

Windows 10 supports four commonly used VPN protocols. Each protocol offers different characteristics and age. Typically, the newest protocol will be the most secure.

■ **Point-to-Point Tunneling Protocol (PPTP)** The oldest and what is considered one of the least secure of all supported VPN protocols. It can be used successfully, however, in low-security scenarios because it is very easy to set up, and still offers more protection than using PPP over the Internet.

- PPTP creates the tunnel, and then can use several user-based authentication methods, including the Microsoft Challenge Handshake Authentication Protocol versions 1 and 2 (MS-CHAP v1 and MS-CHAP v2), Extensible Authentication Protocol (EAP), and Protected Extensible Authentication Protocol (PEAP). If EAP is used, certificates can be used with PPTP, otherwise they are not necessary.

- **Layer 2 Tunneling Protocol (L2TP)**   This protocol uses the IP security extensions (IPsec) for encryption and encapsulation. L2TP encapsulates the messages with IPsec, and then encrypts the contents using the Data Encryption Standard (DES) or Triple DES (3DES) algorithm. The encryption keys are provided by IPsec using Internet Key Exchange (IKE). L2TP/IPsec can use pre-shared keys or certificates for authentication. Using a pre-shared key is useful during testing and evaluation, but should be replaced with a certificate in a production environment.

  - L2TP/IPsec is widely supported on all versions of Windows since Windows XP

- **Secure Socket Tunneling Protocol (SSTP)**   This is a recent protocol introduced with Windows Server 2008 and supported on Vista SP1 or later. It encapsulates PPP traffic using the Secure Sockets Layer (SSL) protocol, which is widely supported on the Internet and because it passes through TCP port 443, which is the same as SSL, it will typically not be blocked by firewalls and can be used from almost any location. Using the Extensible Authentication Protocol-Transport Layer Security (EAP-TLS) authentication protocol together with certificates makes SSTP a very versatile and widely used protocol.

- **Internet Key Exchange, Version 2 (IKEv2)**   IKEv2 is most useful for mobile users and is the default protocol for Windows 10 and Windows 8.1 when trying to connect to remote access servers. This protocol is partially supported on Windows 7 and later versions of Windows, and provides support for IPv6 traffic and the IKEv2 Mobility and Multi-homing (MOBIKE) protocol through the Windows VPN Reconnect feature, which allows automatic reconnection if a VPN connection is lost. Authentication is offered using EAP, PEAP, EAP-MSCHAPv2, and smart cards.

  - IKEv2 will not support older authentication methods, such as Password Authentication Protocol (PAP) and Challenge-Handshake Authentication Protocol (CHAP), which offer low protection.

Windows 10 will seek to negotiate a common VPN type and, by default, the type is set to Automatic, with the option to select one of the four supported VPN types, as shown in Figure 7-2.

FIGURE 7-2 Adding a VPN connection

Authenticating remote users

Windows users authenticate using Kerberos when accessing the local network, but for remote authentication, this is not suitable, and a separate protocol, which protects against network intrusion, must be used. During the initial negotiation sequence (using PPP) when a client connects to the remote computer, each party must agree on a shared authentication protocol to use. By default, Windows 10 will use the strongest protocol that both parties have in common.

In the Add A VPN Connection Wizard, Windows 10 offers three sign-in options when configuring a VPN, such as:

- User name and password
- Smart card
- One-time password

In addition to these options, you can also configure Windows 10 to use the common authentication protocols:

- **EAP-MS-CHAPv2** This is a protocol that uses Extensible Authentication Protocol (EAP), which offers the default and most flexible authentication option for Windows 10 clients. It offers the strongest password-based mechanism for the client side, with certificates being used on the server side. Authentication can be negotiated based on certificates or smart cards, and EAP-MS-CHAPv2 is likely to be further extended and developed as technology advances. Windows 10 will aim to use this method for authentication connections where possible. IKEv2 connections must use EAP-MS-CHAPv2 or a certificate.

- **PAP** This is the least secure protocol because it uses plaintext passwords. It is not considered secure and should only be used whenever other authentication methods cannot be negotiated.

- **CHAP** Used for down-level client compatibility, and has been surpassed by MS-CHAP v2. This protocol uses a pre-shared key between the client and server to enable encryption to take place.

- **MS-CHAP v2** Stronger than the CHAP protocol, with significantly improved security when partnered with EAP to enable encryption of the password.

Creating a VPN connection

Windows 10 provides two methods of creating a VPN connection and configuring the VPN and authentication. The traditional method is found using the Set Up A New Connection Or Network Wizard within the Network And Sharing Center.

The modern method of creating a VPN is as follows:

1. Search for VPN, and click Change Virtual Private Networks (VPN).

2. In the Settings app, click Add A VPN Connection.

3. In the Add A VPN Connection dialog box, configure the options:

   A. VPN provider, for example, Windows (Built-in)

   B. Connection Name, for example, Work VPN

   C. Server Name Or Address, for example, vpn3.adatum.com

   D. VPN type, for example, Automatic

   E. Type of sign-in information and choose User Name And Password

   F. Type of sign-in info, for example, user name, and password

   G. Click Save

4. On the VPN page in the Settings app, click Change Adapter Settings.

5. Select the Work VPN, and then click Change Settings Of This Connection.

6. Click the Security tab in the Work_VPN Properties dialog box, and in the Authentication section, click the radio button to Allow These Protocols.

7. Ensure the Microsoft CHAP Version 2 (MS-CHAP v2) is selected, as shown in Figure 7-3.

8. Click Advanced Settings.

9. In Advanced Properties dialog box, type the L2TP pre-shared key, and click OK twice.

FIGURE 7-3 VPN security properties

Once you have created a VPN connection, you can launch the VPN by opening the Action Center, clicking the VPN tile, choosing the VPN connection in the Network And Internet dialog box, and then clicking Connect. You can also navigate to Network Connections via Network And Internet in the Control Panel, select the VPN icon, and then click Start This Connection.

> *NOTE* **MODERN VS TRADITIONAL METHOD OF CREATING A VPN**
>
> For the exam, you need to be familiar with creating and modifying both protocols and authentication options for a VPN connection using the traditional as well as modern methods.

Additional new VPN features introduced in Windows 10 include the following:

- **Always On** This feature enables Windows to automatically connect to a VPN. The Always On feature can be triggered by sign-in, when the desktop is unlocked, and on network changes. When the Always On profile is configured, VPN remains always connected unless the user disconnects manually or logs off the device. The profile is optimized for power and performance, and the profiles can be pushed and managed on devices using mobile device management (MDM) tools.

- **App-triggered VPN** Previously known in Windows 8.1 as "On demand VPN," this active VPN profile can be triggered by the user launching one of the applications that have been configuring a list of applications.

- **Traffic Filters** To protect the server from a remote attack, an administrator can configure policies on a Windows 10 device to inspect and, if necessary, filter VPN traffic before it is enabled to travel over the VPN. There are two types of Traffic Filter rules available:

- **App-based rules** An app-based rule will only enable VPN traffic originating from applications that have been marked as being allowed to traverse the VPN interface.

- **Traffic-based rules** Enterprise-level traffic-based rules enable fine-tuning of what type of traffic is allowed. By using the industry-standard rules covered by 5 tuple policies (protocol, source/destination IP address, source/destination port), administrators can be very specific on the type of network traffic that is allowed to travel over the VPN interface.

  An administrator can combine both app-based rules and traffic-based rules.

- **LockDown VPN** The LockDown VPN profile is used to enforce the use of the VPN interface. In this scenario, the device is secured to only allow network traffic over the VPN, which is automatically always on and can never be disconnected. If the VPN is unable to connect, then there will be no network traffic allowed. The LockDown profile overrides all other VPN profiles, and must be deleted before other profiles can be added, removed, or connected.

Enable VPN Reconnect

VPN Reconnect has been available since Windows 7 and uses the IKEv2 protocol with the MOBIKE extension, to automatically re-establish a lost VPN connection without user intervention. For mobile users, the prevalence of dropped WiFi or LTE connections can be frequent, due to volatile signal strength. It is best to use and configure VPN Reconnect for your mobile users because this will reduce the frustration of having to manually reconnect, and it will also increase productivity.

The network outage time can be configured from five minutes up to an interruption of eight hours.

To enable VPN Reconnect, follow these steps:

1. Search for VPN, and click Change Virtual Private Networks (VPN).

2. In the Settings app, click Change Adapter Settings.

3. Select the Work_VPN, and then click Change Settings Of This Connection.

4. Click the Security tab in the Work_VPN Properties dialog box, and click Advanced Settings.

5. In the Advanced Properties dialog box, check the Mobility option on the IKEv2 tab.

6. Modify the Network Outage Time as necessary, as shown in Figure 7-4.

7. Click OK twice.

FIGURE 7-4 Configuring the Network Outage Time for VPN Reconnect

Configure broadband tethering

Windows 10 devices are becoming lighter and more mobile. Often users have multiple connected devices, including laptops, tablets, and cellular phones. Virtually ubiquitous Internet connectivity enables users to adopt an "always on" lifestyle. When users face situations where traditional connections, such as corporate WiFi or Ethernet, are not available, they will look for other forms of connectivity. This connectivity includes WiFi hotspots, or mobile devices used to connect to the Internet.

Broadband tethering introduced in Windows 8.1 enables users to share their own Internet connection with others by enabling the device to function as a wireless "hotspot." Similarly, users can connect to other users' shared personal "hotspots," provided they have the necessary credentials.

To connect to a shared mobile hot-spot connection, follow these steps:

1. Click the WiFi icon in the notification area.
2. Select the shared hotspot.
3. Click Connect.
4. Enter the network security key, as shown in Figure 7-5.
5. Click Connect.
6. The network should now be connected.

FIGURE 7-5 Connecting to a shared connection

WiFi services

When connecting to public or private WiFi hotspots, Windows 10 will find and connect your device to open WiFi hotspots that are nearby.

This feature uses crowdsourcing from your device and other Windows devices to source information about the local networks, such as whether the WiFi is open and high quality. If you are in range of the network, Windows 10 will automatically connect to it without being required to enter or know the WiFi password.

The feature is not available in all countries or regions and if WiFi Services is available, this feature is disabled by default.

> *NOTE* **OPT OUT OF WIFI SERVICES**
>
> If you manage an open WiFi network, or if you add the text _optout somewhere in the WiFi network name (SSID) Windows 10 will not automatically connect devices to the network.

To allow Windows 10 to automatically connect to open WiFi hotspots that it knows about through crowdsourcing, follow these steps:

1. Select the WiFi icon on the taskbar.

2. Select Network & Internet settings.

3. From the list on the left, select WiFi.

4. Under WiFi services, turn on Connect To Suggested Open Hotspots as shown in Figure 7-6.

FIGURE 7-6 Managing WiFi settings

At the top of the WiFi page is an option to manage all known networks that the device has connected to. Where a network is password-protected and this has been stored, there is an option to forget the connection that deletes the information and you will need to re-enter the password to reconnect.

Users who do not have unlimited broadband allowances need to be careful when enabling tethering because they incur excessive charges. They should take care to review the bandwidth used regularly, so that their usage does not exceed their allowed quota as defined by the service provider.

Hotspot 2.0 networks

For connecting to public WiFi networks, Windows 10 supports the Hotspot 2.0 wireless 802.11u WiFi standard. This should make connecting to hotspots in public places such as airports, or coffee shops, easier and more secure.

Your device will attempt to connect you to available public hotspots automatically, in a similar fashion to cellular-style roaming.

Although the standard is still new, there are several benefits to using Hotspot 2.0:

- Public Hotspots become easier and more secure—your device will detect which WiFi network is authentic and connect automatically.

- Network Providers can partner with other providers. This will allow great network coverage, and allow cellular-style roaming.

- Encryption is enforced and uses enterprise-grade WPA2 encryption.

When you attempt to join a Hotspot 2.0 network for the first time, Windows 10 presents an Online Sign-Up screen with a list of available network providers. After you have set an account with one of the providers, your device will be able to connect to other Hotspot 2.0 networks automatically in the future.

Configure Remote Desktop client for Windows 10 Mobile, iOS, and Android

An interactive user seldom manages servers locally. With the many tools available, including PowerShell, Remote Server Administration Tools (RSAT), and Remote Desktop, there is very little necessity (or even the possibility with cloud-based servers) to manage the server in person.

How to use Remote Desktop and how to configure the experience of the Remote Desktop Connection by configuring the available settings in the General, Display, Local Resources, Experience, and Advanced tabs, as shown in Figure 7-7, has been reviewed.

FIGURE 7-7 Remote Desktop Connection configuration options

Any edition of Windows using Windows 7 or newer can initiate a Remote Desktop Connection, but the remote PC must be running one of the following editions of Windows:

- Windows 10
- Windows 8/8.1 Enterprise
- Windows 8/8.1 Professional
- Windows 7 Professional
- Windows 7 Enterprise
- Windows 7 Ultimate
- Windows Server 2008
- Windows Server 2008 R2
- Windows Server 2012
- Windows Server 2012 R2
- Windows Server 2016
- Windows Multipoint Server 2011
- Windows Multipoint Server 2012
- Windows Small Business Server 2008
- Windows Small Business Server 2011

You cannot use the Remote Desktop client to connect to these Windows Versions and Editions:

- Windows 7 Starter
- Windows 7 Home
- Windows 8 Home
- Windows 8.1 Home
- Windows 10 Home

Remote Desktop is an established method of connecting to and controlling PCs and servers remotely. This can come from a remote device by using the Microsoft Remote Desktop client app (available for iOS, Android, Mac, and Windows). When you allow remote connections to your PC, you can use another device to connect to your PC and have access to all of your apps, files, and network resources as if you were sitting at your desk.

To set up the remote PC to allow remote connections follow these steps:

1. On the remote PC or server, open Settings, select System, and then About.
2. Under Related settings on the right hand side, select System Info.
3. Select Remote Settings.
4. On the Remote tab under Remote Desktop, select Allow Remote Connections To This Computer, and then select OK.

You should now be able to connect to the remote computer using the Remote Desktop Connection tool built-in to Windows, or by using one of the Remote Desktop apps discussed on the following pages.

If you prefer, you can automatically configure your PC for remote access, by downloading and running the Microsoft Remote Desktop assistant. This assistant updates your system settings to enable remote access, ensures your computer is available for connections, and checks that your firewall allows Remote Desktop connections.

Once the tool has configured your device, it will provide connection information that you can take to the remote machine to help establish the connection. Optionally, you can copy this info to your clipboard, save the connection information to a file, or scan the provided QR code using your mobile device app to add it as a connection on one of your devices.

> *MORE INFO* **MICROSOFT REMOTE DESKTOP ASSISTANT**
>
> You can download the Microsoft Remote Desktop assistant at: *https://www.microsoft.com/ download/details.aspx?id=50042.*

Remote Desktop app on Windows 10

You can use the Remote Desktop app on any Windows 10 device by following these steps:

1. Download the Remote Desktop app from the Microsoft Store from this URL: *https:// www.microsoft.com/ store/p/microsoft-remote-desktop/9wzdncrfj3ps?rtc=1.*

2. Ensure you your PC or server is configured to accept remote connections.

3. Launch the app and connect to your PC or server using a PC, mobile device or HoloLens.

Use the Remote Desktop client to add a Remote Desktop connection to Remote Desktop on Android

You can use the Remote Desktop on an Android device by following these steps:

1. Download the Remote Desktop client from Google Play from this URL: *https://play. google.com/store/apps/details?id=com.microsoft.rdc.android.*

2. Ensure you your PC or server is configured to accept remote connections.

3. Use the Remote Desktop client to add a Remote Desktop connection to connect directly to the Windows PC or Server.

> *NOTE* **ANDROID SUPPORT FOR REMOTE DESKTOP**
>
> The Microsoft Remote Desktop app can run on Android 4.1 and newer devices as well as on Chromebooks with ChromeOS 53 installed.

Remote Desktop on iOS and Mac

You can also use the Remote Desktop client for iOS and Mac to work with Windows 10 from your iOS device including iPhones and iPads and Macs by following these steps.

1. Download the Microsoft Remote Desktop client for iOS from iTunes at this URL: *https://itunes.apple.com/us/app/microsoft-remote-desktop/id714464092?mt=8 or for the Mac at this URL: https://itunes.apple.com/us/app/microsoft-remote-desktop/id715768417?mt=12&ls=1.*

2. Ensure your PC or server is configured to accept remote connections.

3. Use the Remote Desktop client to add a Remote Desktop connection to connect directly to the Windows PC or Server from your iPhone and iPad.

Add a Remote Desktop connection or a remote resource. You use a connection to connect to a directly to a Windows PC and a remote resource to use a RemoteApp program, session-based desktop, or a virtual desktop published on-premises using RemoteApp and Desktop Connections. This feature is typically available in corporate environments.

> **NOTE IOS 6 SUPPORT FOR REMOTE DESKTOP**
>
> The Microsoft Remote Desktop app supports iOS 6.x or newer, and is compatible with iPhone, iPad, and iPod touch devices.

Configure Remote Desktop settings

In addition to using the Remote Desktop Connection found within Windows Accessories, you can use the command-line tool Mstsc.exe to launch the Remote Desktop Connection dialog box, as shown in Figure 7-7. The Mstsc.exe command also enables administrators to launch the tool, with several parameters configured.

The default firewall port that Remote Desktop uses is 3389, and this needs to allow RDP traffic through for Remote Desktop to work. If an administrator changes the firewall port for RDP traffic, the revised port number must be specified in the command-line tool Mstsc.exe when launching the application.

The syntax for mstsc is: `mstsc [<connection file>] [/v:<server[:port]>] [/admin] [/f[ullscreen]] [/w:<width>] [/h:<height>] [/public] | [/span] [/multimon] [/edit "connection file"] [/restrictedAdmin] [/remoteGuard] [/prompt] [/shadow:sessionID> [/control] [/ noConsentPrompt]] [/?]`, and the list of command-line parameters for Remote Desktop Connection are shown in Table 7-1.

TABLE 7-1 Command-line parameters for Remote Desktop Connection

Parameter	Description
<connection file>	Specifies the name of a .rdp file for the connection
/v:<Server[:<Port>]	Specifies the remote computer you want to connect to
/admin	This parameter is used to connect you to a session for the administration of a Remote Desktop Session Host server (The RD Session Host role service must be installed on the remote server).
/edit <"connection file">	Opens the specified .rdp file for editing
/f	Starts Remote Desktop Connection in full-screen mode
/w:<Width>	Specifies the width of the Remote Desktop window
/h:<Height>	Specifies the height of the Remote Desktop window
/public	Runs the Remote Desktop in public mode where passwords and bitmaps are not cached
/span	This enables the Remote Desktop width and height to be matched with the local virtual desktop, spanning across multiple monitors if necessary.
/multimon	Configures the Remote Desktop session monitor layout to render it identical to the client configuration
/restrictedAdmin	Connects to the remote PC or server in Restricted Administration mode which prevents login credentials being sent to the remote PC or server. Functionality and or compatibility may be impacted as the connection is made as local administrator.
/remoteGuard	Utilizes Remote Guard to protect the connection. No credentials are sent to the remote device, however full access is provided.
/ shadow:sessionID	Allows you to specify the SessionID you wish to connect to.
/control	Allows control of the remote session.
/noConsentPrompt	Allows the connection to continue without user consent
/?	Lists the available parameters

Protect remote desktop credentials with Windows Defender Remote Credential Guard

Typically, Remote Desktop client software is used to make a connection to a server for remote administration. This can pose security concerns, since administrator credentials are highly privileged and must be protected.

Windows Defender Remote Credential Guard offers administrators the ability to protect credentials that are typically used over a Remote Desktop connection. This is achieved by redirecting the Kerberos sign on requests (and actively blocking NTLM) back to the device that's requesting the connection. In this way the credentials and credential derivatives are not sent over the network, but instead the target device acquires a Kerberos service tickets on its own, which allows single sign-on experiences for Remote Desktop sessions.

> **EXAM TIP**
> You must be running the Remote Desktop Classic Windows application to use Windows Defender Remote Credential Guard as the Remote Desktop UWP app doesn't support the Windows Defender Remote Credential Guard.

Windows Defender Remote Credential Guard uses the users signed on credentials to connect to the remote computer. The only attack vector available to exploit, is on behalf of the user only when the session is ongoing, which prevents Pass-the-Hash attacks.

Since the credentials are not transmitted, this also prevents the use of credentials after disconnection.

In Windows 10 version 1703, you can configure Remote Credential Guard using Group Policy, as shown in Figure 7-8. To turn on Remote Credential Guard, on the client machine set the Restrict delegation of credentials to remote servers GPO setting found in: Computer Configuration>Administrative Templates>System>Credentials Delegation.

FIGURE 7-8 Remote Credential Guard configuration options

If you prefer to locally configure Windows Defender Remote Credential Guard on, you can use the following parameter to mstsc.exe:

```
mstsc.exe /remoteGuard
```

Enable restricted admin mode for RDP in Windows 8.1 and Windows 2012 R2

Alongside Windows Defender Remote Credential Guard is a more secure method of using Remote Desktop called Restricted Admin mode. This mode prevents users from passing credentials to the remote system and forces them to use local admin privileges on the remote server.

Only users whom possess administrative privileges already can use this feature and an attacker is unable to access any "domain user" credentials because these are not allowed when Restricted Admin mode is used.

Restricted Admin mode must be explicitly enabled on the destination systems which must be running Windows 7 or Windows Server 2008 R2 that have been patched with the Microsoft Security Advisory 2871997 Update which improves credentials protection and management. Supported editions of Windows 8.1, Windows Server 2012 R2, and Windows RT 8.1 and newer, already have the additional protection for the Local Security Authority (LSA) built-in.

> *MORE INFO* **RESTRICTED ADMIN MODE SOFTWARE UPDATE**
>
> For more information relating to the Microsoft Security Advisory 2871997 update that improves credentials protection and management allows Windows 7 or Windows Server 2008 R2 to be configured to use Restricted Admin mode visit this reference: *https://support. microsoft.com/en-gb/help/2871997/microsoft-security-advisory-update-to-improve-credentials-protection-a.*

To enable the Restricted Admin mode you should configure the remote computer using the following steps:

1. Open Registry Editor by running regedit from the Search box.
2. Accept the UAC if prompted.
3. In Registry Editor, create a new registry key as follows:
4. HKEY_LOCAL_MACHINE\System\CurrentControlSet\Control\Lsa
5. Name: DisableRestrictedAdmin
6. Type: REG_DWORD
7. Value: 0
8. Using a value of 0 will enable Restricted Admin mode. Once enabled, the destination system will accept incoming Restricted Admin-enabled connections.
9. Close the Registry Editor.

The setting takes effect immediately and no reboot is required.

To initiate a new connection using Remote Desktop in Restricted Admin mode, run the following command:

```
Mstsc.exe /RestrictedAdmin
```

In Windows 10 version 1703, you can configure Restricted Admin mode using the GPO shown in Figure 7-8. To turn on Restricted Admin mode on the client machine set the option to Require Restricted Admin.

EXAM TIP

You should ensure you are familiar with the new Remote Credential Guard and Restricted Admin mode as these offer enhanced protection for remote connections using the well-known and widely used Remote Desktop protocol.

MORE INFO   WINDOWS DEFENDER REMOTE CREDENTIAL GUARD AND RESTRICTED ADMIN MODE

You can learn more about how to protect Remote Desktop with Windows Defender Remote Credential Guard and restricted admin mode at: *https://docs.microsoft.com/windows/access-protection/remote-credential-guard*.

Troubleshooting Remote Desktop Connections

Remote Desktop is a powerful tool for administrators, which enables them to manage PCs and servers within the enterprise. Some common problems encountered when trying to connect to a remote PC using Remote Desktop, and their resolution, are listed in Table 7-2.

TABLE 7-2 Troubleshooting Remote Desktop Connections

Problem	Possible resolution
The remote PC can't be found	■ Make sure you have the correct PC name ■ Try using the IP address of the remote PC
There's a problem with the network	■ Ensure that the router is turned on (home networks only) ■ Make sure that the Ethernet cable is plugged into your network adapter (wired networks only) ■ See that the wireless switch on the PC is turned on (devices using wireless networks only) ■ Make sure your network adapter is functional
The Remote Desktop port might be blocked by a firewall	■ Contact your system administrator to check that Remote Desktop is not blocked ■ Allow the Remote Desktop application through Windows Firewall ■ Make sure the port for Remote Desktop (usually 3389) is open
Remote connections might not be set up on the remote PC	■ In the System Properties dialog box, under Remote Desktop, select the Allow Remote Connections To This Computer button
The remote PC might only enable PCs that have Network Level Authentication set up to connect	■ Upgrade to Windows 7, Windows 8 or Windows 8.1, or Windows 10, which support Network Level Authentication
The remote PC might be turned off	■ You can't connect to a PC that's turned off, asleep, or hibernating ■ Turn on the remote PC

Remote Desktop Connection Zoom support

Many devices with very high dots per inch (DPI) resolutions are now available. When using a device, such as a Surface Pro, to connect to older versions of Windows, such as Windows 7 and Windows Server 2008, the display content might appear very small and hard to read. Windows 8.1 enabled support for host-side dynamic display scaling, but this is not available for older versions of Windows. In Windows 10, a new feature has been introduced to enable the user to zoom their session display on the client.

The new Zoom option can be found in the system menu in the Remote Desktop Connection session window, as shown in Figure 7-9.

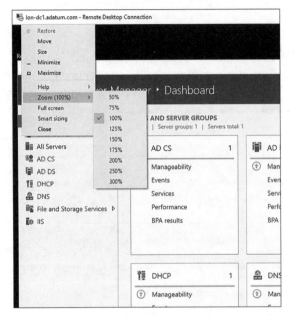

FIGURE 7-9 Using Zoom in Windows 10 Remote Desktop Connection

With the session zoomed in, the screen text and icons become larger, and are more readable and usable for sessions with older versions of Windows.

> **NOTE REMOTE DESKTOP SCALING**
>
> Remote Desktop scaling will not necessarily render the display as clear and crisp as would happen in the case of local scaling.

Remote Desktop Connection pen support

The Remote Desktop Connection within Windows 10 supports pen remoting when connecting from a Windows 10 client to a host system that is running Windows 10 or Windows Server 2016. There was some limited pen support in a Remote Desktop session in Windows 8.1, but that has been enhanced to provide a near-local experience, without any configuration. If the local device supports pen and it is running Windows 10, the user can write or draw in the Remote Desktop session.

This feature is useful for administrators using touch-enabled devices, such as the Surface Book, to connect to a remote application server using their tablet.

Remote Desktop Connection Manager

Administrators who want to manage multiple remote desktop connections can download Remote Desktop Connection Manager (RDCMan). This tool is useful for managing server labs or large server farms, such as within a datacenter. It is similar to the Remote Desktops Microsoft management console (MMC) snap-in found on Windows Server, but more flexible. The current version enables many feature improvements, including virtual machine connect-to-console support, smart grouping of remote machines, support for credential encryption with certificates, and connectivity to virtual machines within Microsoft Azure.

> **MORE INFO** **REMOTE DESKTOP CONNECTION MANAGER 2.7**
>
> You can download the Remote Desktop Connection Manager 2.7 at: *http://www.microsoft.com/download/details.aspx?id=44989*.

Skill 7.2: Configure mobility options

Working from home, or away from the traditional office environment, is not suitable for all corporations or employees. Where feasible, mobile working is very popular, and as technology continues to improve, the trend is likely to grow. Windows 10 embraces mobility and offers several enhancements that increase productivity and collaboration, with Anywhere Access to business tools and information.

You need to understand the options available to enable and support mobility for users, so that they can be productive, working either at the office or away from the office.

This section covers how to:

- Configure offline file policies
- Configure power policies
- Configure Windows To Go
- Configure sync options
- Configure WiFi Direct

Configure offline file policies

When a user is travelling away from the office, there are often occasions when network availability is insufficient for them to be able to connect their device to the corporate network. Until they can re-establish a VPN connection, they are able to use a feature called Offline Files, which will enable them to continue to access corporate data, which is securely cached on their device, and enable this data to be automatically re-synced to the corporate network once they are able to reconnect.

You need to understand how to enable the feature and create policies to manage Offline Files in an enterprise.

Data that is made available over the network has the ability to be shared. A user might not be able to access the Offline Files feature in the following situations:

- An administrator has prevented offline copies on the folder or files.
- The user might not have NTFS permissions to access the files.

Users can choose which shared folders they want to make available offline. They could choose to make many folders available, but in practice, this is not recommended because the sync process will take longer if thousands of files and folders need to be synced each time the user leaves and rejoins the corporate network.

When a user is connected to the network, they can work with online files accessed directly from the network server. If they enable Offline Files, Windows 10 will cache a local copy of the files onto the local device. These files will be kept in sync with the network versions, and if the user must work offline, the Offline Files feature will automatically be used whenever the user needs to work with a networked file that they have previously made available offline.

Windows will also monitor the network for latency and disconnection, and will automatically switch to using the cached files, so that the user does not lose productivity.

> **NOTE** **CLIENT-SIDE CACHE**
>
> When using Offline Files, Windows creates a local copy of the file in the %windir%\CSC directory, which is a hidden folder, and is only accessible by the system.

Windows 10 will automatically switch to Offline Mode when one of the following situations occurs:

- The files are no longer available on the network, for example, the server is unavailable due to a server malfunction, or the server is turned off.
- The files are no longer available on the network due to a network outage, or the user has disconnected his device from the network.
- The files are no longer available on the network due to a network outage, such as the WiFi or VPN connection being lost.
- The network connection speed is slower than the minimum bandwidth specified in Group Policy.

- Always Offline Mode has been configured in Group Policy.

Two of the recent policies settings relating to slow or metered networks are Enable Always Offline Mode and Enable File Synchronization On Costed Networks. Offline Files has been supported by Windows for many years, and for the exam, you need to review the most recent Offline Files Group Policy settings, including the following:

- Configure Slow-link Mode
- Configure Slow-link Speed
- Synchronize All Offline Files Before Logging Off
- Synchronize All Offline Files When Logging On
- Enable Transparent Caching
- Enable File Synchronization On Costed Networks

> *NOTE* **WINDOWS 10 GUI CHANGES**
>
> Changes to Offline Files in the Windows 10 GUI are very minor, for example, the text shown in the Network tab within Control Panel Offline Files has been slightly modified.

There are several new features available to enterprises using Windows Server 2012 and Windows 8 or later. By configuring Group Policy, administrators can enable additional features not found within the GUI, which support more efficient use of Offline Files, as follows:

- **Always Offline Mode**   Provides faster access to cached files and uses less bandwidth by making users work offline even when they are connected through a high-speed network connection. By configuring Group Policy to enable the Configure Slow-Link Mode setting, the latency to 1 (millisecond) causes supported client devices to use the Always Offline Mode.

- **Background file synchronization on costed networks**   Will enable Offline Files to be synchronized in the background, even over costed networks. You need to disable or not configure this setting, so that Windows will track roaming and bandwidth usage limits while the device is using a metered connection. When the client is near or over their usage allowance, Windows will disable background synchronization to prevent users from incurring excessive usage charges.

To enable the Always Offline Mode, you should carry out the following steps:

1. Open Group Policy Management.
2. In the console tree, navigate to Computer Configuration\Policies\Administrative Templates\Network\Offline Files.
3. Double-click Configure Slow-Link Mode.
4. Click Enabled.
5. In the Options box, next to UNC Paths, click Show.

6. In the Value Name box, specify the file share for which you want to enable Always Offline Mode, or to enable Always Offline Mode on all file shares, type *****.

7. In the Value box, type **Latency=1** to set the latency threshold to one millisecond, as shown in Figure 7-10.

8. Click OK twice.

FIGURE 7-10 Configuring Group Policy to enable Always Offline Mode

To disable background file synchronization of Offline Files on metered networks, you should carry out the following steps:

1. Open Group Policy Management.

2. In the console tree, navigate to Computer Configuration\Policies\Administrative Templates\ Network\Offline Files.

3. Double-click Enable File Synchronization On Costed Networks.

4. Click Disabled.

5. Click OK.

You need to also review the following additional enterprise features that can be configured and deployed using Group Policy settings that relate to Offline Files, Folder Redirection, and Roaming User Profiles:

- Deploy Folder Redirection With Offline Files
- Deploy Roaming User Profiles
- Deploy Primary Computers For Folder Redirection And Roaming User Profiles

Configure power policies

Windows 10 continues to enable users and administrators to fine-tune the power settings for individual elements on Windows devices. For mobile users, battery consumption and power conservation can be a critical issue when users are away from the office, without the device charger.

On a mobile device, the battery percentage remaining will be displayed in the notification area, as shown in Figure 7-11, with an option to modify the device Power & Sleep Settings, and options to change the screen brightness.

FIGURE 7-11 Power tile in the notification area

Clicking on the Power & Sleep Settings option will launch the Settings page, as shown in Figure 7-12, which shows the default settings applied to the device.

FIGURE 7-12 Power & Sleep options

NOTE REVIEW POWER OPTIONS ON A MOBILE DEVICE

When preparing for the exam, you should try to use or borrow a laptop to review the power settings and options available within Windows 10 as many options, including the screen brightness, battery life, sleep, or WiFi options are not available when using a desktop or virtual machine.

You define power settings in addition to the user-centric options. You can access Power Options by clicking the Additional Power Settings link on the Power & Sleep settings page, or by using the Power Options Control Panel.

Users can configure many options and choose, modify, or save a power plan, and make amendments to key power-related activities, including:

- Choose what the power button does.
- Choose what closing the lid does.
- Create a power plan.
- Change when the computer sleeps.

Administrators can configure additional advanced power-plan settings, and both types of users can restore plans back to their default settings.

On mobile devices, Windows 10 also includes a useful Windows Mobility Center, which can be used to review mobility settings, all in one location. Depending upon your system, some or all of the following settings might be available on your mobile device:

- **Brightness**   Enables you to temporarily adjust the brightness of your display.
- **Volume**   Enables you to adjust the speaker volume of your device, or select the Mute check box.
- **Battery Status**   Lets you view how much charge is remaining on your battery.
- **Screen Orientation**   Lets you change the orientation of your device screen from portrait to landscape, or vice versa.
- **External Display**   Enables connection to an additional monitor to your device.
- **Sync Center**   Enables you to sync with external data sources, such as Offline Files.
- **Presentation Settings**   Lets you turn on presentation settings during a presentation, and temporarily disable the following:
    - Disables popups and notifications area popups (such as from Outlook)
    - Prevents Windows from going into sleep mode
    - Prevents Windows from turning the screen off

Mobility Center is only available on mobile devices, such as laptops and tablets.

Using Group Policy to configure power policies

In addition to the power options in the GUI interface, administrators can configure the same options by using Group Policy.

The Power Management GPOs are located in the following container:

```
Computer Configuration\Policies\Administrative Templates\System\Power Management
```

There are seven nodes under Power Management: Button Settings, Energy Saver Settings, Hard Disk Settings, Notification Settings, Power Throttling Settings, Sleep Settings, and Video And Display Settings. Each has several GPOs that you need to explore to ensure that you appreciate the various aspects of the power options that can be configured using Group Policy. Although most of the settings are duplications of those found within the Control Panel, the following Sleep Settings are an example of power settings that are not available within the Control Panel:

- Specify The System Sleep Timeout (Plugged In)
- Specify The System Sleep Timeout (On Battery)
- Require A Password When The Computer Wakes (Plugged In)
- Require A Password When The Computer Wakes (On Battery)
- Allow Standby States (S1-S3) When Sleeping (Plugged In)
- Allow Standby States (S1-S3) When Sleeping (On Battery)

Using powercfg.exe

If you have configured the power options for your device, you can save the entire power-management plan as a custom plan to a file. To do this, you need to use the Powercfg.exe command-line tool, which can export and import settings from one computer, which you can then deploy to other devices using the command line or using Group Policy.

Use the Powercfg.exe -list command in a command prompt to get a list of the power plans that are currently available on your device. On a Windows 10 PC, you should see the default plan(s) and any custom plans that you have created, as shown in Figure 7-13.

To export a power plan, make a note of the GUID value, which uniquely identifies the power plan. To export the policy, type **powercfg.exe -export power.pow GUID** (where the GUID value is the GUID that you noted previously). Figure 7-13 shows the completed listing, export, and verification that the .pow file has been created.

To import a custom power plan, type **powercfg.exe /import c:\temp\power.pow**, where c:\temp\power.pow represents the path and file name.

> **NOTE COMMAND PROMPT: COPY AND PASTE**
>
> You can use shortcut keys CTRL-C (Copy) and CTRL-V (Paste) to copy and paste within a Windows 10 command prompt.

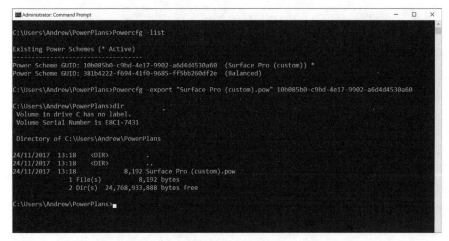

FIGURE 7-13 Using Powercfg.exe at an administrative command prompt

> **NOTE EXPORT REQUIRES ELEVATED PRIVILEGES**
>
> To view the power plans, you can use a normal command prompt, but to import or export a power plan, you need to use an administrative command prompt.

In Figure 7-14, the Power Management Group Policy settings are visible. In the right pane, you can see the highlighted options, which can be used to apply a custom power plan. These are Specify A Custom Active Power Plan and Select An Active Power Plan. You need to ensure that the power plan has been first deployed, using Powercfg.exe, to the device using powercfg. exe /import c:\scheme.pow.

FIGURE 7-14 Power Management Group Policy settings

There are a number of specialist powercfg commands, which are more relevant to mobile devices and can be used to troubleshoot battery issues, such as abnormal battery drain, hibernation behavior, or to determine the expected life of the device battery. You need to review all of these commands for the exam, but if you have a battery-powered device, such as a Surface, it is worthwhile viewing the output of some of the commands shown in Table 7-3.

TABLE 7-3 Troubleshooting energy issues with powercfg.exe

Command	Description
powercfg /energy	Generate an Energy Report
powercfg /a	Identify the available sleep and standby states that your device supports
powercfg -devicequery wake armed	Identify what last caused your device to wake from sleep or hibernation
powercfg /batteryreport	Generate a Battery Report
powercfg.exe /hibernate on	Make hibernation available
powercfg.exe /hibernate off	Makes hibernation unavailable
powercfg /sleepstudy	Generate a Connected Standby Sleep Study; by default, it will generate a report for the last 3 days, but this can be extended up to 28 days by using the / duration 28 argument.

The powercfg /batteryreport is particularly useful for viewing the state of the battery, on a mobile device. The report shows power cycles and the battery performance and degradation over its lifetime.

Configure Windows To Go

Computing continues to evolve, and devices are getting smaller and smaller and more portable, while at the same time packing more features and more power.

Windows To Go offers users a paradigm shift in thinking about a PC. Instead of installing, configuring, and "owning" the PC that they use, the user of a Windows To Go workspace simply inserts a special USB drive into the host PC and boots directly to it. All Windows 10 operations are carried out natively on the USB drive, and essentially, the workspace acts like a parasite or guest using the hosts' hardware except for the hard drive, which is disabled.

You need to regard Windows To Go as a specialist option to enable Windows 10 to be deployed in alternative workplace scenarios. Example scenarios could include travelling ultra-light without a laptop or tablet, or where there are a lot of employees, such as airline staff who use the same device, or staff on short contracts, which would make the provision of hardware uneconomical.

Windows To Go has the following features as well as differences when compared to a typical installation of Windows:

- **Hardware requirements** A Windows To Go workspace should only be used on PCs that meet the Windows 7 or later hardware requirements.

- **Licensing restrictions** Windows To Go is only available in the Enterprise and Education editions of Windows 10.

- **Internal disks are offline** Internal hard disks on the host computer are offline by default.

- **Trusted Platform Module (TPM) is not used** If BitLocker Drive Encryption is used to encrypt a Windows To Go drive, it cannot use the TPM since the TPM is tied to a specific computer, and not to the Windows To Go drive.

- **Hibernate is disabled by default** Hibernation is disabled by default to prevent possible corruption of the Windows To Go drive if it is moved to another device while using hibernation. Hibernation can be re-enabled in Group Policy. Windows To Go supports all other power states.

- **Windows Recovery Environment is not available** To reduce size on the drive, the RE is not available.

- **Refreshing or resetting a Windows To Go workspace is not supported** The feature is disabled; if necessary you should re-image it with a fresh image.

- **Upgrading a Windows To Go workspace is not supported**   Older Windows 8 or Windows 8.1 Windows To Go workspaces cannot be upgraded to Windows 10 workspaces.
- **Architecture and firmware**   The Windows To Go drive must be compatible with the processor architecture and firmware type. For example, 32-bit versions of Windows To Go will not work on 64-bit computers. Windows To Go is not supported on the ARM architecture, and Windows RT is not supported.

Roaming with Windows To Go

Windows To Go drives can be booted on multiple computers. When a Windows To Go workspace is booted on a new host computer, it will detect all hardware on the computer and install any needed drivers. If the Windows To Go workspace returns to the same host computer again, it will load the correct set of drivers automatically.

Some applications do not support roaming as they bind to the computer hardware, which can cause difficulties if the workspace is being used on multiple host computers.

> **MORE INFO WINDOWS TO GO FREQUENTLY ASKED QUESTIONS**
>
> The following article provides an overview about the Windows To Go feature: *https://docs.microsoft.com/windows/deployment/planning/windows-to-go-overview.*

Hardware considerations for Windows To Go

Certified Windows To Go devices have been specially optimized to meet the necessary requirements for booting and running a full version of Windows 10 from a USB drive.

Windows To Go drives are optimized as follows:

- Built for high random read/write speeds
- Support the thousands of random access I/O operations per second
- Tuned to ensure they boot and run on hardware certified for use with Windows 7 and later
- Built to last under normal usage, despite the high performance requirements

> **NOTE HOST USB 2.0 PORTS**
>
> Windows To Go is supported on both USB 2.0 and USB 3.0 ports on PCs certified for Windows 7 or later. A Windows To Go drive, running on a USB 3.0 port, will operate considerably faster on USB 3 than on USB 2.0.

Certified Windows To Go drives

The drives listed in Table 7-4 are currently certified Windows To Go drives.

TABLE 7-4 Certified Windows To Go drives

Windows To Go drive	Vendor Website
IronKey Workspace W500	http://www.ironkey.com/windows-to-go-drives/ironkey-workspace-w500.html
IronKey Workspace W700	http://www.ironkey.com/windows-to-go-drives/ironkey-workspace-w700.html
IronKey Workspace W300	http://www.ironkey.com/windows-to-go-drives/ironkey-workspace-w300.html
Kingston DataTraveler Workspace for Windows To Go	http://www.kingston.com/wtg
Spyrus Portable Workplace	http://www.spyruswtg.com
Spyrus Secure Portable Workplace	http://www.spyruswtg.com
Spyrus Worksafe	http://www.spyruswtg.com
Super Talent Express RC4 for Windows To Go	http://www.supertalent.com/wtg
Super Talent Express RC8 for Windows To Go	http://www.supertalent.com/wtg
Western Digital My Passport Enterprise	http://www.wd.com/wtg

NOTE **CERTIFIED DRIVES**

Using a Windows To Go USB drive that has not been certified is not supported.

Administrators can provision Windows To Go drives using the Windows To Go Workspace Wizard or PowerShell scripts to target several drives and scale out the deployment for a large number of Windows To Go drives. A USB duplicator can be used to rapidly duplicate Windows To Go drives after it has been provisioned. Do not enable BitLocker Drive Encryption on Windows To Go drives if you are planning to use a USB duplicator because drives protected with BitLocker will use the same encryption key if duplicated.

Creating a workspace with the Create A Windows To Go Workspace Wizard

To create a Windows To Go workspace on a certified USB drive, use the Windows To Go Workspace Wizard using these steps:

1. Launch the Windows To Go Workspace Wizard by typing Windows To Go in the Search bar.

2. Insert the certified Windows To Go 3.0 USB drive into an available USB 3.0 port.

3. You'll be asked to Choose The Drive That You Want To Use. Select the certified Windows To Go workspace, and click Next.

4. Choose a Windows 10 image. Select the image, or select Add Search Location, and browse to a location that contains the required Windows 10 Enterprise .wim image file (such as install.wim).

5. Click Next.

6. Check the box next to Set A BitLocker Password (Optional), or click Skip.

7. The Create A Windows To Go Workspace Wizard will now apply the Windows image to the drive, as shown in Figure 7-15.

Once completed, the wizard will optionally configure the host PC to boot to the new Windows To Go workspace.

FIGURE 7-15 Applying the Windows To Go image

Creating a workspace with Windows PowerShell

PowerShell cmdlets can perform the same function as the Create A Windows To Go Workspace Wizard. Because there is no visual confirmation as in the wizard, you need to ensure that only the USB drive you want to provision as a Windows To Go Workspace is connected to the provisioning PC.

The PowerShell script should be run in an elevated Windows PowerShell prompt. The script required to configure the Windows To Go Workspace is quite long, and includes the following stages:

1. Partition a master boot record (MBR) disk with a FAT32 system partition and an NTFS-formatted operating system partition.

2. Apply the Windows 10 .wim file that contains a sysprepped generalized image using the Deployment Image Servicing and Management (DISM) command-line tool.

3. Use the Bcdboot.exe command-line tool to move the necessary boot parts to the system partition on the disk.

4. Apply the new SAN policy setting OFFLINE_INTERNAL - "4" to prevent Windows 10 from automatically bringing online any internally connected disk.

5. Create and deploy an answer file (unattend.xml) that disables the use of Windows Recovery Environment with Windows To Go.

There isn't enough space in this book to include the scripts required, but you can view a sample PowerShell script at: *https://docs.microsoft.com/windows/deployment/deploy-windows-to-go*.

Configure sync options

The number of devices that users own has risen significantly over the last few years. It is typical for a user to have personal equipment at home, and also be provided with devices, such as a smartphone and a computer, by their employer. A few users have multiple tablets, laptops, and desktop PCs. With the rising trend of Bring Your Own Device (BYOD), whereby users bring their own devices to the workplace, users can find it difficult to manage their identity and consistency across multiple devices, and still remain productive on each.

Windows 10 builds on the sync settings that were introduced with Windows 8, and helps you with synchronization between your devices whether those are at home or at the workplace. You can sync settings, such as your desktop theme, browser settings, and passwords, so that they will appear on all your Windows 10 devices. This synchronization is not automatic; unless you sign in with a Microsoft account and turn on the syncing for each device.

Even if you sign in with a Microsoft account, you can disable syncing, or review each of the available options and enable or prevent them one by one.

In Windows 10, the sync settings are found in the Sync Your Settings section under the Accounts page in Settings. The default settings are that sync is turned on, as shown in Figure 7-16.

FIGURE 7-16 Syncing your settings to other devices

There are seven choices for the user to configure relating to syncing settings between your devices:

- **Sync Settings**   If this is turned off, no changes are made to any of the settings on your other devices when you sign in with your Microsoft account.
- **Theme**   This lets you sync your color and background choices. Turning this setting off enables each device to retain its own theme.
- **Internet Explorer Settings**   This lets you sync Internet Explorer browser settings.
- **Passwords**   Any passwords saved on your Windows 10 device will be securely synced to the other devices that you sign in to with your Microsoft account.
- **Language Preferences**   This is useful if you require multilingual support.
- **Ease Of Access**   Any accessibility options that are applied to one machine will sync to all your Windows 10 devices.
- **Other Windows Settings**   Syncs other settings and preferences, such as taskbar settings and position, search preferences, mouse pointer speed, printer preference settings, File Explorer Quick Access settings, and many more.

Deleting your personal settings from the cloud

You have seen that when you use a Microsoft account to sign in to Windows 10, the settings and app data that you choose to sync are saved in your Microsoft account, or more specifically, they are stored in your secure OneDrive cloud.

If you stop synchronizing your settings between your devices, the data will not be removed from OneDrive; you need to delete the PC settings from OneDrive. To stop synchronizing your settings and delete the settings from OneDrive, carry out the following steps:

1. Sign in to your device with your Microsoft account.
2. Open Settings, click Accounts, and then click Sync Your Settings.
3. Set the Sync Settings toggle to Off.
4. Repeat this action on all devices that use the same Microsoft account.
5. If you have a Windows 8.1 phone, navigate to Settings, then tap Sync My Settings, and click Turn Off Synchronization For All Settings.
6. To delete your settings from OneDrive, you need to launch OneDrive.com.
7. Click the Settings/Options gear in the top right corner of the screen.
8. Select Device Backups.
9. For all devices, click Delete.

> *NOTE* **MULTIPLE ACCOUNTS**
>
> If you use associated multiple devices with your Microsoft account, you need to perform the removal task for each device.

Sync Center and configuring sync options

Previous versions of Windows included options to create a sync partnership between Windows and mobile phones, portable music players, or other mobile devices, but the most common use for Sync Center is to sync with Offline Files. If you have enabled Offline Files, as explored earlier in this chapter, Windows will display a sync partnership in Control Panel Sync Center, as shown in Figure 7-17.

FIGURE 7-17 Windows Sync Center

When working with Offline Files, you can use Sync Center to perform tasks. For the exam, you need to review all options, and pay particular attention to the Manage Offline Files option, which opens a dialog box that enables you to configure settings, including:

- Disable Offline Files.
- Open Sync Center.
- View Your Offline Files.
- Check Disk Usage For Your Offline Files.
- Change Disk Usage Limits For Your Offline Files.
- Delete Temporary Files.
- Encrypt Or Unencrypt Your Offline Files.
- Set The Threshold, in minutes, of how often Windows checks the speed of your network connection. By default, this is configured as five minutes.

If you right-click the Offline Files icon in the center of the Sync Center screen, as shown in Figure 7-17, you can select Schedule For Offline Files. This will launch the Offline Files Synchronization Schedule Wizard.

In the Offline Files Synchronization Schedule Wizard, you can modify the default schedule for when you want Windows to synchronize your offline files. If you choose synchronization at a scheduled time, you can set a start date, time, and whether the synchronization should repeat and at what frequency, such as hourly, weekly, or other.

You can choose the events or actions that will automatically synchronize Offline Files, such as when:

- You log on to your computer
- Your computer is idle
- You lock Windows
- You unlock Windows

You can also choose additional scheduling options by clicking the More Options button, as shown in Figure 7-18.

FIGURE 7-18 More synchronization scheduling options

When working with offline files, you need to take care that they are carefully managed in order to reduce the likelihood of sync conflicts. When Windows has two copies of the same file stored in separate places and a conflict occurs, the sync will not succeed unless you decide which of the files to keep. No conflict would normally occur when you are working away from the office and syncing the newer files from your device back to the network location.

Conflicts arise when multiple users are accessing the same files and folders. For example, if you had worked on a file remotely and so had another user, Windows will ask you how to address the conflict. If you accept the option to keep the latest version, you could potentially lose any amendments to your work, if this was not previously saved to the networked version.

Depending upon the number of conflicts that you encounter, it is preferable to use the Offline Files feature on files that are not shared with other users.

Use Work Folders

Work Folders is the enterprise feature which enables administrators to create a special folder called a sync share. It requires Windows Server 2012 R2 or Windows Server 2016, and is available to Windows 8.1 and Windows 10 users. Sync shares have characteristics similar to that of Offline Folders. Multiple devices can connect to the same sync share, but each user has their own single connection. Furthermore, sync shares can be accessed by non-domain joined computers that are owned or used by domain users, such as a home device or BYOD.

As this is an enterprise feature, you only need to understand how the basics of Work Folders are used and the functionality they provide.

Work Folders are available on Windows 7 and newer versions of Windows, and via an app on an Apple iPad or Android device. The functionality is as shown in Table 7-5.

TABLE 7-5 Work Folders functionality

Functionality	Availability	Description
Work Folders integration with Windows	Windows 10 Windows 8.1 Windows RT 8.1 Windows 7 (download required)	Work Folders item in Control Panel Work Folders integrated into File Explorer to enable access to files stored in Work Folders Work Folders sync engine
Work Folders app for devices	Apple iPad (iOS 10.2 and later) Android 4.4 KitKat and later	A Work Folders app that enables access to files in Work Folders

Once the feature has been installed and configured on a Windows Server 2012 R2 or Windows Server 2016 domain computer, the user needs to launch Manage Work Folders within Control Panel and follow the Set Up Work Folders Wizard to connect to the corporate sync share.

There are three methods by which a device can be configured to use Work Folders:

- **Auto Discovery** Users only need to enter their corporate email address, and Work Folders will auto discover the correct path to the sync share using the DNS entry, which will look similar to *workfolders.contoso.com*.

- **Custom URL** This is provided by an administrator. Work Folders will use the uniform resource identifier (URL), which will be similar to *workfolders.contoso.com*.

- **Group Policy** This method can be deployed to devices that are part of the domain in which you want to use Work Folders. You can add Custom URL to the Specify Work Folders Group Policy Object (GPO), which is found at User Configuration\Policies\ Administrative Templates\Windows Components\Work Folders. You need to provide a Work Folder URL, such as *https://workfolders.contoso.com/sync/1.0,* in the GPO, as shown in Figure 7-19. If the setting to force automatic setup is checked, users are not asked where they want to store the Work Folders data on the local device, instead this is stored in the %USERPROFILE%\WorkFolders location.

FIGURE 7-19 Configuring Work Folders using Group Policy

You need to know the following limitations and requirements about Work Folders, although you are not expected to have configured the infrastructure on Windows Server 2012 R2 or Windows Server 2016:

- Windows Server 2012 R2 or Windows Server 2016 are required to host sync shares.
- NTFS file system is required to store user files.
- Server certificates from a trusted certification authority (CA), such as a public CA, are required for each Work Folders file server host. A server needs to be accessible from the Internet, such as a network gateway.
- A registered domain name resolvable from users over the Internet.
- Ability to create a public DNS Host(A) record called workfolders.
- The max size for individual files is 10 GB.
- Work Folders uses the: %USERPROFILE%\Work Folders location by default.
- PCs and devices must be running one of the operating systems shown in Table 7-5.

Configure WiFi Direct

WiFi Direct is a new standard developed with the WiFi Alliance, is fully supported by Windows 10, and enables WiFi Direct devices to connect seamlessly to one another. This can be achieved using Miracast over Infrastructure, which uses Ethernet if a network access point or secure ad-hoc WiFi network is available, or over a private ad-hoc wireless network as and when required.

WiFi Direct enables you to interact with other hardware, for example, print to a wireless printer or send your PowerPoint presentation to an external display.

Devices that are using WiFi Direct include mobile phones, cameras, printers, TVs, PCs, and gaming devices, such as Xbox One.

WiFi Direct is very similar to Bluetooth, but only 10x faster (WiFi Direct transfers data at up to 250 Mbps, whereas Bluetooth 4.0 transfers data at up to 25 Mbps).

As the technology continues to mature, Microsoft has upgraded and enhanced the application program interface (API) support with Windows 10 for developers to use when writing their software. Original equipment manufacturer (OEM) vendors are gradually incorporating WiFi Direct into their devices, such as printers using WiFi Direct. Unlike Bluetooth, only one device needs to support WiFi Direct, though they will still pair in much the same way as Bluetooth. For example, Miracast enables a Windows device to wirelessly display on to a projected screen, such as a TV or projector. Ideal for enabling screens that do not have built-in support for WiFi Direct, Miracast uses a High-Definition Multimedia Interface (HDMI) adapter, which plugs into the remote screen. Windows 10 can wirelessly connect to the Miracast adapter.

To use the WiFi Direct technology, a user will turn on or enable the WiFi Direct device, such as a Miracast adapter or printer, and Windows 10 will locate the device wirelessly and connect. Once connected, application files that are required for the user interface, such as display or printer dialog screens, are received directly from the WiFi Direct device.

Some characteristics of WiFi Direct are listed below:

- **Distance between devices (ad hoc WiFi)**   Compared to Bluetooth, which creates a Personal Area Network of just a few feet, WiFi Alliance states that WiFi Direct devices can reach each other over a maximum distance of up to 656 feet.

- **Security**   WiFi Direct uses either WPA2-PSK or WPA2-Enterprise security, which uses AES 256-bit encryption with a key-based encryption and authentication method.

- **Speed**   WiFi Direct claims device-to-device transfer speeds of up to 250Mbps.

- **Services**   WiFi Direct Send, WiFi Direct Print, WiFi Direct for DLNA, Miracast, and Miracast over Infrastructure are the five services that currently utilize the WiFi Direct standard.

The following steps provide an example of how to connect to a WiFi Direct TV screen:

1. Turn on the TV and select Screen Mirroring, Miracast, or other wireless input source on your TV.
2. On your Windows 10 device, open Settings and click Devices.
3. Select Bluetooth and other Devices.
4. Click Add Bluetooth or other Device, and you should see a list of the following types of devices that Windows 10 can search for:
   A. Bluetooth
   B. Wireless display or dock
   C. Everything else

After selecting Wireless display or dock, Windows 10 should be able to locate your TV, as shown in Figure 7-20.

5. To project your screen, open the Action Center and click the Connect tile.

6. Select the WiFi Direct device from the list of wireless display and audio devices.

7. Windows will now establish the connection and your screen should now be mirrored.

FIGURE 7-20 Connecting to an external display

MORE INFO **WIFI ALLIANCE**

The WiFi Alliance is the worldwide authority that maintains the WiFi standard. More information can be found at *http://www.wi-fi.org/*.

Thought experiments

In these thought experiments, demonstrate your skills and knowledge of the topics covered in this chapter. You can find the answers to these thought experiments in the next section.

Scenario 1

Your CEO has asked you to research possible solutions for providing members of the sales team with access to company files, which can be synced to their devices over the Internet. The technology deployed should be available when you are at home or visiting clients. Your infrastructure includes Windows Server 2016.

Answer the following questions regarding your research:

1. What possible technologies can you use to provide access to company files over the Internet?

2. The Sales Manager uses an Apple iPad. Which solution would enable iPad to access and sync the files?

3. Your sales team needs to access and be able to present a PowerPoint slideshow. The slideshow is updated each day by the marketing team. Which solution would enable access to the updated file?

Scenario 2

You have been asked to help provide assistance to a helpdesk operator who is encountering some difficulties when connecting to devices using Remote Desktop Connection. You have several devices, including the following:

- Desktop PC running Windows Vista Business edition at your home office
- Windows 7 laptop running Home edition at your home office
- Windows 10 Surface Book running Enterprise edition provided by your employer
- Twenty five Windows 2016 Servers located in a private data center

Answer the following questions about Remote Desktop Connection:

1. You try to connect to your home devices from your workplace using Remote Desktop. You can successfully connect to the desktop PC, but you're unable to make a connection to your laptop. You need to access the laptop using Remote Desktop. What can you do?

2. When you connect to the desktop PC, using your Surface Book, the screen size is very small. What can you do?

3. You find it laborious to connect to the individual servers at the datacenter using the RDP client, one at a time. What can you suggest?

Thought experiment answers

This section provides the solutions for the tasks included in the thought experiments.

Scenario 1

1. Answers vary and possible solutions include Work Folders, OneDrive, OneDrive for Business and Offline Files. While Remote Desktop, , and VPNs can be used, they are not valid answers because they are not sync technologies.

2. Remote Desktop, Work Folders, OneDrive, and OneDrive for Business enable file access by an Apple iPad, but of these options, only Work Folders represents a solution that sync the files.

3. Work Folders is a sync technology, enabling access to the updated file.

Scenario 2

1. Answers vary, but because you're having some success, it is likely that your home router is correctly configured to enable port forwarding to the internal network. Even if there are other issues found with the configuration, the home laptop is running an edition of Windows that does not support Remote Desktop connection. The laptop needs to be upgraded to either Windows 10 Pro or Windows 10 Enterprise version.

2. Because the Surface Book offers very high DPI resolutions, use the Scaling feature within the Remote Desktop Connection application.

3. You need to download and install the Remote Desktop Connection Manager in order to be able to quickly and seamlessly change from one server in the data center to another.

Chapter summary

- Windows 10 includes remote access capabilities that enable users to connect to a remote network using dial-up or VPN connections.

- Windows 10 supports four commonly used VPN protocols. These are Point-to-Point Tunneling Protocol (PPTP), Layer 2 Tunneling Protocol (L2TP), Secure Socket Tunneling Protocol (SSTP), and Internet Key Exchange, Version 2 (IKEv2).

- Windows 10 uses common authentication protocols including EAP-MS-CHAPv2, PAP, CHAP and MS-CHAP v2.

- VPN Reconnect is a feature supported when using IKEv2, which enables VPN connections to be automatically re-established if they are broken. VPN Reconnect uses the IKEv2 tunneling protocol with the MOBIKE extension.

- Always On, App-triggered VPN, and LockDown VPN profiles are new VPN features in Windows 10 that enable administrators to implement enterprise-grade VPN requirements.

- Broadband tethering enables Windows 10 to connect devices to ad-hoc wireless networks.

- WiFi Services enables access to password-protected networks and hotspots shared through crowdsourcing.

- Windows Defender Remote Credential Guard allows administrators to protect credentials that are typically used over a Remote Desktop connection.

- Remote Desktop improves the support for devices with pens, and also introduces a new feature that enables users to configure session zoom scaling, which can be used to compensate for screens with high DPI resolutions.

- Offline Files and Work Folders enable users to continue to work with shared files even when they are not connected to the network.

- The Sync Center offers a centralized location to configure actions that will trigger the synchronization of sync partnerships.

- Users can modify existing device power plans or create new ones to fine-tune their battery consumption and manage battery life. Administrators can use the Powercfg. exe command line tool and Group Policy to export, import, and apply power plans to devices.

- Windows Mobility Center offers users of mobile devices quick access to configuration settings that are often modified by mobile users.

- Windows To Go workspaces enable users to travel without their own device, and use a Windows To Go certified USB drive to boot to Windows 10 on a host computer.

- Work Folders enable users to access and sync company sync shares from external devices that include domain-joined and non-domain joined devices.

- WiFi Direct enables Windows 10 devices to interact with other hardware, such as printers, TVs, PCs, and gaming devices, such as Xbox One.

CHAPTER 8

Manage apps

U sers require applications for every task they perform; this includes editing documents, querying databases, and generating reports. Supporting the operation of applications is a critical part of the desktop support role, and you will encounter questions on the exam regarding app management. This chapter examines the different methods for presenting apps to the end user, and how those apps can be supported in Windows 10.

Skills in this chapter

- Skill 8.1: Deploy and manage RemoteApp apps
- Skill 8.2: Support desktop apps

Skill 8.1: Deploy and manage RemoteApp apps

Traditionally, support staff in IT departments deploy apps to users' devices. This means that the app is physically present on a user's device. However, you can also make apps available by using Remote Desktop Services. RemoteApp in Windows Server 2016 enables you to publish apps to users' devices. These apps are presented as if they are installed locally, but run on the RD Session Host server. There are a number of advantages to using RemoteApp apps. These include:

- Supporting branch offices, where there is limited local IT support.
- Enabling users that want to access programs remotely.
- Providing the ability to deploy your line-of-business (LOB) apps to a variety of devices types and architectures.
- Enabling "hot desking" workspaces, where users do not own their designated computers.
- Being able to deploy multiple versions of an app.

Configure RemoteApp prerequisites

Before you can deploy RemoteApp apps, you must perform a number of procedures on your Windows Server 2016 server computer.

- Install the RD Session Host Role Service

- Install apps

Note that the specifics of the process for deploying the required server roles might vary based on your organization's specific requirements. To provide the necessary services for a small organization using a single RD Session Host Role server, use the following guidance.

Installing the RD Session Host role service

To install the RD Session Host role service (and any required services), sign in to your Windows Server 2016 server computer as a member of the local Administrators group. Open Server Manager, and then complete the following procedure:

1. In Server Manager, on the Dashboard, click Add roles and features.

2. Click Next, and then, on the Installation Type page, click Remote Desktop Services installation, and then click Next.

3. On the Select deployment type page, click Quick Start, as shown in Figure 8-1. This deployment option enables you to deploy Remote Desktop Services on a single server, and creates a collection and publishes RemoteApp apps. This option deploys the RD Connection Broker, RD Web Access, and RD Session Host role services to the same server.

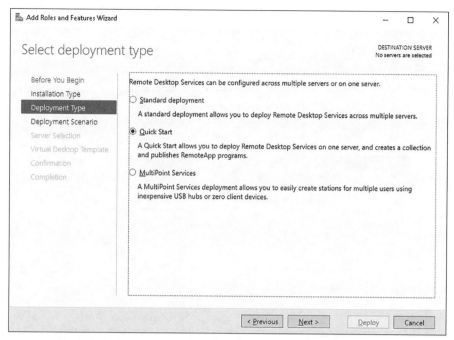

FIGURE 8-1 Deploying Remote Desktop Services

> **NOTE** **ADDITIONAL ROLE SERVICES**
>
> Depending on your existing Remote Desktop Services configuration, you might need to in-stall one or more of the additional role services listed: Remote Desktop Connection Broker, Remote Desktop Gateway, Remote Desktop Licensing, Remote Desktop Virtualization Host, and Remote Desktop Web Access. For more information, visit the Microsoft website: *https:// docs.microsoft.com/en-us/windows-server/remote/remote-desktop-services/welcome-to-rds*

4. On the Select deployment scenario page, click Session-Based Desktop Deployment.

5. On the Select A Server page, ensure that the local server is in the Selected list. Click Next.

6. On the Confirm Selections page, select the Restart The Destination Server Automati-cally If Required check box, and then click Deploy. The installation proceeds, as shown in Figure 8-2.

FIGURE 8-2 Completing the Remote Desktop Services deployment

7. Restart your server computer and then sign in as a member of the local Administrators group. After you sign in, configuration completes without further intervention.

Install apps

After you have installed the Remote Desktop Session Host, you can install apps on the server. You install apps in a similar way that you do on a local desktop. For example, to make Microsoft Office 2016 available as a RemoteApp, install the app on the Remote Desktop Session Host computer.

To ensure that apps work properly on an RD Session Host, you must use Control Panel to install them. Use the following procedure:

1. Open Control Panel and click Programs.

2. On the Programs page, click Install Application On Remote Desktop, as shown in Figure 8-3.

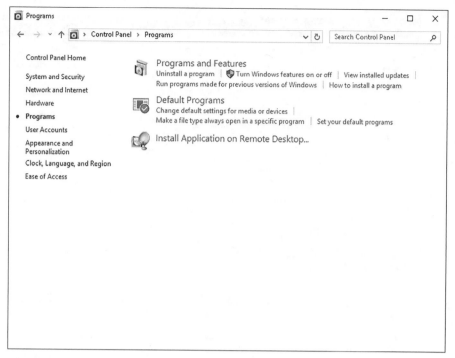

FIGURE 8-3 Installing an app for RemoteApp deployment

3. In the Install Program From Floppy Disk Or CD-ROM dialog box, click Next.

4. Browse to the location of the setup file for the application. Select the installer, and click Next.

5. The app installation process starts. Follow the on-screen installation prompts to install the app.

6. After the app is installed, in the Finish Admin Install dialog box, click Finish.

After you have installed the apps that you want to make available to your users through Remote Desktop Services, you must publish the app. To do this, open Server Manager, and then complete the following procedure:

1. In Server Manager, click Remote Desktop Services.

2. In the Remote Desktop Services window, click the QuickSessionCollection node.

3. In the RemoteApp Programs section, click Tasks, and then click Publish RemoteApp Programs.

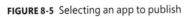

FIGURE 8-4 Publishing an app to RemoteApp collection

4. Scroll down and select the app that you just installed, as shown in Figure 8-5, and then click Next.

Publish RemoteApp Programs

Select RemoteApp programs

- RemoteApp Programs
- Confirmation
- Publishing
- Completion

Select the RemoteApp programs to publish to the QuickSessionCollection collection. To add a RemoteApp program to the list, click Add.

The RemoteApp programs are populated from EU-RTR.ADATUM.COM.

	RemoteApp Program	Location
☐	System Configuration	%SYSTEMDRIVE%\Windows\system32\msconfi...
☐	System Information	%SYSTEMDRIVE%\Windows\system32\msinfo3...
☐	Task Manager	%SYSTEMDRIVE%\Windows\system32\taskmgr....
☐	Windows Defender	%SYSTEMDRIVE%\Program Files\Windows Defe...
☐	Windows Media Player	%SYSTEMDRIVE%\Program Files (x86)\Windows...
☐	Windows Memory Diagnostic	%SYSTEMDRIVE%\Windows\system32\MdSche...
☐	Windows Speech Recognition	%SYSTEMDRIVE%\Windows\Speech\Common\s...
☐	WordPad	%SYSTEMDRIVE%\Program Files\Windows NT\...
☑	XML Notepad 2007	%SYSTEMDRIVE%\Program Files (x86)\XML Not...

Add...

Verify that the program is installed on all the RD Session Host servers in the collection.

< Previous | Next > | Publish | Cancel

FIGURE 8-5 Selecting an app to publish

5. On the Confirmation page, click Publish.

6. When prompted, click Close. The newly published app is displayed in the RemoteApp Programs list.

Configure RemoteApp and Desktop Connections settings

RemoteApp and Desktop Connections enables you to provide specific RemoteApp apps to users. RemoteApp And Desktop Connections is enabled by default on a Windows 10 computer. To access RemoteApp and Desktop Connections:

1. Click Start, type **RemoteApp and Desktop Connections**.

2. Click RemoteApp And Desktop Connections. The RemoteApp And Desktop Connections window will appear, as shown in Figure 8-6.

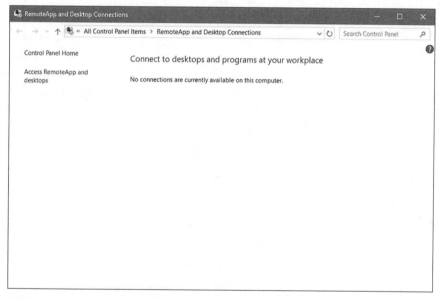

FIGURE 8-6 The RemoteApp And Desktop Connections window

3. Click Access RemoteApp and desktops.

4. In the Access RemoteApp And Desktops Wizard, enter the connection URL to the server that hosts the apps, as shown in Figure 8-7, and click Next.

FIGURE 8-7 Entering a connection URL

5. On the Ready To Set Up The Connection page, shown in Figure 8-8, click Next.

FIGURE 8-8 Confirming the URL

6. After the connection is successfully set up. As shown in Figure 8-9, the Finish page displays the URL used, and lists the number of available programs.

FIGURE 8-9 Viewing the successful establishment of a URL connection

You can now access these programs from Start, as shown in Figure 8-10. They are listed as (Work Resources).

FIGURE 8-10 Selecting RemoteApp programs from Start

You can also check the configuration of your RemoteApp And Desktop Connections as shown in Figure 8-11.

FIGURE 8-11 Viewing the RemoteApp And Desktop Connections configuration

---

NOTE CERTIFICATES

In order to subscribe to a desktop connection feed, your server administrator must have installed a digital certificate on the Remote Desktop Session Host computer. This certificate must be trusted by the client computers that will connect to it. The certificate subject name must also match the URLs used to access the desktop connection feeds. To edit the certificate settings used, sign in on your server computer and open Server Manager. In the Remote Desktop Services node, on the Overview page, under the DEPLOYMENT OVERVIEW heading, click TASKS and then click Edit Deployment Properties. Click Certificates in the navigation pane. In the Manage certificates pane, you can view and configure the certificate settings.

Configure Group Policy Objects for signed packages

RemoteApp programs are typically digitally signed. To ensure that users can access RemoteApp programs that are digitally signed, you must configure client computers to recognize those programs as coming from a trusted publisher by using Group Policy.

In most cases, the Group Policy changes will be made to a domain-based Group Policy environment. You can do this by using the Group Policy Management console on a domain controller or another computer running the Remote Server Administration Tools connected to a domain controller.

The following Group Policy settings allow you to control the behavior of client computers when opening a digitally signed RDP file from RemoteApp. They are all found in Computer Configuration\Policies\Administrative Templates\Windows Components\Remote Desktop Services\Remote Desktop Connection Client.

■ Specify SHA1 thumbprints of certificates representing trusted RDP publishers.

■ Allow RDP files from valid publishers and user's default RDP settings.

■ Allow RDP files from unknown publishers.

Subscribe to the Desktop Connections feeds

To subscribe to additional Desktop Connections feed, do the following:

1. From Control Panel, open the RemoteApp And Desktop Connections window.

2. In the RemoteApp And Desktop Connections window, click Access RemoteApp And Desktops.

3. In the Connection URL box, type the URL for the connection that your administrator provided to you.

4. Click Next.

5. On the Ready To Set Up The Connection page, click Next.

6. After the connection is successfully set up, note the name of the connection, and then click Finish.

7. Close RemoteApp and Desktop Connections.

8. To access the connection, click Start, type **RemoteApp and Desktop Connections**, click RemoteApp And Desktop Connections, and then click the name of the connection (for example, Adatum).

9. The programs and remote desktops that are available as part of the connection are listed under the connection name. Click the program or remote desktop that you want to use.

Support iOS and Android

Clients always access RemoteApp programs by using the Remote Desktop Connection app. This app is included by default in Windows clients, so no additional installation is required. However, to support iOS and Android clients, you must install the Microsoft Remote Desktop app in order to access RemoteApp programs.

Install and configure Remote Desktop app on iOS

To install the Remote Desktop app on an iOS device, perform the following steps:

1. Open the App Store app on your iOS device.

2. Locate and install the Microsoft Remote Desktop app.

3. Open the Microsoft Remote Desktop app.

4. Tap the plus (+) icon and then select RemoteApp.

5. Enter the URL to the RemoteApp server.

6. Enter your Microsoft credentials associated with the RemoteApp deployment.

7. Select the invitations listed on the screen to accept the associated RemoteApp programs.

8. After accepting your invitations, the list of apps you have access to will be downloaded to your device and made available. Tap one of the apps to start using it.

Install and configure Remote Desktop app on Android

To install the Remote Desktop app on an Android device, perform the following steps:

1. Open the Play Store app on your Android device.

2. Locate the Microsoft Remote Desktop app.

3. Click the INSTALL button.

4. After the app has installed, open the Microsoft Remote Desktop app.

5. Tap the plus (+) icon and then select RemoteApp.

6. Enter the URL to the RemoteApp server.

7. Enter your Microsoft credentials associated with the RemoteApp deployment.

8. Select the invitations listed on the screen to accept the associated RemoteApp programs.

9. After accepting your invitations, the list of apps you have access to will be downloaded to your device and made available. Tap one of the apps to start using it.

Configure Remote Desktop Web access for distribution

Remote Desktop Web Access (RD Web Access) enables users to access applications through a special website. RD Web Access provides a secure way to present remote applications to users who do not wish to use a single device to access RemoteApp programs, or who need access from a web browser. A typical URL is *https://rds.Adatum.com/RDWeb*.

> **NOTE CHANGING THE RD WEB ACCESS URL**
>
> To view the URL used by RD Web Access, sign in on your server computer and open Server Manager. In the Remote Desktop Services node, on the Overview page, under the Deployment Overview heading, click Tasks and then click Edit Deployment Properties. Click RD Web Access in the navigation pane, and the URL is displayed on the right.

After they sign in, users can access a secure site, and establish a secure socket layer (SSL) session between the client and the RD Web Access server. After authentication, users see a list of any RemoteApp apps that they have permission to use, as shown in Figure 8-12.

FIGURE 8-12 Viewing available RemoteApp apps via a web browser

Skill 8.2: Support desktop apps

Although Windows 10 supports a growing set of Microsoft Store apps, many organizations rely on traditional desktop apps to fulfill business needs and enable user productivity. A number of issues can arise while supporting desktop apps. For example, the desktop app might not be fully compatible with Windows 10. In this case, you can use the Application Compatibility tools to determine how widespread the problem is and learn how to fix it before proceeding with an organization-wide installation of Windows 10 or the application.

Other issues include the need to run two or more versions of an app side-by-side, and in these cases and similar scenarios, you might opt for technologies such as Hyper-V, RemoteApp, and AppV. You might also opt to run a problematic or noncompliant app virtually or remotely. Other options available for additional desktop app scenarios and functionality include User Experience Virtualization (UE-V) and Microsoft Intune (discussed in this section).

> **This section covers how to:**
> - Support desktop app compatibility by using Application Compatibility Tools
> - Support desktop application co-existence
> - Install and configure User Experience Virtualization
> - Deploy desktop apps by using Microsoft Intune

Support desktop app compatibility by using Application Compatibility Tools

The Application Compatibility Tools are included with the Windows Assessment and Deployment Toolkit (Windows ADK) and can be used to help you diagnose and fix application compatibility problems. The Application Compatibility Tools consists of two components: Compatibility Administrator and Standard User Analyzer.

> **MORE INFO** **WINDOWS ADK FOR WINDOWS 10**
>
> For more information about the Windows ADK for Windows 10, including download links, visit: *https://docs.microsoft.com/en-us/windows-hardware/get-started/adk-install*.

Fix problems

When application compatibility problems are uncovered, you have to decide how you will deal with them. It might be time to move from a little-known office application suite to something more mainstream, such as Microsoft Office. It might be time to simply retire an application, or you might decide (and likely will in most cases) to fix the problem and continue to use the application. Fixing the problem can involve modifying the code or applying shims.

A common way to fix a compatibility issue is to alter the app code. Microsoft recommends this in preference to changing Registry settings or trying other potentially risky or short-term workarounds. Changing the code requires resources (like money and time) on the front end, but the result might be worth it. If altering the app code is not an option, or if you need a short-term workaround, another option to consider is to create a shim.

UNDERSTAND SHIMS

If you opt to use the Shim Infrastructure, you can apply the fix (shim) to a specific application and application version only. Shims you create remain independent of the core Windows functions.

Technically, Shim Infrastructure involves application programming interface (API) hooking; the shim redirects API calls from Windows to some other code, which is the shim itself. Windows manages and secures shims just as it would the original application code. Thus, you can't use shims to work around security mechanisms already in place by the operating system, including User Account Control (UAC) prompts. You also can't use a shim to fix kernel-mode code, specifically to fix issues with device drivers. Shims can fix compatibility issues and are often applied as the desired solutions to compatibility problems.

KNOW WHEN TO USE SHIMS

Deciding to use shims is a process like anything else. You must first decide whether the problem merits a shim and is worth the time it takes to create it. Here are a few reasons you might opt for a shim:

- The vendor who created the application is out of business and no updates are available. The source code isn't available either, so shims are the only option.

- Your company created the application. If you don't have the time available to rewrite the code, a shim is the next best alternative.

- The vendor is still in business, but has yet to create an update or fix. Alternatively, a company-created application can be modified in the future, but no immediate update is available. In these cases, a shim can work temporarily, until an update becomes available in the future.

USE COMPATIBILITY ADMINISTRATOR

One tool you might opt to use to resolve application compatibility issues is the Compatibility Administrator. This tool provides:

- Compatibility updates, compatibility modes, and AppHelp messages that you use to resolve specific compatibility issues.

- Tools that enable you to create your own customized compatibility updates, compatibility modes, AppHelp messages, and compatibility databases.

- A tool that you can use to query and search for installed compatibility updates on your organization's computers.

To use this tool to fix an application compatibility issue, use the following:

1. Sign in to your computer where you installed the Windows ADK Application Compatibility Tools with a user account that belongs to the local Administrators group.

2. Click Start, expand Windows Kits, and then click Compatibility Administrator (64-bit). Note that there is also a 32-bit version available.

3. In the Compatibility Administrator (64-bit) – New Database (1) [Untitled_1]* dialog box, right-click New Database(1) [Untitled_1]*, and then click Rename.

4. Type an appropriate name for the database, as shown in Figure 8-13, and then press Enter.

FIGURE 8-13 Creating a database in the Compatibility Administrator

5. In the Compatibility Administrator window, right-click your newly named database, click Create New, and then click Application Fix.

6. In the Create New Application Fix Wizard, in the Name Of The Program To Be Fixed text box, type the application name.

7. Click Browse, and in the Find Binary window, browse to the suspect application's launch file, and then click Open.

8. In the Create New Application Fix Window, click Next.

9. On the Compatibility Modes page, shown in Figure 8-14, select the Run This Program In Compatibility Mode For check box, click the drop-down list box, and then select a suitable mode, if required.

FIGURE 8-14 Selecting a Compatibility Mode for a app

NOTE **COMPATIBILITY MODES**

You can configure a compatibility mode for an app. This forces the app to run as if installed on the selected operating system. This is useful for older apps.

---

10. Some older apps require that they run in administrative mode. If this is the case with your suspect app, in the Additional Compatibility Modes section, scroll down, select the RunAsAdmin check box, and then click Next.

11. On the Compatibility Fixes page, click Next.

NOTE **COMPATIBILITY FIXES**

Built-in to the Compatibility Administrator are a number of predefined compatibility fixes. These can be selected in this list.

---

12. On the Matching Information page, click Finish.

13. In the Compatibility Administrator window, shown in Figure 8-15, click Save.

FIGURE 8-15 Ready to create an application fix, or shim

14. In the Save Database window, browse to a suitable location, type a name in the File name box, and then click Save. The file has an .sdb extension.

15. Close the Compatibility Administrator window.

After you have created the fix, you can distribute the application fix, or shim, to your users. They can install it by running the following command:

Sdbinst C:\Suspect_App_Fix.sdb

You can also distribute the fix by using a script, or with Group Policy Objects.

Support desktop application co-existence

You can further test and run applications on new operating systems by using technologies such as Hyper-V, RemoteApp, and App-V. Hyper-V lets you run applications on virtual machines (VMs) in a dedicated space that you can easily manage. RemoteApp lets you access applications remotely through Remote Desktop Services, and the apps themselves are housed and managed on network servers. App-V lets you virtualize applications so that you can use the applications side-by-side on the same system. All three options let you test applications in various scenarios before deployment. You can then make decisions based on what solution and environment works best in your enterprise.

Support Hyper-V

With Windows 10 Pro and Windows 10 Enterprise, you can create virtual machines that are housed inside a single operating system on a single computer. These virtual machines can run their own operating systems, and you can separate and secure them with virtual switches. A hypervisor keeps these "child" operating systems separate from the parent operating system.

This enables network administrators to combine multiple machines into one, which saves money, power consumption, resources, and space. In Windows 10, this technology is called Client Hyper-V and is a free element. With regard to supporting applications, you will install applications that you want to test in these environments to check compatibility, perhaps after shims or other updates are applied.

To use Hyper-V, you'll need the following:

- Windows 10 Pro or Windows 10 Enterprise, 64-bit
- A processor with Second Level Address Translation (SLAT) support
- 4 GB of RAM
- BIOS-level hardware virtualization support

If you have a compatible computer, you can create and configure a virtual machine.

> **NOTE SYSTEMINFO**
>
> You can use SystemInfo.exe to verify whether your computer meets the Hyper-V requirements.

You must first enable Hyper-V from Control Panel, however, under Programs And Features. Click Turn Windows Features On Or Off, locate Hyper-V, and select all related entries (see Figure 8-16). When it's enabled, click OK and restart the computer. After restarting, you'll have access to two new apps when you log on as an administrator: Hyper-V Manager and Hyper-V Virtual Machine Connection.

FIGURE 8-16 Installing the Hyper-V features

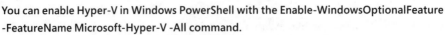
Understanding and supporting RemoteApp

Remote Desktop Services (RDS) lets you virtualize a computing session. You can opt to virtualize the entire desktop or, in this chapter, only individual applications. You use RemoteApp tools and technologies to virtualize applications. When you do, applications look and feel as though they're running on the computer a user is sitting in front of, but in reality the app is being hosted elsewhere. As you might guess, this could be used to resolve compatibility problems with specific apps, as well as provide another means to test the apps before deployment. You can use RemoteApp with local apps, and they can be added to the Start screen.

RemoteApp programs are stored on an RD Session Host server; virtual desktops are hosted on an RD Virtualization Host server. These virtual environments can be accessed remotely from a configured client machine. The Windows server running the RDS role must have the following services configured and available:

- RD Session Host enables a server to host the desired applications (and perhaps full desktops). Users connect to this server to run the programs. Users also save files and access other network resources available on the server, as applicable.

- RD Virtualization Host, with Hyper-V, hosts the virtual machines and makes them available to users as virtual desktops. These virtual desktops can be provided in a pool on a first-come, first-served basis, or you can assign a specific desktop to a specific user.

- RD Web Access enables users to access RemoteApp and Desktop Connection through a web browser.

- RD Licensing is used to manage the RDS client access licenses. A license must exist for a user to connect to the RD Session Host server.

- RD Gateway enables users to access the internal enterprise network remotely from an Internet-connected device such as a tablet or laptop.

- RD Connection Broker helps manage session load balancing and reconnection. It also provides access to the RemoteApp programs and virtual desktops.

Here are other reasons to use RDS:

- You can consolidate all apps to manage them more easily. When an app needs to be updated or otherwise serviced, you can perform the needed work on the RD Session Host server instead of on every client desktop.

- You can simplify deployment when applications are difficult to manage, perhaps because they are updated often or prone to problems.

- You can use fewer resources on client computers and simplify management by hosting rarely used applications.

- You can allow access to company applications remotely, for instance, from home, from tablets or other limited hardware, or while traveling on business.

Understand and support App-V

In some instances, you might need to run several applications side-by-side on a single computer. Doing so is generally okay, unless those applications conflict with one another. Such a conflict almost always occurs when you need to run multiple versions of the same application.

This could certainly happen and is common in testing environments. In other cases, applications simply don't work well together. This might not have anything to do with versioning and could be caused by something completely different and difficult to diagnose. App-V helps you resolve these kinds of problems. Specifically, App-V lets you virtualize an application so that it remains independent of others, but can still live on the same machine without causing conflict.

Application virtualization, as you've already learned, can also mean that users can access an application that's installed elsewhere from almost anywhere an Internet connection and compatible hardware can be used. Virtualization keeps applications off client machines, which means that the users' computers remain "clean" and administrators can manage the apps centrally (rather than having to manage every client in the enterprise). After App-V is set up and configured for use, a Windows 10 Enterprise user can install App-V client software to access and use the desired applications. As with other virtualization technologies, the running apps appear to the user to be installed and running on their own machines.

EXAM TIP

As soon as apps are virtualized, authorized users can access them through the App-V client application. If more than one app is available, a list appears from which they can select. Administrators set the required limitations on users and the apps they can access.

You must perform plenty of steps before end users can access virtualized applications. Setting up the actual infrastructure is beyond the scope of this book and is best left to experienced network administrators, but you must understand the fundamental task sequence and the hardware, software, and services required.

USE MICROSOFT DESKTOP OPTIMIZATION PACK (MDOP)

App-V is available from Microsoft Desktop Optimization Pack (MDOP). MDOP is available as a subscription for Software Assurance (SA) customers, although you can download an evaluation to experiment with if you are an MSDN or TechNet subscriber. To work through this part of the chapter, you'll need to download and install MDOP before continuing.

Specifically, you need these elements, which are all part of App-V Server:

- App-V Management Server for managing App-V
- App-V Publishing Server to host virtual applications

- App-V Reporting Server to run and view applicable reports
- App-V Reporting Database Server to work with database deployments and report management

Beyond the required software, the hardware must also meet minimum requirements. The computer on which MDOP is installed must have the following:

- Microsoft .NET Framework 4.5
- Windows PowerShell 3.0
- Update for Windows KB2533623

Each element must also meet specific requirements. For example, the App-V client, Remote Desktop Services client, and the App-V server must all have the applicable Microsoft Visual C++ Redistributable Package installed. To see all requirements, refer to this article on TechNet at: *http://technet.microsoft.com/en-us/library/jj713458.aspx*.

> **NOTE SOFTWARE ASSURANCE (SA)**
>
> Software Assurance is generally associated with an enterprise's ability to obtain the next version of Windows software as part of their enterprise agreement as a fee associated with qualified products. Some of the most popular additional benefits are free technical training, licenses for home users, online training, and 24/7 support. SA also provides deployment planning services and other benefits.

INSTALL THE APP-V SEQUENCER AND GETTING READY FOR SEQUENCING

You should install MDOP and the App-V Sequencer on a 64-bit Windows 10 Enterprise computer. From the MDOP installation folder, navigate to App-V, Installers, 5.1 (or applicable version), and then run the setup program. As soon as it's installed, obtain the installer files for the application that you want to sequence. Copy those files to the computer that's running the sequencer. Create a new VM to use for the sequencing tasks, and make a backup copy of it before you start.

When you're ready, locate the Microsoft Application Virtualization Sequencer from the All Apps section of the Start menu. Click to open.

You can now do the following:

- Create virtual packages that can be deployed to computers that run the App-V client.
- Upgrade and edit configuration information for packages you've already created.
- Convert virtual packages.

Creating a package also creates the following:

- An MSI file that you'll use to install the virtual package on client computers.
- A Report.xml file that contains all issues, warnings, and errors that were discovered during sequencing (in case you need to troubleshoot the package).
- An APPV file, which is the virtual application file.

- A deployment configuration file that regulates how the virtual application is deployed.
- A user configuration file that regulates how the virtual application runs.

SEQUENCE AN APPLICATION

You can create virtualized application packages for standard applications, add-ons or plugins, and middleware. Creating packages for standard applications is the most common and what is detailed here. The following steps create one of the simplest types of packages. They don't configure every aspect available, including the option to stream the virtualized application; that experimentation is up to you. From the computer that has the sequencer installed, use these steps:

1. From the Start menu, type App-V, and in the results click Microsoft Application Virtualization Sequencer.

2. Click Create A New Virtual Application Package.

3. Select Create Package (Default), and then click Next.

4. Click Refresh and, if all problems are resolved, click Next.

5. Select the Standard Application (Default) check box, and then click Next.

6. Click Browse to find the installation file for the application. (If the application doesn't have an associated installer file, select the Perform A Custom Installation check box, and then click Next. Continue as prompted.)

7. Type a name for the package.

8. Click Browse to find the Primary Virtual Application Directory. Navigate to the location where the file would be installed by default, perhaps C:\ProgramFiles\<application name>. Note that you are navigating to this in the VM you already created.

9. Click Next three times. At the Create A Basic Package Or Customize Further page, select Customize, and then click Next.

10. Click Next to bypass the option to run the program briefly.

11. Select Allow This Package To Run Only On The Following Operating Systems, and then select Windows 10 32-bit and Windows 10 64-bit. Notice the other options, such as the option to Allow The Package To Run On Any Operating System.

12. Click Next.

13. Click Create.

14. When the Package Completed page appears, click Close.

With the package created, you are now ready for deployment. You can deploy App-V packages by using an Electronic Software Distribution (ESD) solution. When you opt for an ESD, you eliminate the need for an App-V 5.1 management server, management database, and publishing server. Alternatively, you can use Windows PowerShell to deploy a virtualized application. You can also opt to install the virtual application on a single computer, deploy it through Group Policy, or use it with Configuration Manager.

MORE INFO DEPLOYING VIRTUAL APPLICATION PACKAGES

To learn more about deploying App-V packages via ESD, refer to this article on TechNet at: *https://technet.microsoft.com/en-us/library/mt346570.aspx.*

Install and configure User Experience Virtualization

Users are more mobile than ever, and the trend will continue. Making the user experience the same no matter where the users log on whether it's on a laptop, desktop, or tablet would be valuable to users and enhance productivity. Network administrators have been doing so for quite some time by incorporating roaming user profiles, making the user's files and folders available offline, configuring syncing when a user reconnects to the network, and incorporating folder redirection. However, User Experience Virtualization (UE-V) provides a different approach to maintaining a consistent user experience.

Microsoft UE-V monitors the Windows operating system, monitors apps and application settings that are applied when users are at their computers, and captures those settings. The information is saved to a defined storage location such as a network share folder. (This data isn't saved to OneDrive, a USB drive, or similar mechanism.) The settings are then applied to the different computers and devices assigned to the user. What is synchronized and what apps and applications are included is determined by the settings location templates that the network administrator creates and configures, in combination with what the applications' developers make available for synchronization.

Here are a few additional things to understand about UE-V:

- A user can change personal settings from any device included in the UE-V synchronization group. Those changes will be applied to the other computers the next time the user logs on to them.

- The user can use UE-V with a Windows 7 or newer computer. Applicable and compatible settings will sync automatically.

- Changes are saved to a file, and the file is synced on log on. Nothing is actually virtualized.

- Application settings that can be synced can come from applications installed on the device, applications that are sequenced with App-V, and RemoteApp applications.

- Settings can be used as part of a recovery process when a machine is reimaged or reinstalled.

- You can incorporate Windows PowerShell and windows management instrumentation (WMI) to configure and deploy UE-V agents. Refer to this article to learn more at: *http://technet.microsoft.com/en-us/library/dn458904.aspx.*

- UE-V includes application settings templates for various editions of Microsoft Office, Internet Explorer, Windows Accessories, desktop settings, ease of use settings, and more.

Several elements must be in place for UE-V to work. A UE-V Agent must be used. This agent watches what changes and saves those changes as applicable. A settings package is also necessary to store the application and operating system settings and application template information. Finally, a UE-V Generator must exist where you can create your own custom templates. A lot of planning and resources are required to put this technology into place. A deployment includes the following:

1. Deploy the Settings Storage Location.

2. Deploy the UE-V Agent. (This is included in Windows 10).

3. Install the Group Policy templates.

4. Install the Agent Generator.

5. Deploy the Settings Template Catalog.

6. Deploy Settings Location Templates.

7. Administer UE-V and understand how to:

   - Manage frequency of scheduled tasks.

   - Restore application and Windows settings.

   - Configure applicable Group Policy objects.

   - Manage settings packages.

   - Incorporate App-V applications.

   - Incorporate Configuration Manager as applicable.

Deploy desktop apps by using Microsoft Intune

Not all companies have the money, time, or resources to set up and maintain an intricate server infrastructure, the ability or know-how to set up personal VMs, or the ability to set up a UE-V substructure to synchronize various user settings. Keeping applications off users' desktops, especially with so many of them mobile and using multiple devices, can lighten the load required of network administrators (as well as support staff). This is where Microsoft Intune can provide significant benefits. Any size company can use Microsoft Intune to virtualize applications.

In this section you'll review just enough about Microsoft Intune to understand what it is and how you can use it. With Microsoft Intune, a company can:

- Use a single web-based administrator console to manage computers and mobile devices via the cloud.

- Simplify the management of various devices, including Windows laptops, desktops, tablets, and phones and even Apple iOS and Android devices.

- Make following company guidelines easier by using the cloud to manage all devices.

- Download Microsoft Intune client software when necessary, using a Microsoft account and password, from the administration page. (Client software can be deployed in many ways, including manually, through Group Policy and by using Configuration Manager.)

- Make software available to users, requiring all users to have the software or making it optional, while at the same time requiring no user interaction for installing it.

- Make software available through the company portal so that Windows RT users can install applications as needed.

- Create, upload, publish, and deploy software packages; configure and manage security policies; manage inventory; and create inventory reports when combined with Configuration Manager.

Unlike most of what you've seen so far in this section, you can get a free 30-day trial of Microsoft Intune even if you don't have a Software Assurance plan. After you set it up (and possibly install Microsoft Silverlight if you didn't have it already), go to *https://manage.microsoft.com*, log on, and work through the setup processes. Your logon name should look something like *administrator@yourname*.onmicrosoft.com. Figure 8-17 shows the Microsoft Intune Administrator Console with System Overview selected.

FIGURE 8-17 The Microsoft Intune Administrator Console

If you've set up a free trial of Microsoft Intune, you can find out about how to upload and distribute apps via Microsoft Intune, as shown in Figure 8-18, by reading Chapter 1, "Manage identity."

FIGURE 8-18 The Microsoft Intune Apps page

Thought experiments

In these thought experiments, demonstrate your skills and knowledge of the topics covered in this chapter. You can find the answers to these thought experiments in the next section.

Scenario 1

Your organization must deploy an application to users in North America and India. You do not have application deployment tools in place for the India locations, and the application must be available to a group of users in North America who need to access the app from their Android smart phones.

1. How can you deploy this app to all users by using only one deployment method?

2. How will your Android users access the app?

Scenario 2

You have been commissioned by a large organization to help prepare for an enterprise-wide rollout of Windows 10. Company employees use a myriad of desktop applications, two of which were written by a developer who's no longer in business. The company wants you to help test the applications to see whether they are or can be made compatible with Windows 10.

1. What tool will you choose to determine whether the applications in question are compatible?

2. What's the first thing you must do when you begin to test the compatibility of an app with this tool?

3. You discover that the apps ran successfully on Windows XP when a user was signed in as an administrator. What must you do?

4. After creating a fix for the apps, how might the users install the fix?

Thought experiment answers

This section provides the solutions for the tasks included in the thought experiment.

Scenario 1

1. You can publish the app and use RemoteApp to make the app available to all users.

2. The Android users will need to download the Microsoft Remote Desktop app from the Google Play Store.

Scenario 2

1. The Compatibility Administrator.

2. Create a database.

3. Configure the Compatibility Mode to Windows XP and enable the RunAsAdmin option.

4. The users could be emailed the fix (an .sdb file), which they can install using the sdbinst. exe program.

Chapter summary

- RemoteApp allows you to publish apps to your users over multiple platforms.

- Group Policy can be used to configure how clients will respond to signed packages.

- You can use RemoteApp and Desktop Connections or RD Web Access to access Remote-App programs.

- You can determine application compatibility and deal with problems that arise in many ways, including using the Application Compatibility Tools and creating shims.

- Applications can coexist with others that would usually cause compatibility issues or simply aren't compatible with the current operating system. The technologies to consider include Hyper-V, RemoteApp, and App-V. Each offers something unique and is used in specific circumstances to provide solutions.

- You can give users a consistent desktop and user experience with UE-V.

- You can use Microsoft Intune to host applications and manage computer inventory, even if you don't have a server structure in place.

CHAPTER 9

Manage updates and recovery

To keep your personal and enterprise Windows 10 computers secure, you need Windows 10 patched from known threats such as malware, system vulnerabilities, and security risks. The process of using the Microsoft and Windows Updates mechanism ensures that Windows systems are protected. This process is recommended by Microsoft for the complete lifespan of Windows, especially since threats continue to increase in both complexity and frequency.

Microsoft has built up the stability of the new kernel originally developed for Windows Vista, continuously improving it to provide Windows 10 with a very stable and reliable platform for users. Windows 10 features improve reliability and reduce the likelihood of crashes occurring, such as the self-healing file system used for Storage Spaces, in place memory conservation, and improved anti-malware protection.

The drive toward using the Cloud more extensively has allowed Microsoft to develop and implement new solutions for recovering from operating system failures. In much the same way as the Previous Versions feature empowered end users to recover overwritten or damaged files, in Windows 10 end users can simply and efficiently recover a failed or unresponsive system without lengthy downtime. This releases administrators from recovering individual files from tape backups.

Skills in this chapter:

- Skill 9.1: Configure system recovery
- Skill 9.2: Configure file recovery
- Skill 9.3: Configure and manage updates

Skill 9.1: Configure system recovery

It is rare that Windows 10 will suffer from a system crash in a corporate environment where each computer is managed by an administrator. System instability can arise from unstable device drivers, a failed internal module such as a system drive or memory failure, or poorly written third-party software.

Resolution from a system failure may be quick or slow, depending upon the nature of the failure and also any precautions in place at the time of the failure. If you install a faulty device driver you can remove it by simply performing a driver rollback, and troubleshoot a system that will not boot by allowing Windows to apply automatic repairs during startup. Some features from earlier versions of Windows are retained in Windows 10, but others such as Last Known Good Configuration have been deprecated.

Windows 10 helps users remain productive by safeguarding against system failure and incorporating tools that speed up the recovery process after a failure has occurred.

> **This section covers how to:**
> - Configure a recovery drive
> - Configure system restore
> - Perform a refresh or recycle
> - Perform a driver rollback
> - Configure restore points

Configure a recovery drive

Most Windows 10 PCs will have a recovery partition to contain a full image of the system. The contents of the recovery partition can also be copied to a removable storage device so that in the event that your recovery partition becomes inaccessible or corrupted you will still be able to recover your system.

Disk drive space on many small form factor devices and tablets is often smaller than that available on a laptop or PC, and this can limit the availability for an original equipment manufacturer (OEM) to include a recovery partition on devices shipped with Windows 10. If there is no recovery partition, you can still create a bootable Universal Serial Bus (USB) recovery drive that can boot into the Recovery Environment (RE). You will then need to access a system image that you have created or that is provided by the OEM.

To create a recovery drive, follow these steps:

1. Search for Recovery Drive and select Create A Recovery Drive.
2. Accept the User Account Control (UAC) prompt and provide the necessary credentials, if required.
3. Check the Backup System Files To The Recovery Drive option.
4. Click Next. Windows 10 will prepare the recovery image.
5. If you have not already connected a backup device to the system, on the Connect A USB Flash Drive page, connect a drive that has at least 8 GB capacity.
6. On the Select The USB Flash Drive page, select the drive for the recovery drive and click Next.

7. On the Create The Recovery Drive page, read the warning that the USB drive contents will be deleted and click Create. The Creating The Recovery Drive page appears with a progress bar, which will indicate the phase of the process that is being performed. The process can take up to 30 minutes depending on the performance of the PC and the media.

8. The tool performs the following actions:

   A. Prepares the drive

   B. Formats the drive

   C. Copies Recovery Drive utilities

   D. Backs up system files

9. On the last page, click Finish.

When the recovery drive has been provisioned on the removable media you will see the confirmation screen as shown in Figure 9-1. If your device has a recovery partition, you will see a link on the confirmation screen to delete the recovery partition from your PC. This relates to the Windows 10 device recovery partition and not the newly created recovery drive. If you want to free up the space on your device, you need to select this option. It is important to store the recovery drive in a safe place because you will not be able to recover your device if you have lost the recovery drive and you have deleted the recovery partition.

FIGURE 9-1 Creating a recovery drive

NOTE SDHC MEMORY CARDS

Some devices will support the use of Secure Digital High-Capacity (SDHC) memory cards. The Recovery Drive Wizard can use a SDHC card as an alternative to using a USB flash drive.

You should carefully label your Recovery Drive media after they have been created. A 64-bit (x64) recovery drive can only be used to reinstall a device with 64-bit architecture. The Windows 10 Recovery Drive cannot be used to repair down-level versions of Windows.

Configure system restore

You might have used System Restore in a previous version of Windows, such as Windows XP or Windows 7, to restore a computer that has become unstable. System Restore has been retained in Windows 10 and it offers a familiar and reliable method of recovering systems by restoring the operating system to a restore point created during a period of stability.

Once enabled, System Restore will automatically create restore points at the following opportunities:

- **Whenever apps are installed**   If the installer is System Restore compliant.
- **With updates**   Whenever Windows 10 installs Windows updates.
- **Based on a schedule**   Windows 10 includes scheduled tasks, which can trigger restore point creation.
- **Manually**   You can create a System Restore from the System Protection screen.
- **Automatically**   When you use System Restore to restore to a previous restore point, Windows 10 will create a new restore point before it restores the system using the selected restore point.

To turn on System Restore and manually create a System Restore point, follow these steps:

1. Search for System and click the System Control Panel item.
2. On System, select the System Protection link in the left pane. The System Properties dialog box appears with the System Protection tab open.
3. To turn on the System Restore feature, select the Local Disk (C:) (System) drive, and then click Configure.
4. On the System Protection For Local Disk (C:) dialog box, select Turn On System Protection.
5. Under Disk Space Usage, move the slider for the Max Usage to allow room on the restore points to be saved (five percent is a reasonable amount) as shown in Figure 9-2.
6. Click OK twice.

FIGURE 9-2 Configuring System Restore properties

You can also use PowerShell to configure System Restore. Some of the available cmdlets that you should review include the following:

- **Enable-ComputerRestore**   Enables the System Restore feature on the specified file system drive.

- **Disable-ComputerRestore**   Disables the System Restore feature on the specified file system drive.

- **Get-ComputerRestorePoint**   Gets the restore points on the local computer.

- **Checkpoint-Computer**   Creates a system restore point.

The following command enables System Restore on the C: drive of the local computer:

```
PS C:\> enable-computerrestore -drive "C:\"
```

> **NOTE SYSTEM RESTORE REQUIRES NTFS AND USES VOLUME SHADOW COPY SERVICE**
>
> System Restore uses the Volume Shadow Copy Service (VSS) and is only available on drives that are formatted with NTFS.

If the amount of space allocated for the restore points becomes full, System Restore will automatically delete the oldest restore points. If you require more restore points to be available, you need to allocate a larger proportion of the hard disk to the feature.

Once the system has created restore points, you are protected and the system should be recoverable.

To recover your system, you can launch the System Restore Wizard from either:

- **System Protection**   If your system will allow you to sign in to Windows, you can launch System Restore from the Windows 10 graphical user interface (GUI).

- **Windows Recovery Environment (Windows RE)**   If the system will not allow you to sign in, you can boot to the Windows RE and launch the System Restore Wizard from the Advanced options.

> *NOTE* **WINDOWS RE**
>
> Windows RE is built on Windows Preinstallation Environment (Windows PE), which is a cut down version of Windows and offers only limited functionality.

Identify affected apps and files

When using System Restore to restore the computer to an earlier state, the wizard will allow you to scan the restore point and advise you which apps and files will be affected by performing the operation. To perform a System Restore on Windows 10, follow these steps:

1. Search for System and click the System Control Panel item.

2. On the System, select the System Protection link in the left pane. The System Properties dialog box appears with the System Protection tab open.

3. Click System Restore.

4. On the Restore System Files And Settings page, click Next.

5. On the Restore Your Computer To A State It Was In Before The Selected Event page, choose the restore point that you want to be restored as shown in Figure 9-3.

FIGURE 9-3 Applying a System Restore point to your system

6. Optionally, click Scan For Affected Programs, or click Next.

7. On the Confirm Your Restore Point page, click Finish.

8. On the warning screen, click Yes.

9. The System Restore will now prepare your computer and restart. The System Restore process can take some time to complete.

10. When the process is complete, the system will restart and you can sign in to Windows.

11. You will be presented with a summary of the system restore status, and a confirmation that your documents have not been affected.

12. Click Close.

> **NOTE** **SYSTEM RESTORE WITHIN WINDOWS RE**
>
> When using System Restore within Windows RE, as a protection against unauthorized access to the system, you need to select a user account and provide the user's password before you can use the System Restore feature.

Modify the task schedule

After you have enabled the System Restore feature, you can modify the default task schedule for when you want automatic restore points to occur by modifying the SR scheduled task. Use the following steps to modify the System Restore task schedule:

1. Search for Task, and click the Task Scheduler item.

2. In the Task Scheduler Microsoft Management Console (MMC), expand the node on the left to locate Task Scheduler Library\Microsoft\Windows\SystemRestore.

3. Double-click the SR task in the middle pane.

4. On the SR Properties (Local Computer) dialog box, click the Triggers tab.

5. On the Triggers tab, click New.

6. In the New Trigger dialog box, configure the schedule that you require. For example, you can configure Windows to create a daily System Restore point at noon.

7. Ensure that the Enabled check box is selected, and click OK.

8. On the Triggers tab, click OK.

9. In the Task Scheduler MMC, the trigger is now displayed and enabled.

10. Close the Task Scheduler MMC.

Launch Windows Recovery Environment

To launch the Windows RE and use safe mode or other advanced troubleshooting tools, you can attempt to start Windows 10 in advanced troubleshooting mode by using one of the following options:

- If available, select Restart Now under Advanced Startup in the Recovery section of the Settings App.

- Recovery from the menu. Restart the device using the Recovery Drive.

- Boot the device using Windows 10 installation media, and select the Repair Your Computer option.

- Press the Shift key and select the Restart option on the Start menu.

In addition to the methods above, Windows will automatically start in the WinRE after detecting the following issues:

- Two consecutive failed attempts to launch Windows.

- Two consecutive unexpected shutdowns that occur within two minutes of boot completion.

- A Secure Boot error

- A BitLocker error on touch-only devices.

Once Windows 10 boots to the advanced troubleshooting mode, you need to click Troubleshoot, then on the Advanced Options screen you can access some or all of the following options as shown in Figure 9-4.

- **System Restore**   Use a System Restore point to restore Windows.

- **System Image Recovery**   Recover Windows using a system image file.

- **Startup Repair**   Fix problems that are preventing Windows from loading.

- **Command Prompt**   Used for advanced troubleshooting.

- **Startup Setting**   Change Windows startup behavior.

- **Go back to the previous build**   Revert to a previous Windows build for Windows Insiders.

If your system has a unified extensible firmware interface (UEFI) motherboard you will also be offered an additional option:

- **UEFI Firmware Settings**   Used to modify UEFI settings.

FIGURE 9-4 Windows 10 Advanced Troubleshooting Mode

NOTE **WINDOWS 10 DOES NOT SUPPORT F8 AT STARTUP**

Unlike versions prior to Windows 10, you can't access the advanced troubleshooting mode by pressing F8 during the startup process. You can re-enable the F8 support by modifying the BCD.

The advanced troubleshooting mode shown in Figure 9-4 allows you to select the Startup Settings,. which restarts Windows in a special troubleshooting mode that might be familiar to users of other versions of the Windows operating system. The Startup Settings boot trouble-shooting mode presents you with the following options:

- **Enable debugging mode**   Start Windows 10 in troubleshooting mode, monitoring the behavior of device drivers to help determine if a specific device driver is causing Windows 10 to behave unexpectedly.

- **Enable boot logging mode**   Windows 10 creates and writes to a file named Ntbtlog.txt to record the device drivers installed and loaded during startup.

- **Enable low-resolution video mode**   Start Windows 10 in a low-resolution graphics mode.

- **Enable Safe Mode**   Windows 10 starts with a minimal set of drivers, services, and ap-plications to allow you to troubleshoot the system using the GUI. Safe mode does not include network connectivity.

- **Enable Safe Mode with Networking**   Safe mode with networking enables network connectivity.

- **Enable Safe Mode with command prompt** Safe mode using a command prompt window rather than the Windows GUI.

- **Disable driver signature enforcement** Allows you to load device drivers that do not have a digital signature.

- **Disable early-launch anti-malware protection** Start Windows 10 without the early launch anti-malware functionality running. This mode is useful for identifying whether early launch anti-malware is affecting a driver or app from being loaded.

- **Disable automatic restart on system failure** Stops Windows 10 from automatically restarting after a system failure occurs.

You can cancel and reboot your system normally by pressing Enter. To select an option that you require, you need to press the number key or function key F1-F9 that corresponds to the list of items as shown in Figure 9-5.

Startup Settings

Press a number to choose from the options below:

Use number keys or functions keys F1-F9.

1) Enable debugging
2) Enable boot logging
3) Enable low-resolution video
4) Enable Safe Mode
5) Enable Safe Mode with Networking
6) Enable Safe Mode with Command Prompt
7) Disable driver signature enforcement
8) Disable early launch anti-malware protection
9) Disable automatic restart after failure

Press F10 for more options
Press Enter to return to your operating system

FIGURE 9-5 Windows 10 Startup Settings

If you press F10, you are taken to another screen with the option to launch the recovery environment. This option reboots the system and returns you to the Advanced Options screen as shown in Figure 9-4.

Perform a reset

If other methods of recovering your system fail or your problems reoccur, you can revert your system to the state similar to how it was when you purchased it or when Windows 10 was first installed. Typical issues that prevent the use of other tools mentioned in this chapter could include a damaged hard drive or a malware attack that encrypts the drive.

Windows 8 first introduced the option to refresh or recycle your computer; Windows 10 has improved the performance and reliability of this feature. You will see the words *recycle* and *reset* used interchangeably by Microsoft to mean the same thing, although the Windows interface options typically use the term *reset*. The Reset This PC option consolidates the two options (Refresh Your PC and Reset Your PC) that were available in Windows 8 and Windows 8.1.

For enterprise users who suffer from an unstable or corrupted system, often the quickest remediation is to deploy a fresh system image from the deployment server to the device. Home users and small organizations can use a similar solution, but rather than use a deployment server on the network such as Windows Deployment Services (Windows DS), Windows 10 is able to re-image the device itself. Selecting the Reset This PC option effectively reinstalls the Windows 10 operating system and allows you to either keep your files or remove everything.

To start the recovery process, follow these steps:

1. Launch Settings.
2. Click Update & Security.
3. Select Recovery.
4. On the Reset This PC page, click Get Started.

   The screen will be dimmed and you will be presented with the options shown in Figure 9-6 as follows:

   - **Keep My Files**   Removes apps and settings, but keeps your personal files.
   - **Remove Everything**   Removes all of your personal files, apps, and settings.

5. Select Keep My Files.

   A warning appears informing you that your apps will be removed; it lists any apps that will need to be reinstalled.

6. Click Next.

   On the Ready To Reset This PC page, you are reminded that resetting the PC will remove apps and reset all settings back to defaults.

7. Click Reset to restart the PC and allow the reset process to begin.

FIGURE 9-6 Reset This PC options

After the reset process has completed and you've signed in, you will have a list of removed apps on the desktop.

The second option asks you if you want to clean the drives also. This allows you to remove all settings, apps, and personal files and restore the operating system to the factory settings,, which is to the same state when you first installed or upgraded to Windows 10. If you plan on selling or disposing of the device, you can choose to remove the files and to clean the drive during the reset process and the hard disk will be fully erased and the disk will be overwritten prior to the automated reinstallation of Windows 10. This option is ideal if you are seeking to recycle your PC and want to make it difficult for someone to recover your removed files.

When the system reset is complete, you are offered the out-of-box experience (OOBE). You will need to configure the device, install any apps, and modify any settings that you would like.

Your device manufacturer may have included the ability to restore your Windows 10 device to the factory installed OEM image and settings. This action restores the operating system to the original factory settings and is also available if you upgraded from Windows 8.1 to Windows 10. Selecting this option provides an automated reinstallation of Windows 10 and presents the OOBE that is provided by the OEM.

After the reset process, if you sign in with the same Microsoft account you were using before, the Microsoft Store apps that you have purchased will be available to reinstall by using the following steps:

1. Open the Microsoft Store.

2. Select the three dots in the top right corner and then click My Library.

3. Select the apps you want to install, and select Install.

EXAM TIP

In versions of Windows prior to Windows 10, you could use a utility called Recimg.exe to capture an image of your computer after you installed applications and made customizations. You could then export this image and use it as a recovery image, but this utility has been deprecated in Windows 10.

Perform a Fresh Start

With the Creators Update, Windows 10 provides a new way to reset the system called Fresh Start. This is included in both the Recovery section of the Settings app and within the Windows Defender Security Center. Fresh Start performs three actions:

- Reinstalls Windows 10 while retaining your data.
- Removes all installed apps and bloatware.
- Installs the latest security updates.

You can access the Fresh Start feature using the following steps:

1. Launch Settings, and click Update & Security.

2. Select Recovery.

3. Under More Recovery Options, click the Learn how To Start Fresh With A Clean Installation Of Windows.

4. On the pop up dialog, click Yes to Switch Apps.

5. Alternatively, launch Settings, and click Update & Security.

6. Select Windows Defender and click Open Windows Defender Security Center.

7. On the Windows Defender Security Center screen, select Device Performance and Health and then under Fresh Start click Additional Info.

8. On the Fresh Start page click Get Started and accept the UAC prompt.

The screen will be dimmed and you will be presented with the warning as shown in Figure 9-7.

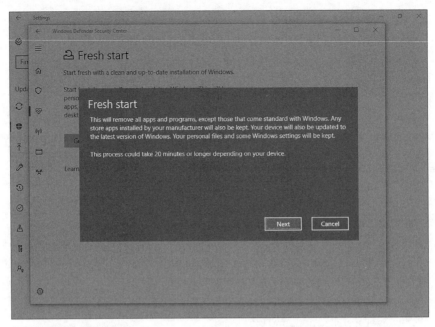

FIGURE 9-7 Fresh Start options

1. On the Fresh Start page, to proceed, click Next.

2. Fresh Start will then display a list of apps that will be removed. Fresh Start saves a list of apps removed, called Removed Apps, which will be found on the desktop once the process is completed.

3. Click Next.

4. If you recently upgraded to Windows 10, click Next on the warning regarding the previous version of Windows.

5. On the Let's Get Started page, click Start.

6. The PC is then reset which can take up to 20 minutes.

> *NOTE* **PREVIOUS VERSION OF WINDOWS WILL BE REMOVED**
>
> When performing a Fresh Start, if the device was recently upgraded to Windows 10, you won't be able to go back to the previous version of Windows.

When the PC restarts after the Fresh Start has completed, you can log in with the same username and password and all your data will be retained. Any applications that you use will need to be reinstalled, but crucially any third-party apps or bloatware that came preinstalled on your system by the OEM will have been removed. If you need access to the list of removed apps, a file is created during the process and this is found on the desktop after you sign in to the device. Within the Fresh Start page in Windows Defender Security Center, you will see a history of when the Fresh Start feature has been used, and a link to the list of Removed Apps.

Perform a driver rollback

You know that device drivers allow Windows to control and communicate with the majority of hardware found in and attached to a device. Because a device driver allows the operating system to use the hardware, device drivers are a critical part of the operating system. You will have reduced device functionality if its driver is unavailable, corrupted, or not installed.

Device driver software is maintained by the hardware OEM and they often produce improved drivers that can be made available throughout the lifetime of the device. New device drivers often make improvements or remove errors from previous versions. So, it is recommended that you allow Windows to update device driver software whenever a new version is available. Thankfully in Windows 10, this process is automatic by default, although you can disable all updating of device drivers as shown later in this chapter.

You need to be aware that device drivers run at the kernel level and have access to all system resources within the operating system. To prevent malicious code from been granted access to your system, you need to ensure that only drivers that are signed with a digital signature from a trusted authority are allowed to be installed on your system. The 64-bit versions of Windows 10 enforces device driver signing, but the 32-bit versions of Windows 10 permit their use and will warn users about the danger of using unsigned drivers.

Drivers are often bundled as a set of files known as a driver package and can contain the following modules:

- **Driver files**   A driver is a dynamic-link library (DLL) with the SYS file name extension.

- **Installation files including INF**   A device setup information (.inf) file that is copied to the %SystemRoot%\Inf directory during installation. Every device must have an INF file, which provides information that the system needs for device installation.

- **Installation files including CAT files**   A driver catalog file (.cat) contains a cryptographic hash of each file in the driver package to verify that the driver package has not been altered after it was published.

- **Other Files**   A driver package can also contain additional files, including device installation apps, device icon, device property pages and device stage metadata.

When a device driver is installed manually, Windows 10 updates the driver store with the driver, within the FileRepository folder, using a trusted location located at %SystemRoot%\System32\DriverStore.

Drivers can be copied to the Driver Store prior to device installation, for example, by using Group Policy or during initial system deployment. In this way, standard users can connect known hardware to their Windows 10 devices and the system will automatically install the driver software from the driver store without help from the IT helpdesk. To manually install driver packages to the driver store, use the command line tool Pnputil.exe, which has the following syntax: pnputil.exe -a path\drivername.inf, as shown in Table 9-1.

TABLE 9-1 Pnputil.exe parameters

Parameter	Description
-a or /add-driver	Adds the INF file specified
-d or /delete-driver	Delete the INF file specified
-e or /enum-drivers	Lists all third-party INF files
-f or /force	Force the deletion of the identified INF file. Cannot be used together with the -i parameter.
-I or /install	Installs the identified INF file. Cannot be used together with the -f parameter
/?	Displays help

An example command to add the INF file specified by the DEVICE.INF is:

```
pnputil /add-driver C:\%SystemRoot%\System32\DriverStore\Device.inf
```

In addition to the Pnputil.exe, you can use the following Windows PowerShell cmdlets:

- **Enable-PnpDevice**   Enables a Plug and Play (PnP) device.
- **Disable-PnpDevice**   Disables a PnP device.
- **Get-PnpDevice**   Displays information about PnP devices.
- **Get-PnpDeviceProperty**   Displays detailed properties for a PnP device.

An example PowerShell command to enable the device specified by the instance ID 'NET\VI D_6986&;PID_4466&;MI_00\8&;&;0020' is as follows:

```
PS C:\> Enable-PnpDevice -InstanceId
 'NET\VID_6986&;PID_4466&;MI_00\8&;&;0020'
```

If a new device driver causes system instability or problems using some hardware, you can use the Driver Roll Back feature to revert a particular driver to the previous version of the device driver within Device Manager.

You can only use the Driver Roll Back feature if you have previously updated the default driver, that is, if you have not installed a newer driver, the option within Device Manager will be unavailable. Using Driver Roll Back will overwrite the current device driver. After using this feature, the previous device driver is no longer available unless you manually reinstall the driver.

> *NOTE* **NO ROLL BACK DRIVER FOR PRINTERS**
>
> Although Printers and Print queues appear in the Device Manager, you are not able to use the driver Roll Back feature for these devices.

To use Roll Back Driver, complete the following steps:

1. Open Device Manager.
2. Right-click the device to roll back, and then click Properties.
3. In the Device Properties dialog box, click the Drivers tab.

4. Click Roll Back Driver.

5. In the Driver Package Roll Back dialog box, provide feedback to Microsoft and then click Yes as shown in Figure 9-8.

FIGURE 9-8 Device Driver Roll Back

> *NOTE* **SAFE MODE**
>
> **If you are unable to start Windows 10 following a recent device driver upgrade, you can start the computer in safe mode and then attempt to Roll Back the driver. This will reinstate the previous driver and allow the system to start.**

Configure restore points

Included with Windows 10 is the Backup And Restore (Windows 7) tool, which allows you to create a system image of your computer. Although this feature was deprecated in Windows 8 and removed in Windows 8.1, it has returned in Windows 10. The reappearance of this feature is useful for users upgrading from Windows 7 directly to Windows 10. Any backups that were created on a Windows 7 machine can be accessed on your Windows 10 computer and you can also use it to back up your Windows 10 PC using the familiar tool.

The backup tool allows you to create backups of files contained in folders, libraries, and whole volumes. You can also create a system image and manually create a system repair disk. The backups can be saved onto external USB drives, network drives, or onto a local disk if it is different from the disk on which Windows 10 is installed.

The Backup And Restore (Windows 7) tool is found in the System And Security section of Control Panel, or you can search for "backup and restore" and select the Backup and Restore (Windows 7) item listed in Settings.

Create a backup and system image

To create a backup of your files and folders and a system image follow these steps:

1. Search for Backup And Restore, and select the Backup And Restore (Windows 7) item listed in Settings.

2. On Backup And Restore (Windows 7), click Set Up Backup.

3. On the Select Where You Want To Save Your Backup page, choose the location and click Next.

4. On the What Do You Want To Back Up page, click the Let Windows Choose (Recommended) option, and click Next.

5. On the Review Your Backup Settings page, click the Change Schedule Link.

6. On the How Often Do You Want To Back Up page, leave the Run Backup On A Schedule (Recommended) check box selected, and choose when you want the back up to be performed.

7. Click OK.

8. On the Review Your Backup Settings page, click Save Settings And Run Backup.

    The backup will begin. The first backup will take the longest time because this is a full back up and subsequent backups are incremental backups.

> **NOTE ADVANCED BACKUP SCHEDULING**
>
> Backup And Restore (Windows 7) allows you to create a simple backup schedule. If you modify the Automatic Backup task in Task Scheduler, you can specify a more complex backup schedule, for example, to backup multiple times per day, or to back up when your workstation is in the locked state.

You can allow Windows to choose what to back up, which will include all files and folders in your user profile (including libraries) and a system image. You can specify the frequency and time when Windows 10 will perform backups, or retain the default backup schedule of Sunday at 7 P.M. every week.

If you require more specific scheduling, you can modify the triggers within Task Scheduler after you have enabled scheduled backups. Available options to trigger a scheduled backup include:

- On a schedule
- At log on
- At startup
- On idle

- On an event
- At task creation/modification
- On connection/disconnect to a user session
- On workstation lock/unlock

Volume Shadow Copy Service (VSS) is used by Backup And Restore (Windows 7) to create the backups. The initial backup creates a block level backup of files to a backup file using the new virtual hard disk (.vhdx) file format. You can mount the VHDX file stored in the backup folder in File Explorer. VSS greatly enhances the performance of the backup operation because subsequent backups will copy only the data that has changed since the previous backup, which is often a smaller amount of data. Therefore, the incremental backup will be created much faster than the initial backup.

Each time you run a backup, the Backup And Restore (Windows 7) tool creates a new restore point that can be used by the Previous Versions feature in File Explorer, which we will cover later in this chapter. These restore points are not the same as the System Restore points created using System Protection.

Within an elevated command prompt you can use the Wbadmin.exe tool to back up and restore your system, volumes, files, folders, and applications. You need to be a member of the Backup Operators or the Administrators group to use this tool. To list the backups available on your system, run the following command in an elevated command prompt:

```
wbadmin get versions
```

The output will display the backup metadata, including the time, target location and what the backup can be used for, such as Volume, Files, Applications, Bare Metal Recovery and System State.

System Image Recovery

When you use the System Image Recovery process within Windows Recovery Environment, Windows 10 replaces your computer's current operating system state with the system image that has been created by the Backup And Restore (Windows 7) tool.

You should only use System Image Recovery if other recovery methods are unsuccessful because it will overwrite data on your computer. During the restore process, you can't choose individual items to restore. All of the apps, system settings, and files are replaced. Any data files stored locally on your computer that you have created or modified since the system image was created will not be available after you use the System Image Recovery unless you have saved them onto another location such as OneDrive.

To recover a device with a Restore Point, follow these steps:

1. Launch Settings, and click Update & Security.
2. Select Recovery.
3. Under Advanced Startup, click Restart Now
4. On the Choose An Option page, select Troubleshoot.

5. On the Troubleshoot page, select Advanced Options.

6. On the Advanced Options page, select System Image Recovery.

7. Allow the system to reboot and Windows will prepare for System Image Recovery.

8. On the System Image Recovery page, select your user account.

9. On the System Image Recovery page, enter your password and click Continue.

10. On the Re-image Your Computer page, verify the system image is correctly selected as shown in Figure 9-9, and click Next.

FIGURE 9-9 Using the System Image Recovery Wizard

11. On the Choose Additional Restore Options page, click Next, and then click Finish to start the restoration process.

12. In the Re-image Your Computer dialog box, read the warning, and then click Yes. The Re-image Your Computer process will now proceed.

13. Once competed, Windows will need to restart. Click Restart Now, or you can wait and allow Windows to automatically restart. When Windows restarts, you will be presented with the sign in screen.

Create a system repair disk

You can create a system image and a system repair disk using the Backup And Restore (Windows 7) tool, which can be used with the advanced troubleshooting mode to recover Windows 10 in the event of a drive or other catastrophic failure.

A system image can be incorporated into any backup when using the Backup And Restore (Windows 7) tool, however to create a system repair disk requires that you manually create a repair disk as follows:

1. Search for Backup And Restore and select the Backup And Restore (Windows 7) item listed in Settings.

2. Insert a blank writable CD or DVD into your device.

3. On Backup And Restore (Windows 7), click the Create A System Repair Disc link.

4. On the Create A System Repair Disc page, click Create Disc.

5. Click Create disc, as shown in Figure 9-10.

FIGURE 9-10 Creating a system repair disc

The system repair disc is useful if Windows 10 will not automatically boot in the advanced startup options. In this scenario, insert the system repair disk and your computer will boot from the recovery media automatically. If it doesn't, you might need to change the boot order.

Skill 9.2: Configure file recovery

Empowering users to quickly recover lost, corrupted, or accidently deleted files is built into Windows 10. Users are constantly protected from accidental data loss and they now have the ability to help themselves when recovering files, a task which was typically requested through an enterprise IT helpdesk.

Whether the data is stored on local computers, on networked drives, or in the cloud using OneDrive, the data can be monitored for changes or deletions that can then be reverted should the need arise.

Many users who have upgraded from Windows 7 might not have seen the Previous Versions feature or encountered File History, or the Recycle Bin feature within OneDrive.

This section covers how to:

- Configure File History
- Restore previous versions of files and folders
- Recover files from OneDrive

Configure File History

File History is file recovery method that provides users with a very easy and user friendly method of retrieving files after they have been accidently deleted or modified. Once enabled, File History will automatically create a backup of all user files that have been modified on an hourly schedule. So long as the backup destination location does not become full, the File History can continue to store changes indefinitely.

To turn on File History, follow these steps:

1. Launch Settings, click Update & Security, and select Backup.
2. Under Back up using File History, click the Plus (+) icon labeled Add A Drive.
3. File History will search for drives.
4. In the Select A Drive dialog box, select the external hard drive that you want to use for File History.
5. On the Back Up Using File History page, verify that the Automatically Back Up My Files toggle is On.

Once enabled, File History will save copies of your files for the first time. This will happen as a background operation and you can continue to work normally.

File History saves your files from your user profile and all the folders located in your libraries, including OneDrive, that are synced to your device if OneDrive is used. You can manually include or exclude folders on the Backup Options page. To manually include additional folders to be monitored by File History, you need to perform the following steps:

1. Open Settings, click Update & Security, and select Backup.
2. Click the More Options link.
3. On the Backup Options page, click Add A Folder.
4. Select the folder that you want to back up and click Choose This Folder as shown in Figure 9-11.
5. Ensure that the folder is listed in the list of folders under Back Up These Folders.

6. Close the Backup Options page.

FIGURE 9-11 Configure File History Backup Options

There are two other methods for adding a folder to the File History list of folders:

- **Add folders to one of the existing libraries already backed up by File History** File History will protect these folders.
- **In File Explorer** Select the folder and click History in the Home ribbon, and then click the Include It In Future Backups link.

You can configure many of the File History settings multiple ways and you need to be familiar with each of them:

- File History in Control Panel
- Backup within the Settings app
- History item on the File Explorer ribbon

Within the advanced settings screen of File History, accessed from the See Advanced Settings link on the Backup Options page, you configure the following:

- Modify the frequency of the File History backup from every 10 minutes to daily.
- Share the backup drive to other HomeGroup members.
- Open File History event logs to view recent events or errors.
- Define the length of time to keep saved versions of your files.

- Manually clean up older versions of files and folders contained in the backup to recover space on the backup drive. You could also use the command line tool FhManagew.exe to delete file versions based on their age stored on the File History target device.

> **NOTE** **FILE HISTORY RESTORE POINTS**
>
> Previous Versions is a feature that uses the File History restore points and allows you to select one of the file version histories and is accessed within File Explorer. Previous Versions is covered later in this chapter.

File History file recovery

You can launch File History file recovery, as shown in Figure 9-12in several ways:

- **History icon**   Open File Explorer and navigate to the folder that contains a modified or deleted file, and then click History on the Home ribbon. The File History page will open and you can view the recoverable files.

- **Restore personal files**   Open File History in Control Panel and select the Restore Personal Files link on the left side.

- **Restore files from a current backup**   The Restore Files From A Current Backup link is at the bottom of the page within the following location: Settings\Update & security\ Backup\More options\Backup Options.

FIGURE 9-12 Restore your personal files using File History

When the File History page is in view, you can navigate through each restore point by using the left and right arrow buttons. Each restore point has a date and time to help you decide which version of the file or files to restore. You can select one or more files to revert, and select which version of the file by navigating through the backups that have been made by File History. If you right-click the file or folder, you can preview the file to view the contents. If you want to proceed to recover the file, click the green button on the File History screen. The file or files selected will be restored and File Explorer will open with the restored files displayed.

> **NOTE** **FILE HISTORY BACKUP LOCATION**
>
> You can navigate to the backup files that File History creates. They are stored on the backup drive in a folder hierarchy. The files backed up in Figure 9-12 would be found at the following location: F:\FileHistory\Demo\SSTE-212\Data\C\Travel Plans\Seattle.

File History support for encryption

Protecting files and folders using Encrypting File System (EFS) is supported on NTFS when using Windows 10 Pro and Windows 10 Enterprise versions. File History supports backing up files that are encrypted using the EFS so long as the drive selected for the backup is formatted as a NTFS volume. Without NTFS, data cannot be encrypted using EFS and therefore if the destination drive does not use NTFS, File History will not back up encrypted files.

If you use BitLocker Drive Encryption to protect your data on your PC and use File History to back up this data to a removable drive, the data will no longer be protected. You should consider enabling BitLocker To Go on the removable drive to protect the contents. The File History is designed to back up on a per-user basis and is performed using the local user account, which means only files and folders that you have access to will be backed up.

> **NOTE** **TURN OFF FILE HISTORY**
>
> There is only one Group Policy Object (GPO) relating to File History, located at Computer Configuration\Administrative Templates\Windows Components\File History\Turn off File History. When enabled, File History cannot be turned on.

Restore previous versions of files and folders

Previous Versions has been reintroduced in Windows 10, and is a file and folder feature that enables users to view, revert or recover files that have been modified or deleted by mistake. Previous Versions uses the File History feature or restore points created during backups in Backup And Restore (Windows 7). One of these features must be configured to use the Previous Versions feature.

After you have enabled File History or created a Backup And Restore (Windows 7) backup, you need to browse in File Explorer to the location where the modified or deleted files are. If one of these methods has "protected" the file or folders being browsed, the Previous Versions tab shown in File Explorer will list the available restore points for your data. Until one of these tasks has been performed, the Previous Versions tab will be empty.

VSS is used by Previous Versions to monitor and preserve copies of modified files on an automatic schedule. You saw earlier in the chapter that the Backup And Restore (Windows 7) tool also creates a restore point each time you create a backup. After the initial File History restore point has been created, subsequent restore points may take only a few minutes to complete.

> **NOTE   PREVIOUS VERSIONS RESTORE POINTS**
>
> In the Previous Versions tab, a message is displayed which states that the previous versions come from File History and from restore points. The Previous Versions feature uses the restore points that are created by the Backup And Restore (Windows 7) tool and not the restore points that System Restore creates.

If you configure File History and also use the Backup And Restore (Windows 7) tool, multiple restore points will be available in the Previous Versions tab. The Previous Versions feature is available on all file systems if File History is used. The Backup And Restore (Windows 7) can only be used to back up data using New Technology File System (NTFS) volumes.

To revert files to a previous version, use the following steps:

1. Ensure that File History is turned on.

2. Create a folder on your computer, for example, "C:\Travel Plans\York", and then create or save a text file called "Things to do.txt" into the folder.

3. In File History, click Run Now.

4. Open Test.txt and modify the contents, save, and exit the file.

5. In File History, click Run Now.

6. Right-click Test.txt and select Restore Previous Versions.

7. On the Previous Versions tab, note that the Test.txt file has one previous version listed, which is the original file. Modify the file again. There will not be another Previous Version listed until the next Restore Point is created by File History.

8. To manually create a new Restore Point, return to File History and click Run Now. Return to the Test.txt file and notice that it now has two file versions listed, as shown in Figure 9-13.

FIGURE 9-13 Restore previous versions of files and folders in File Explorer

9. Delete the Things to do.txt file.

10. To recover the last version of the file that was saved by File History, right-click the "C:\ Travel Plans\York", folder and select Restore Previous Versions.

11. On the Previous Versions tab, select the Travel Plans folder, and drop down the Open menu item, and select Open in File History.

12. File History launches. Double-click the folder that contained the deleted file.

13. Select the deleted file, and choose the green restore button.

14. Verify that the Things to do.txt file has been restored to the This "C:\Travel Plans\York" folder.

Recover files from OneDrive

OneDrive allows you to store your files online. You can sync files between your PC and One-Drive. You can access files from OneDrive.com from just about any device that is connected to the Internet. There are a couple of ways you can recover files from OneDrive that have gone missing.

If you accidentally delete a file stored in your OneDrive account, you can recover files by using the Recycle Bin, which is available with OneDrive.com.

The OneDrive Recycle Bin can retain deleted items for a minimum of three days and up to a maximum of 90 days. The actual retention period is dependent on the size of the Recycle Bin, which is set to 10 percent of the total storage limit by default. If the Recycle Bin is full, old items will be deleted to make room for new items as they are added to the Recycle Bin and this may have an impact on the 90-day retention period.

To recover deleted files from your OneDrive.com, follow these steps:

1. Browse to your OneDrive.com, or right-click the cloud icon in the notification area and click View Online.

2. On the left side of the page, select the Recycle Bin.

3. If the Recycle Bin is not visible, click the three horizontal lines in the top left corner of the screen and select Recycle Bin.

4. Select the items that you want to recover.

5. Click Restore on the menu.

OneDrive will restore the items and they will be removed from the Recycle Bin.

At present you are not able to modify the retention settings or increase the size of the Recycle Bin for OneDrive.com. If you are using the Recycle Bin often and you are concerned about whether your deleted files will be protected by the Recycle Bin, you could consider increasing the space provided to the Recycle Bin by upgrading to a paid OneDrive storage plan such as Office 365 Personal. If space is limited, you could also review the items currently in the Recycle Bin and selecting items for permanent deletion to free up space as shown in Figure 9-14.

FIGURE 9-14 Permanently deleting items from the OneDrive Recycle Bin

When you delete files using the OneDrive.com interface or from your OneDrive folders within File Explorer, the deleted files will be automatically synchronized to the OneDrive.com Recycle bin and the File Explorer Recycle Bin (or Trash if you are using OneDrive on a Mac).

If you use the Restore All or Empty Recycle Bin options you need to be aware that these tasks are irreversible.

The Search feature within OneDrive.com is a powerful method of locating files stored in your OneDrive. Search results do not include items in the OneDrive Recycle bin or the File Explorer Recycle Bin.

OneDrive document version history

For Office documents, such as Microsoft Word and Microsoft Excel, OneDrive.com maintains previous versions of these documents where available. To view the available versions stored in OneDrive, navigate to the Office file right-click and choose Version History. OneDrive will open the file in a new browser tab. You can then see the list of available versions on the left pane, and review the contents of each file as shown in Figure 9-15.

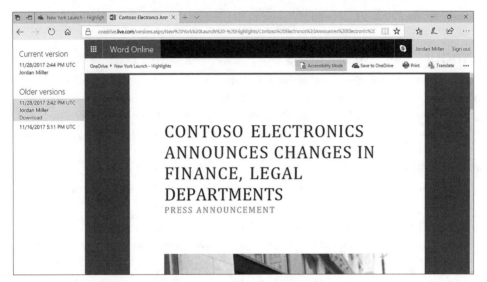

FIGURE 9-15 Microsoft Office previous versions available in OneDrive

The older versions are listed together with the date and time of when the file was last saved. If you select an older version of the document from the list of older versions in the left pane, OneDrive will open the older file into the tab and display the name of the modifier. You can choose to Download this older version from the links displayed in the left pane.

Skill 9.3: Configure and manage updates

Most IT professionals are vigilant against attacks, but most end users are not. Within an enterprise, end users' machines are highly managed and they must rely on proper safeguards being in place. All employees should be encouraged to review appropriate training and education relating to updates, data security, malware threats, and social engineering attacks.

This section focuses on the understanding that it is essential that computers are not left unprotected and open to being compromised. Windows Updates offers enterprises and end users a reliable and proven method of reducing the ever present threat of malicious attack.

This section covers how to:

- Configure update settings
- Configure Windows Update policies
- Manage update history
- Roll back updates
- Update Microsoft Store apps

Configure update settings

Keeping Windows fully updated and secure is the aim of the update mechanism built into Windows 10. On the second Tuesday of each month, known as "Patch Tuesday," Microsoft typically releases a bundle of new updates, updated drivers, and other enhancements to their operating systems. More recently "Patch Tuesday" is referred to as Update Tuesday. In addition, non-security updates for Microsoft Office are released on the first Tuesday of each month and firmware updates for the Surface devices are released on the third Tuesday of every month.

If urgent threats occur during the intervening time, additional "Zero-Day" updates will also be released to counter exploits that cannot wait until the next regular update.

Unlike previous versions of Windows where the user had the ability to disable updates, Windows Update with Windows 10 will check for and install updates automatically. The user has several options available to modify this behavior as follows:

- **Change Active Hours** This setting allows the user to identify the period of time when they expect the device to be in use. Automatic restarts after an update will occur outside of the active hours.

- **Restart Options** Updates will automatically be installed on your system. Windows will ask you to schedule a restart of your device to complete the installation of updates. The installation can be completed at a particular time and day within the following seven days. Users can also see more reminder notifications to prompt them to restart their PCs.

- **Advanced Options** There are three areas that can be configured within the advanced options as shown in Figure 9-16.

    - **Choose How Updates are Installed** Users can choose to include updates for other Microsoft products in addition to Windows, and use the users sign in info to automatically sign back into the device to complete the installation following an update.

    - **Choose when updates are installed** Updates are issues in servicing rings, or branches. Users can choose which servicing ring they want the device to adopt and also defer feature updates for up to 365 days, and quality updates which include security improvements for up to 30 days.

- **Pause Updates** A user can temporally pause updates from being installed onto their device for up to 35 days. After the device is un-paused it will automatically receive and install updates and cannot be paused again until these complete.

FIGURE 9-16 Windows Update Advanced Options

NOTE ADMINISTRATORS CAN SPECIFY THE MAXIMUM ACTIVE HOURS RANGE

Administrators can configure active hours max range through Group Policy using the Specify active hours range for auto-restarts GPO found at Computer Configuration\Administrative Templates\Windows Components\Windows Update.

It is good practice to allow Windows to automatically download and install new driver software and updates for your devices as they become available; this setting is enabled by default. Although the option is not found easily within Devices And Settings in Control Panel, it can be found using search. While it isn't recommended, you can disable automatic updates and choose to never install driver software from Microsoft Update by following these steps:

1. Search for Device Installation.

2. Click the Change Device Installation Settings to launch the Device Installation Settings in Control Panel.

3. Click the No as shown in Figure 9-17, and click Save Changes.

FIGURE 9-17 Modifying the Device Installation Settings

4. Accept the UAC.

Delivery Optimization for Windows 10 updates

In Windows 10 you have several options regarding how Windows updates and Microsoft Store apps are delivered to the computer. By default, Windows obtains updates from the Microsoft Update servers, computers on the local network, and on the Internet. Windows Update Delivery Optimization allows the application of updates more quickly than previous versions of Windows. Once one PC on your local network has installed an update, other devices on the network can obtain the same updates without downloading directly from Microsoft.

This process is similar to popular peer-to-peer file sharing apps. Only partial file fragments of the update files are downloaded from any source, which speeds up the delivery and increases the security of the process. If you allow delivery optimization to take place, you then can choose how your PC will obtain updates and apps from other PCs:

- **PCs on your local network** Windows will attempt to download from other PCs on your local network that have already downloaded the update or app.

- **PCs on your local network and PCs on the Internet** Windows will attempt to download from the PCs on your local network, and also looks for PCs on the Internet that are configured to share parts of updates and apps.

If Delivery Optimization is enabled, your computer can also send file parts of apps or updates that have been downloaded using Delivery Optimization to other PCs locally or on the Internet.

To configure the additional sources, complete the following steps:

1. Open Settings, click Update And Security, and then click Windows Update.

2. Click the Advanced Options link.

3. Click Choose How Updates Are Delivered and review the available options as shown in Figure 9-18.

FIGURE 9-18 Choose How Updates Are Delivered page of Windows Update

4. Turn on update seeding, and chose the method:

    ■ PCs on my local network.

    ■ PCs on my local network and PCs on the Internet.

5. Close the Choose How Updates Are Delivered page.

The default options for Delivery Optimization are different depending on which edition of Windows 10 is used, as follows:

■ **Windows 10 Enterprise and Windows 10 Education** Use the The PCs On Your Local Network option by default.

■ **All other editions of Windows 10** Use the The PCs On Your Local Network And PCs On The Internet option by default.

With the Creators Update of Windows 10, several new delivery optimization features are available, which allow you to modify the behavior. These are found in Group Policy under Configuration\Policies\Administrative Templates\Windows Components\Delivery Optimization and can be found in Table 9-2.

TABLE 9-2 Delivery Optimization options

GPO Setting	Description
Minimum RAM (inclusive) allowed to use Peer Caching	Specifies the minimum RAM size in GB required to use Peer Caching, with the default value is 4 GB.
Minimum disk size allowed to use Peer Caching	Specifies the required minimum disk size for the device to use Peer Caching, with the default value is 32 GB.
Minimum Peer Caching Content File Size	Specifies the minimum content file size in MB enabled to use Peer Caching.
Enable Peer Caching while the device connects via VPN	Determines whether a device will be allowed to participate in Peer Caching while connected to VPN.
Allow uploads while the device is on battery while under set Battery level	Specifies the battery levels at which a device will be allowed to upload data whilst on battery. Devices can download from peers whilst on battery regardless of this policy. By default, devices will not upload while using battery power.

You can also use two new PowerShell cmdlets to review the performance of Delivery Optimization, such as the real-time snapshot of all current Delivery Optimization jobs and obtain key performance data.

These are:

```
Get-DeliveryOptimizationStatus
Get-DeliveryOptimizationPerfSnap
```

> **MORE INFO CONFIGURING DELIVERY OPTIMIZATION**
>
> You can find out more information about configuring Delivery Optimization for Windows 10 updates by visiting: *https://docs.microsoft.com/windows/deployment/update/waas-delivery-optimization*.

Deferring upgrades

The Professional, Enterprise, and Education editions of Windows 10 have the ability for users to defer feature upgrades. With this setting enabled, you can defer upgrades, including new Windows features. This will not permanently disable the upgrade, but it defers the download and installation for up to a year. All security updates will continue to be downloaded and installed, although these can also be deferred, but only for up to 30 days.

Some users will prefer to delay upgrades to their system, so that they can be reassured that any issues present with the installation can be resolved before the deferred upgrade is triggered. Others may be working on a project, and they do not want updates being installed during a project.

Devices using Windows 10 Home will automatically download the latest upgrades and these will be installed at the next reboot. Users can schedule a reboot to install them within the next seven days, but users cannot disable or defer feature upgrades.

Windows Update for enterprise customers

Businesses face a tradeoff between application compatibility and keeping systems secure and protected. By allowing devices to be fully patched and updated they run the risk that key enterprise software, or bespoke apps may be incompatible with the latest Windows 10 feature or quality update. With new malware and security vulnerabilities detected daily, it is important to strike a balance between maintaining systems in an up to date and protected state which remains fully compatible with hardware and software configurations.

With Windows 10, Microsoft has introduced several different Windows 10 servicing "branches" for businesses to consider and decide which option is the most appropriate from the following options:

SEMI-ANNUAL CHANNEL

- All Windows 10 PCs are on this servicing option by default, and will receive feature upgrades and security updates automatically.

- A new Windows version will be made available in March and September of each year, and the year/month will be used in the version name such as Windows 10 Enterprise, Version 1703.

- Each release will be supported and updated by Microsoft for 18 months from the time of its release.

- Business customers that use Professional, Enterprise, and Education versions of Windows 10 can delay feature updates for any time up to a maximum of 365 days. By allowing businesses the option to delay the adoption of the feature upgrades, they can perform extra testing to ensure that new features can be verified for quality and application compatibility and fit within their production environment.

- At any time before the updates are installed, users can also pause the installation for up to 35 days. Windows 10 Home edition users are not able to delay feature updates.

LONG TERM SERVICING CHANNEL (LTSC)

- The long-term servicing option is available only in the Windows 10 Enterprise LTSC edition.

- During the installed life of LTSC, Windows 10 will not receive feature updates, but will be provided with security updates.

- The 10 years of support includes five years for mainstream support and then five years of extended support.

- Systems identified that would be suitable candidates for using LTSC rely on ultimate stability such as systems powering hospital emergency rooms, air traffic control centers, financial trading systems, and factory areas.

- Microsoft will release a new LTSC version of Windows 10 every 2-3 years, and the year will designate the version, such as Windows 10 Enterprise 2016 LTSB.

WINDOWS INSIDER

- During the build up to the release of Windows 10, Microsoft created a special beta program that allowed IT pros to access early release versions of Windows 10.

- This program was hugely popular, with over 10 million subscribers.

- The Windows Insider Program continues and members can install, and deploy preproduction code to their test machines, allowing them to test, evaluate and provide feedback the Microsoft product team on any issues they encounter.

From mid-2017, Windows 10 adopted new servicing naming terms that allow both Windows 10 and Office 365 ProPlus servicing to be aligned as shown in Table 9-3.

TABLE 9-3 Servicing process name changes

OLD NAME	NEW NAME
Current Branch	Semi-Annual Channel*
Current Branch for Business	Semi-Annual Channel
Long-Term Servicing Branch	Long-Term Servicing Channel

The Semi-Annual Channel replaces the Current Branch and Current Branch for Business concepts. During the transition period, you may see the Current Branch referred to as the Semi-Annual Channel (Targeted).

Since some systems may have updates deferred, or delayed, you may notice that this change may not be reflected in all installed systems.

There are various update features built into Windows 10. Customers can also use established update methods. Administrators will have full control over the internal distribution of security updates and can use existing management solutions such as System Center Configuration Manager (SCCM), Windows Server Update Services (WSUS), or Windows Intune. Alternatively, administrators can leave the users to receive these updates automatically via Windows Update.

Configure Windows Update policies

Within Group Policy there are multiple settings that can be configured to modify the behavior of Windows Update. Using Group Policy Objects (GPOs) is the most efficient method of modifying the default settings of your computers within Active Directory Domain Services (AD DS) domain environment.

This section focuses on the three nodes that contain Windows Update GPO settings for Windows 10 devices as follows:

- Computer Configuration\Administrative Templates\Windows Components\Windows Update as shown in Table 9-4.
- Computer Configuration\Administrative Templates\Windows Components\Data Collection And Preview Builds as shown in Table 9-5.
- Computer Configuration\Administrative Templates\Windows Components\Delivery Optimization as shown in Table 9-6.

To set a GPO to configure Windows Update, complete the following steps:

1. In the Search box, type **gpedit.msc**, and then click gpedit.msc.
2. In the Local Group Policy Editor, navigate to one of the three nodes, which relate to Windows Update.
3. In the right pane, select the GPO setting and configure the setting as required.
4. Click OK and close Local Group Policy Editor.

TABLE 9-4 Windows 10 GPO settings in the Windows Update node

GPO Setting	Description
Turn off auto-restart for updates during active hours	Allows you to specify the active hours during which the PC won't restart.
Specify active hours range for auto-restarts	Allows you to specify the maximum number of hours that active hours can be set. Between 8 and 18 hours.
Specify deadline before auto-restart for update installation	Allows you to enforce a restart between 2-14 days after a restart is scheduled.
Configure auto-restart reminder notification for updates	Allows you to specify when auto-restart reminders are displayed.
Turn off auto-restart notifications for update installations	Allows you to turn off all auto restart notifications.
Configure auto-restart required notifications for updates	Allows you to specify how the restart notifications are dismissed. By default this is automatic after 25 seconds.
Configure Automatic Updates	Configure whether Windows Update to enable automatic updates on your computer. If this setting is enabled you must select one of the four options in the Group Policy setting (note there is no option 1): 2 = Notify for download and auto install 3 = Auto-download and notify for install 4 = Auto-download and schedule the install 5 = Allow local admin to choose setting If you select option 4 you can also modify a recurring schedule, otherwise all installations will be attempted every day at 03:00.
Specify intranet Microsoft update service location	Configure whether Windows Update will use a server on your network to function as an internal update service.
Do not allow update deferral policies to cause scans against Windows Update	Allows you to prevent update deferral policies to cause scans against Windows Update.
Remove access to use all Windows Update features	Enabling this policy removes user access to Windows Update scan, download and install features.
Specify Engaged restart transition and notification schedule for updates	Enabling this policy allows you to configure setting related to PC restart following a period of time when auto restart settings have being configured.
Do not include drivers with Windows Updates	If you enable this policy setting, Windows Update will not include drivers with Windows quality updates.
Configure auto-restart warning notifications schedule for updates	Controls when users receive notification reminders and warnings to restart their device following an update installation.
Update Power Policy for Cart Restarts	For educational devices that remain on charging carts overnight, so that they will receive update reboots during the scheduled install timeframe.
Defer Windows Updates\Select when Feature Updates are received	Controls the type of feature updates to receive and when based on branch readiness level.
Defer Windows Updates\Select when Quality Updates are received	Controls the type of quality updates to receive and when based on branch readiness level.

There are seven GPOs that relate to the Windows 10 Preview Builds as described in Table 9-5.

TABLE 9-5 GPO settings in the Data Collection And Preview Builds node

GPO Settings	Description
Toggle user control over Insider builds	Whether users can access the Insider build controls in the Advanced Options for Windows Update.
Allow Telemetry	Determines the amount of diagnostic and usage data reported to Microsoft by Preview Build users as follows. 0= Security (Enterprise, educational, Server and IoT Operating Systems will send minimal telemetry data to Microsoft) 1= Basic (Limited amount of diagnostic and usage data) 2= Enhanced (Sends enhanced diagnostic and usage data). 3= Full (Sends enhanced diagnostic and usage data plus additional diagnostics data during a crash).
Configure the Commercial ID	Allows you to define the identifier used to uniquely associate the device for when telemetry data is being sent to Microsoft.
Configure Authenticated Proxy usage for the Connected User Experience and Telemetry service	Allows you to block or allow the Connected User Experience and Telemetry service from automatically using an authenticated proxy to send data back to Microsoft.
Disable pre-release features or settings	Determines the level to which Microsoft can experiment with the product to study user preferences or device behavior as follows: 1 = Allows Microsoft to configure device settings only. 2= Allows Microsoft to conduct full experimentations.
Configure Connected User Experiences and Telemetry	Forward Connected User Experience and Telemetry requests to a proxy server.
Do not show feedback notifications	Allows you to prevent devices from showing feedback questions from Microsoft.

The final table of GPO settings allows you to modify the Delivery Optimization settings in Windows 10 so that you can fine tune, and regulate peer caching of updates.

TABLE 9-6 GPO settings in the Delivery Optimization node

GPO Settings	Description
Absolute Max Cache Size (in GB)	Allows you to limit the maximum size in GB for the Delivery Optimization cache. The default size is 10 GB.
Enable Peer Caching while the device connects via VPN	Can allow the device to participate in Peer Caching while connected via VPN to the domain network to download from or upload to other domain network devices, whilst either on the VPN or via the corporate network.
Download Mode	Configure the use of Windows Update Delivery Optimization for downloads of Windows apps and updates as follows: 0= HTTP only: No peering 1= LAN: HTTP blended with peering behind the same NAT 2=Group: HTTP blended with peering across a private group. 3=Internet: HTTP blended with Internet Peering. 99=Simple: Download mode with no peering. 100=Bypass mode: Do not use Delivery Optimization and use BITS instead.
Group ID	Used to create a group ID to which that the device belongs to. Used to limit or group together devices.
Max Cache Age (in seconds)	Specifies the maximum time in seconds that each file is held in the Delivery Optimization cache after downloading successfully. Default setting is 3 days.
Max Cache Size (percentage)	Specifies the maximum cache size that Delivery Optimization uses as a percentage of available disk size. Default is 20%.
Maximum Download Bandwidth (in KB/s)	Specifies the maximum download bandwidth that the device can use across all concurrent download activities using Delivery Optimization.
Max Upload Bandwidth (in KB/s)	Defines the maximum upload bandwidth that a device will utilize for Delivery Optimization.
Minimum Background QoS (in KB/s)	Specifies the minimum download QoS (Quality of Service or speed) for background downloads. Default is 500KB/s
Allow uploads while the device is on battery while under set Battery level (percentage)	Specify the value between 1 and 100 to allow the device to upload data to LAN and Group peers while on battery power. The device can download from peers while on battery regardless of this policy.
Minimum disk size allowed to use Peer Caching (in GB)	Specifies the required minimum disk size for the device to use Peer Caching. Default is 32GB.
Minimum Peer Caching Content File Size (in MB)	Specifies the minimum content file size in MB enabled to use Peer Caching. Default value is 100 MB.

Minimum RAM capacity (inclusive) required to enable use of Peer Caching (in GB)	Specifies the minimum RAM size in GB required to use Peer Caching. Default value is 4 GB.
Modify Cache Drive	Specifies the drive Delivery Optimization will use for its cache.
Monthly Upload Data Cap (in GB)	Specifies the maximum total bytes in GB that Delivery Optimization is allowed to upload to Internet peers in each calendar month. Default value is 20 GB.
Maximum Download Bandwidth (percentage)	Specifies the maximum download bandwidth that Delivery Optimization uses. The default value is 0.

Manage update history

Once an update has been downloaded and applied to a device, you can view your update history on the Windows Update page.

When you select the Update History option, you can see the updates that have been applied to your device. The updates are listed in date order. Each update is listed with the following information (see Figure 9-19):

- Update name
- Microsoft Knowledge Base (KB) reference number
- Status of the installation
- Date of the installation

FIGURE 9-19 Update history

You can select the link below an update to display a summary of the update. If you click More Info on the summary of the update page, you will be redirected to a webpage which provides the KB article related to the update.

Roll back updates

When viewing updates in the Update History page, you can click Uninstall Updates and the Installed Updates within Programs And Features in Control Panel will open. You can click an update within Installed Updates to uninstall the update and restart Windows.

When you view the list of updates, you might notice that some updates cannot be uninstalled. If you encounter an update that does not provide you with the uninstall option, you need to review the KB article that relates to the update for more information.

Resolving a problematic device driver or update

You have seen that the user has few choices when it comes to installing Windows updates. Sometimes a device driver or Windows update might cause your system to crash or exhibit instability. If Windows was behaving correctly prior to the update, you can uninstall the driver and prevent the driver or update from being installed again.

To uninstall an unwanted device driver:

1. Launch the Device Manager.
2. Select the device that has the problem driver.
3. Locate the device driver with the problem driver and choose Uninstall.
4. In the uninstall dialog box, select the check box to Delete The Driver Software For This Device.
5. Click OK and close Device Manager.

To uninstall an unwanted Windows Update:

1. Launch Settings, click Update & Security.
2. Select Windows Update and click Update History.
3. On the Update History page, click the Uninstall Updates link.
4. On the Uninstall an Update page, select the unwanted update from the list.
5. Right click the update and if available click Uninstall.
6. Click Yes to uninstall the update.
7. Once completed, you might need to restart your computer.

Until a new or updated fix is made available to replace the problem driver, you can temporarily prevent the driver or update from being reinstalled onto your machine. This is achieved by using the "Show or hide updates" troubleshooter, which you can download from Microsoft. The troubleshooter provides a user interface for either hiding or showing problem Windows Updates and drivers for Windows 10. You can download the Wushowhide.diagcab tool from the Microsoft Download Center.

Once installed, you need to run the troubleshooter and search for updates. You choose either Hide Updates or Show Hidden Updates. If you choose to hide updates, any updates that failed to install correctly on Windows 10 will be displayed. You can select which updates you do not want to be installed again as shown in Figure 9-20.

FIGURE 9-20 Resolving a problematic device driver or update.

By marking the updates as hidden, Windows will not attempt to install them again until you enable them to be shown. In the wizard you are able to review detailed information relating to the updates. The troubleshooter will resolve the problem driver issues by updating the system to prevent the updates from being reapplied while they are hidden.

MORE INFO SHOW OR HIDE UPDATES TROUBLESHOOTER PACKAGE

To download the troubleshooter, visit: *https://support.microsoft.com/help/3073930/how-to-temporarily-prevent-a-driver-update-from-reinstalling-in-window*.

Clean up the Component Store

Some updates such as servicing stack updates are often marked as permanent in their manifest file (metadata) to prevent the update from being removed, which could cause stability issues.

Updates can occupy a large amount of storage space; this can be an issue for smaller devices and tablets. To identify the size of the WinSxS storage folder that contains all Windows updates, you need to open an elevated command window and type: **Dism.exe /Online / Cleanup-Image /AnalyzeComponentStore**.

The output, as shown in Figure 9-21, will advise whether the Component Store should be cleaned, which will allow Windows to reduce the size of the store and free-up some hard disk space.

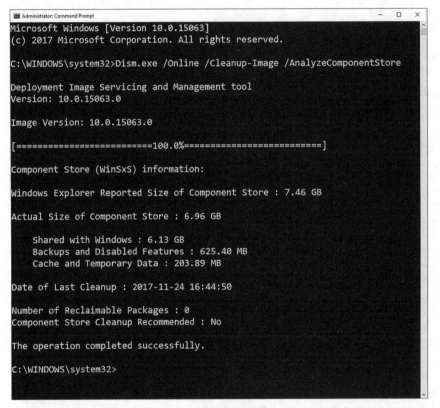

FIGURE 9-21 Dism.exe to analyze the Component Store

Windows will automatically clean up the WinSxS folder for you as a scheduled task in the background, but you can manually reduce the size of the folder by deleting installed package files within the WinSxS Component Store using one of the following methods:

- **Task Scheduler** The StartComponentCleanup task will clean up components automatically when the system is not in use. The task is set to run automatically 30 days after an updated component has been installed before uninstalling the previous versions of the component. To manually run the task, you need to open Task Scheduler and manually start the Task Scheduler Library\Microsoft\Windows\Servicing\StartComponent-Cleanup task. Alternatively, you can invoke the task from the command line by typing:

```
schtasks.exe /Run /TN "\Microsoft\Windows\Servicing\StartComponentCleanup"
```

- **Deployment Image Servicing and Management** Deployment Image Servicing and Management (DISM) is an advanced command line tool that allows you to install, uninstall, configure, and update Windows features, packages, drivers, and international settings. To reduce the size of the WinSxS folder and immediately delete previous versions of updated components using DISM, open an elevated command prompt and type:

```
Dism.exe /online /Cleanup-Image /StartComponentCleanup
```

- **Disk Cleanup** You can also use the GUI tool, Disk Cleanup to reduce space used by temporary files and system files, empty the Recycle Bin, and other files. There is an option to include system files, which includes drivers and updates.

Rolling back Windows

Windows 10 is able to roll back the operating system to a previous version such as a Windows Insider preview build. If you installed a feature update, such as upgrading from Windows 10 (1609) to Windows 10 (1703), you can also go back to the previous version of Windows 10. If you upgraded to Windows 10 from an earlier version such as Windows 7, 8, or 8.1, you will also have an option to roll back the upgrade.

To preserve drive space Windows automatically performs a cleanup of all update files 10 days after updates have successfully been installed. You must therefore evaluate, and if necessary, remove the operating system update before the 10-day period expires and ensure that the manual cleanup process has not taken place during this period.

After 10 days, Windows 10 no longer offer the option to roll back operating system updates to a previous version because the original files will have been deleted to free up space on the hard drive. If you upgraded an earlier version of Windows to Windows 10, the old version is stored in a folder called C:\Windows.old and can take up a lot of space—depending on the previous Windows version and age.

To roll back Windows 10 within 10 days of installation to an earlier version of Windows, use the Go Back To feature using following steps:

1. Open Settings and choose Update & Security.
2. Select the Recovery option.
3. Under the Go Back To Windows 7, select Get Started, as shown in Figure 9-22.
4. Follow the process to begin the rollback procedure, which will involve your system restarting.

FIGURE 9-22 Roll Back Windows to a previous version

> **NOTE ROLL BACK UPDATES ON A PORTABLE DEVICE**
>
> If you're using a portable device, you need to connect it to a power source to roll back up-dates to ensure that the device does not run out of power during the procedure.

Update Microsoft Store apps

Once a Microsoft Store app is installed, it will update itself automatically without any user interaction. You can change this default behavior within Settings and also modify policy using Group Policy. Due to the nature of the Microsoft Store and the extensive testing and validation of all apps prior to being made available in the Store, the updates are regarded as being safe for systems and you are advised to upgrade Store apps to benefit from any increased function-ality and features.

On a daily basis, Windows 10 will attempt to check with the Microsoft Store for app updates. When an update for an installed app is available, it will be automatically downloaded and updated if you are online.

To see how many apps require updating, check for updates, pause updates, or manually update apps, you need to open the Microsoft Store. If you click the three dots to the right of your avatar and select Downloads And Updates, you can view all recent apps update activity.

If you click the Get Updates button, any pending updates will be downloaded immediately, as shown in Figure 9-23.

FIGURE 9-23 Viewing Microsoft Store app downloads and installations

If you have installed apps on another Windows 10 device, they may appear in your library, which is found in the Microsoft Store Settings. Unlike Windows 8.1, apps associated with your Microsoft account, these are not automatically installed on each of your Windows 10 devices; you must manually download and install them from within the My Library option once you have signed in to the Microsoft Store.

Disable automatic app updates in the Microsoft Store

Not everyone will want to take advantage of the updates, for example, a new update may deprecate a desired feature or incur large data consumption over costed networks. For all users except Windows 10 Home, you can opt out of the automatic app updating. To disable automatic Microsoft Store app updates, you can use these steps:

1.   Sign into Windows with your Microsoft account user.

2.   Open the Microsoft Store.

3.   Click the three dots to the right of your avatar and click Settings.

4.   In Settings, enable (default) or disable Update Apps Automatically as shown in Figure 9-24.

5.   Click Home, the back arrow, or close the Microsoft Store.

FIGURE 9-24 Modifying Microsoft Store update settings

By disabling apps, you also conserve bandwidth, but your apps will not be updated. Whenever you have the Store app open, you can update your apps by selecting Downloads from the Settings menu and clicking Check For Updates.

> **NOTE** **WINDOWS 10 HOME USERS ALWAYS RECEIVE STORE APP UPDATES**
>
> Windows 10 Home users will have the disable the Update Apps Automatically option set to On and they are unable to modify this setting.

Once you have installed the Group Policy administrative templates, configure the settings.

For enterprise administrators, Microsoft Store functionality can be configured using the following six GPOs found in the Computer Configuration\Administrative Templates\Windows Components\Store folder:

- Turn off Automatic Download of Updates on Win8 machines.
- Turn off Automatic Download and Install of updates.
- Turn off the offer to update to the latest version of Windows.
- Disable all apps from Windows Store.
- Turn off the Store application.
- Only display the private store within the Windows Store app.

If your enterprise has developed custom Microsoft Store apps and has installed them using the sideloading process, you should upgrade the app in a similar way, using the APPX installer file to replace the existing app, or you can use the command line tool Dism.exe or Windows PowerShell to manage and update sideloaded apps.

If your organization uses many sideloaded apps across the enterprise, you should consider using Microsoft System Center 2012 R2 Configuration Manager or the Microsoft Intune Self-Service Portal to deploy and manage Microsoft Store apps.

Thought experiments

In these thought experiments, demonstrate your skills and knowledge of the topics covered in this chapter. You can find the answers to these thought experiments in the next section.

Scenario 1

You want to use the Backup And Restore (Windows 7) tool to create a backup of your files contained on your computer to a removable USB hard drive or SDHC memory card. You want to create a custom schedule. Answer the following questions relating to the Backup And Restore (Windows 7) tool:

1. What is the default backup schedule for the Backup And Restore (Windows 7) tool?

2. How would you modify the schedule so that you can be more specific, for example, you want to backup the data every 30 minutes?

3. What triggers are available that could be used to begin the backup task?

4. You no longer want to use Backup And Restore (Windows 7) tool for your Windows 10 Pro tablet. What built-in backup tool could you use instead, and how could the data be safeguarded from theft?

Scenario 2

You have been asked to review the backup and restore options available within Windows 10 and OneDrive.com. Your manager is developing a backup strategy and wants to ensure that files are backed up and users can easily access the backed up files for at least six months. Back-ups will be stored offsite. Answer the following backup related questions.

1. How would relying on the OneDrive Recycle Bin feature affect the backup strategy?

2. You want to examine how the Previous Versions feature found in File Explorer works, but you cannot see any Previous Versions listed. How do you enable Previous Versions?

3. Could the Previous Versions feature found in File Explorer offer backup and recovery of files as part of the backup strategy?

Scenario 3

Your organization has 1,300 users distributed across the country in six branch office locations. Each location has high-speed Internet connectivity and there is a small team of IT staff at each office. You are upgrading the Windows 8.1 computers with Windows 10 and you need to research and create a plan for how Windows updates will be deployed across your organization.

Answer the following questions regarding your research:

1. Which edition of Windows 10 will you recommend for the majority of your users?

2. What new feature in Windows 10 could be used to expedite the roll out of Windows updates within the branch offices?

3. What enterprise ready tools could you include in your research for update management within the enterprise?

Thought experiment answers

This section provides the solutions for the tasks included in the thought experiments.

Scenario 1

1. The default backup schedule for the Backup And Restore (Windows 7) tool is every Sunday at 7 P.M.

2. You need to edit the AutomaticBackup task in the WindowsBackup node found in Task Scheduler and configure the task to repeat every 30 minutes by editing the trigger.

3. The triggers available for the task to begin include the following: On a schedule, At log on, At startup, On idle, On an event, At task creation/modification, On connection/disconnect to a user session, On workstation lock/unlock.

4. You would suggest using File History. This feature allows the back up of files and folders to a removable drive such as a USB drive, or SDHC memory card which may be used with the device. The external storage may optionally be encrypted using BitLocker To Go or EFS.

Scenario 2

1. The OneDrive Recycle Bin is not a backup facility. It will only retain files that have been deleted for a maximum of 90 days. This is less than the six months required by the backup strategy.

2. You would need to turn on the schedule to create restore points using either File History or the Backup And Restore (Windows 7) tool. Once the Backup And Restore (Windows 7) tool creates a backup, or when File History runs, previous versions of files will be available on the Previous Versions tab.

3. Previous Versions could provide the longevity of access to the backed up files if the backup storage location does not become full. To ensure that the Previous Versions complied with the backup strategy, you would need File History or the Backup And Restore (Windows 7) tool to save the image to a remote storage location, such as a networked attached drive.

Scenario 3

1. Due to the size of the organization and also the potential benefits of having a licensing agreement using Software Assurance, you will recommend Windows 10 Enterprise.

2. The Windows Update Delivery Optimization feature in Windows 10 Windows to source security updates and app updates from other PCs that already have the updates.

3. Microsoft System Center 2012 R2 Configuration Manager, Windows Server Update Services and Microsoft Intune are three tools that can be used for update management within the enterprise.

Chapter summary

- A Windows 10 recovery drive can be used to recover your system in the event of failure.

- System Restore is part of the system protection, and useful to restore the operating system to a previous point in time if, for example, prior to when your computer became unstable.

- Windows Recovery Environment allows you to access the advanced startup options to troubleshoot Windows 10 startup issues.

- Windows 10 introduces the ability to reset your device. Reset can reinstall Windows 10 and allow you to keep your files.

- A new feature called Fresh Start within the Windows Defender Security Center allows you to keep your personal files and some Windows settings but remove all apps, including third-party apps pre-installed on your device.

- After 10 days following the upgrade to Windows 10, the previous operating system, stored in the Windows.old folder will be deleted. Prior to this happening, users can revert to the previous version of Windows.

- Driver Rollback allows you to revert to a previous device driver after your system begins to suffer the effects of upgrading to a new device driver that is poorly performing.

- Restore points are created when the Backup and Restore (Windows 7) tool creates a backup image. You can use a system image to recover Windows 10 in the event that Windows 10 becomes unstable, such as a hard drive failure and other methods have failed to recover your system.

- Windows 10 File History is the preferred backup option that performs automatic back-ups of files every hour to a non-local storage.

- Previous Versions is a feature that allows you to recover deleted or modified versions of your files directly from File Explorer rather than via a backup or File History. Previous versions are generated whenever File History or the Backup and Restore (Windows 7) tool create restore points.

- OneDrive allows you to recover files you've deleted from OneDrive folders in the File Explorer Recycle Bin and the OneDrive Recycle Bin in the cloud interface. Recovering previously deleted files from either Recycle Bin will allow the files to be available again in OneDrive.

- OneDrive can provide a history of older versions of Office documents that are stored within OneDrive so that you can access, restore, and download previous versions of your files.

- The OneDrive Recycle Bin can retain deleted items for a minimum of three days and up to a maximum of 90 days, and the size of the Recycle Bin is 10 percent of your total storage.

- Windows 10 Home users have Windows Updates automatically downloaded and installed on their devices. Windows 10 Pro, education and Enterprise customers can defer feature updates for up to 365 days, and defer quality updates for up to 30 days.

- Windows 10 Pro, education and Enterprise customers can pause updates for up to 35 days.

- The Semi-Annual Channel brings a new version of Windows 10 twice a year that is supported for 18 months.

- The Long Term Servicing Channel is a special version of Windows 10, available to Enterprise customers only, is supported for up to 10 years and does not receive feature upgrades.

- Windows Update Delivery Optimization is a method of peer-to-peer sharing of Windows update files. This feature significantly reduces the time that a Windows 10 device is vulnerable from zero-day malware attacks. Peer caching can occur between other users on the local network or optionally across the Internet.

- Administrators can use Group Policy to centrally configure and manage Windows Update behavior, location of WSUS servers, and Windows Update Delivery Optimization settings.

- If a driver update causes system stability issues, you can uninstall the update and if necessary disable the automatic application of the update.

- Updating Microsoft Store apps is automatic and ensures that your system has the latest version of apps. Windows 10 Pro, education and Enterprise customers can modify this setting.

Index

A

S

Y

Z

A MODERN INTRODUCTION
TO PHILOSOPHY

THE FREE PRESS TEXTBOOKS
IN PHILOSOPHY

GENERAL EDITOR: *Paul Edwards*